CONSTITUTIONAL RIGHTS AFTER GLOBALIZATION

Constitutional Rights after Globalization juxtaposes the globalization of the economy and the worldwide spread of constitutional charters of rights. The shift of political authority to powerful economic actors entailed by neoliberal globalization challenges the traditional state-centred focus of constitutional law. Contemporary debate has responded to this challenge in normative terms, whether by reinterpreting rights or redirecting their ends, eg, to reach private actors. However, globalization undermines the liberal legalist epistemology on which these approaches rest, by positing the existence of multiple sites of legal production (eg, multinational corporations) beyond the state. This dynamic, between globalization and legal pluralism on one side, and rights constitutionalism on the other, provides the context for addressing the question of rights constitutionalism's counterhegemonic potential. This shows first that the interpretive and instrumental assumptions underlying constitutional adjudication are empirically suspect: constitutional law tends more to disorder than coherence, and frequently is an ineffective tool for social change. Instead, legal pluralism contends that constitutionalism's importance lies in symbolic terms as a legitimating discourse. The competing liberal and 'new' politics of definition (the latter highlighting how neoliberal values and institutions constrain political action) are contrasted to show how each advances different agenda. A comparative survey of constitutionalism's engagement with private power shows that conceiving of constitutions in the predominant liberal legalist mode has broadly favoured hegemonic interests. It is concluded that counterhegemonic forms of constitutional discourse cannot be effected within, but only by unthinking, the dominant liberal legalist paradigm, in a manner that takes seriously all exercises of political power.

Constitutional Rights after Globalization

GAVIN W ANDERSON
University of Glasgow

·HART·
PUBLISHING

OXFORD AND PORTLAND, OREGON
2005

Hart Publishing
Oxford and Portland, Oregon

Published in North America (US and Canada) by
Hart Publishing c/o
International Specialized Book Services
5804 NE Hassalo Street
Portland, Oregon
97213-3644
USA

Hart Publishing is a specialist legal publisher based in Oxford, England.
To order further copies of this book or to request a list of other
publications please write to:

Hart Publishing, Salter's Boatyard, Folly Bridge,
Abingdon Road, Oxford OX1 4LB
Telephone: +44 (0)1865 245533 or Fax: +44 (0)1865 794882
e-mail: mail@hartpub.co.uk
WEBSITE: http//www.hartpub.co.uk

British Library Cataloguing in Publication Data
Data Available
ISBN 1–84113–448–1 (hardback)

Typeset by Hope Services (Abingdon) Ltd.
Printed and bound in Great Britain by
MPG Books, Bodmin, Cornwall

Acknowledgements

I would like to express my deep gratitude to David Beatty, who supervised the doctoral thesis from which this monograph developed, for all his support and encouragement, and in particular for our many vigorous debates which were invaluable in crystallising the arguments presented here. I also wish to acknowledge my considerable intellectual debt to Harry Arthurs, who first showed me that all law is plural, and who has remained an influential, and patient, teacher over the years. I thank the following for giving generously with helpful comments and advice: Upendra Baxi, Damian Chalmers, Sujit Choudhry, David Dyzenhaus, Bob Hancké, Allan Hutchinson, Rod Macdonald, Patrick Macklem, Martin Rhodes, Scott Veitch, and Neil Walker. I am very grateful to Paul Harvey for research assistance and his help in bringing the project to completion. Thanks are also due to the Schools of Law at the Universities of Warwick and Glasgow, where conversations with colleagues were important in shaping the ideas of this book, for study leave, and; to the Faculty of Law, University of Toronto, and the Robert Schuman Centre for Advanced Studies, European University Institute, each for providing a stimulating working environment for researching and writing this book. Special thanks to Alasdair Gray for permission to reprint his illustrations from Lanark on the cover. I would finally like to thank Richard Hart, Mel Hamill and Hart Publishing for their support and assistance in the preparation and publication of the manuscript.

Contents

Table of Cases

AUSTRALIA

CANADA

ENGLAND AND WALES

EUROPEAN COURT OF HUMAN RIGHTS

GERMANY

SOUTH AFRICA

UNITED STATES

Part I: Constitutionalism Beyond the State

1

Constitutionalism in an Age of Globalization

O URS IS A time of globalization. Debates about what globalization is (or is not), its causes, effects, and future trajectory, have achieved a prominent, if not pre-eminent, position in the social sciences.[1] One of the central issues in these debates concerns the extent to which political power any longer resides exclusively, or primarily, in the governmental institutions of the nation state. It is argued that we are witnessing the emergence of significant forms of political authority outside the traditional focus on the public institutions of the state, and that the actors and institutions of the global economy are increasingly setting the terms for the conduct of social life. For some, globalization, and its accompanying reconfiguration of political power, amounts to nothing less than the demise of the paradigm of modernity, making untenable the idea of the nation state as the main organising principle of society.[2]

Lawyers have come somewhat late to the globalization debate,[3] and while there is now a burgeoning literature on law and globalization, there is a sense that this work is peripheral to the main business of understanding national (and international) law. This is no more so than in constitutional law, where much scholarship remains focused on the rules establishing and regulating state institutions, and defining the substance and scope of the rights of citizens vis-à-vis the state. While studies of globalization and constitutional law have in the past followed separate trajectories, exploring the linkages between these two fields now requires the urgent attention of constitutional scholarship.

In this book, I argue that we need to reconfigure our understandings of constitutional law and constitutional rights according to the paradigm of legal pluralism. It is this paradigm that enables us to understand better, and respond to, the challenges facing constitutionalism in an age of globalization. Legal pluralism provides us with the tools for capturing the contemporary reality of the multiple sites of governance. Moreover, it underscores the paucity of those accounts of constitutionalism which focus primarily on the adjudication of

---

[1] See, eg, D Held and A McGrew, *The Global Transformations Reader: An Introduction to the Globalization Debate*, 2nd edn (Cambridge, Polity Press, 2003).

[2] U Beck (trans P Camiller), *What is Globalization* (Cambridge, Polity Press, 2000) 20.

[3] W Twining, *Globalisation and Legal Theory* (London, Butterworths, 2000) 3.

individual rights in addressing the problems raised by the growth of private power. Rather, legal pluralism reveals the political character of our prevailing definitions of constitutionalism and demonstrates how state-centred accounts prevent us from asking questions of accountability with regard to *all* forms of political power. Legal pluralism accordingly shows the importance of effecting a paradigm shift in the field of constitutional law. Furthermore, such a shift becomes imperative in the context of the paradigmatic crisis affecting traditional approaches to constitutionalism, which, being increasingly out of touch with contemporary patterns of power, are unable to deliver their promises of promoting liberty and autonomy.

RIGHTS CONSTITUTIONALISM AND THE GLOBALIZATION OF LIBERAL LEGALISM

From one perspective, claims that constitutional law, and specifically rights constitutionalism, are in paradigmatic crisis appear overblown. Rather, the recent explosion of constitution making would appear to confirm it to be in good health.[4] The adoption of a bill or charter of rights has been a central feature of the transition process for states emerging from totalitarian shadows, whether those in central and eastern Europe, South Africa, or Latin America.[5] In some older constitutions, like Australia's, dormant rights have been given a new lease of life,[6] while in the UK, new constitutional protections for rights have been grafted onto existing structures.[7] Indeed, the successful export of a judicially administered charter of fundamental rights is itself a high profile example of globalization. One important consequence of this has been greater convergence in constitutional practice as a growing number of jurisdictions, often in sharp

---

[4] A representative sample of countries which have undergone major constitutional reform over the past 25/30 years includes: '. . . Eastern Europe (eg, Hungary 1990, Romania 1991, Bulgaria 1991, Poland 1992, the Czech Republic 1993, Slovakia 1993); new democracies in Southern Europe (eg, Greece 1975, Portugal 1976, Spain 1978, Turkey 1982); new democracies in Africa (eg, Mozambique 1990, Zambia 1991, Uganda 1992, Ghana 1993, Ethiopia 1995, South Africa 1993 and 1996); new independent countries in Africa (eg, Zimbabwe 1980, Namibia 1990, Eritrea 1993); other African countries (eg, Egypt 1980); Asian countries and territories (eg, Sri Lanka 1978, the Philippines 1987, Hong Kong 1991, Vietnam 1992, Cambodia 1993); Pacific Islands (eg, Papua New Guinea 1975, Solomon Islands 1978, Cook Islands 1981, Niue 1994, Fiji 1998); Latin American countries (eg, Chile 1980, Nicaragua 1987, Brazil 1988, Colombia 1991, Peru 1993, Bolivia 1994); and industrialised democracies (eg, Sweden 1975, Canada 1982, Israel 1992, New Zealand 1990 and 1993)': R Hirschl, 'The Political Origins of Judicial Empowerment through Constitutionalization: Lessons from Four Constitutional Revolutions' (2000) 25 *Law and Social Inquiry* 91 at 92, fn 1. As Hirschl notes (*ibid* at 92), 'nearly every recently adopted constitution or constitutional revision contains a bill of rights and established some active form of judicial review.'

[5] See A Przeworski et al, *Sustainable Democracy* (Cambridge, Cambridge University Press, 1995).

[6] See G Williams, *Human Rights under the Australian Constitution* (Melbourne, Oxford University Press, 1999).

[7] KD Ewing, 'The Human Rights Act and Parliamentary Democracy' (1999) 62 *Modern Law Review* 79, 92.

contrast to their public law traditions,[8] has accorded a higher prominence to rights discourse and judicial review.[9] The argument that rights constitutionalism has gone global is further supported by the growing use of comparative sources,[10] leading to a more 'cosmopolitan' approach to constitutional adjudication.[11] In its strongest version, it is said that we are witnessing the emergence of universal principles of constitutional law guiding the formation and execution of public policy.[12]

Underpinning rights constitutionalism, and so also achieving global salience, is the dominant paradigm of contemporary western law, namely liberal legalism. This paradigm was born from the Enlightenment ideals of 'rationalism, universalism, certainty and order.'[13] In the liberal philosophy of the moderns, the most rational form of social organisation was one that gave priority to individual freedom.[14] In practice, this was to be delivered through the modern state, which was seen as the exclusive location of both political sovereignty, as this was where political power actually resided, and legal sovereignty, as the state alone had the right to exercise that political power.[15] This close connection between political and legal sovereignty gives us the modern understanding of law as the general and universal commands of the state, in contrast with the particular and personal commands of the monarch in pre-modern times.[16] Moreover, locating both aspects of sovereignty in the state served to protect freedom, as the rule of law would replace arbitrary rule with legal order, enabling citizens to exercise self-government over their own affairs, in the knowledge that the state would protect them from capricious interference with their liberty.

In contemporary terms, the liberal legalist doctrine of the rule of law stands for 'a commitment to autonomy under law.'[17] This rests on both the normative priority of individual freedom, and the belief that the state is not only the best, but the only, institution capable of securing that freedom by laying down clear,

---

[8] See H Klug, *Constituting Democracy: Law, Globalism and South Africa's Political Reconstruction* (Cambridge, Cambridge University Press, 2000) at 76–85 and M Loughlin, 'Rights Discourse and Public Law Thought in the UK' in GW Anderson (ed), *Rights and Democracy: Essays in UK-Canadian Constitutionalism* (London, Blackstone, 1999) 193.

[9] R Hirschl, *Towards Juristocracy: The Origins and Consequences of the New Constitutionalism* (Cambridge MA, Harvard University Press, 2004).

[10] C McCrudden, 'A Common Law of Human Rights? Transnational Judicial Conversations on Constitutional Rights' (2000) 20 *Oxford Journal of Legal Studies* 499, 506–10.

[11] S Choudhry, 'Globalization in Search of Justification: Toward a Theory of Comparative Constitutional Interpretation' (1999) 74 *Indiana Law Journal* 819, 820.

[12] See D Beatty, *The Ultimate Rule of Law* (Oxford, Oxford University Press, 2004).

[13] RA Macdonald, 'Metaphors of Multiplicity: Civil Society, Regimes and Legal Pluralism' (1998) 15 *Arizona Journal of International and Comparative Law* 69, 71.

[14] J Gray, *Liberalism* (Milton Keynes, Open University Press, 1986), ch 2.

[15] See M Loughlin, *Sword and Scales: An Examination of the Relationship Between Law and Politics* (Oxford and Portland, OR, Hart Publishing, 2000), 137.

[16] *Ibid* at 129.

[17] S Veitch, *Moral Conflict and Legal Reasoning* (Oxford and Portland, OR, Hart Publishing, 1999) 140.

consistent and enforceable rules for the conduct of social life. From its origins, constitutional law was thought to perform a special role in this regard, by subjecting relations between the state and its citizens to the rule of law, and so ensuring that the conditions which enable freedom to prosper are maintained.[18] Sometimes this was to be achieved by empowering the state to act to protect freedom, for example by promulgating anti-discrimination laws, or providing basic welfare entitlements. At others (and reflecting liberalism's ambivalent attitude to the state), this required limiting the state's capacity to act in an oppressive manner, for example by preventing legislative, executive and judicial power from being placed in the same hands.

The global spread of rights constitutionalism exemplifies the ideal that the liberal legalist promise of freedom through law is best secured by entrenching individual rights as higher law guarantees enforceable against the state. On this view, courts emerge as the key actors, cast as the repositories of reason and objectivity, charged with 'elaborat[ing] the principles of right conduct,'[19] in contradistinction to the partisan politics of legislatures.[20] Accordingly, liberty and individual autonomy are best protected when the institutions of state act in accordance with the constitutional law declared and enforced by the courts.

The growing hold of this conception of law as right[21] would appear to be confirmed by the prominent role now accorded to lawyers and courts in public discourse. In the academy, constitutional scholarship is increasingly taking the form of normative argument directed to courts, focusing on two principal questions. First, how should the general terms of constitutional texts be interpreted? Secondly, and related, what social outcomes should constitutional adjudication promote? Underlying both questions, and reinforced by their increasing centrality in constitutional discourse, are the liberal legalist assumptions that constitutional law is a coherent and autonomous system of norms that operates as an effective tool of social engineering to promote or protect individual freedom. In the broader political context, we can also see that as the adjudication of rights before courts becomes an increasingly prominent aspect of public discourse,[22] it leads some to argue that we are witnessing the 'judicialization of politics',[23] and the politicisation of law.[24]

---

[18] See SM Griffin, *American Constitutionalism: From Theory to Politics* (Princeton, Princeton University Press, 1996) 13.

[19] Loughlin, above n 15, at 223.

[20] As Jeremy Waldron notes, 'orthodox legal theory tends to view legislative activity in derogative terms, such as "deal-making, horse-trading, log-rolling, interest-pandering and pork-barrelling," in comparison with the more elevated tones reserved for judicial reasoning' (J Waldron, *The Dignity of Legislation* (Cambridge, Cambridge University Press, 1999) 2).

[21] Loughlin, above n 15, at 11.

[22] See AS Stone, *Governing with Judges: Constitutional Politics in Europe* (Oxford, Oxford University Press, 2000).

[23] Hirschl, above n 9, at 211.

[24] See M Loughlin, The Idea of Public Law (Oxford, Oxford University Press, 2004) 162.

GLOBALIZATION AND THE EMPIRICAL CHALLENGE OF PRIVATE POLITICAL POWER

The spread of charters of rights has led to the claim that constitutionalism now stands 'on the brink of a world-wide hegemony.'[25] However, taking a broader empirical perspective shows how constitutionalism is under often intense pressure from shifting patterns of geo-political power. One prominent theme of recent constitutional scholarship concerns how to reconcile existing conceptual structures with forms of social organisation not readily contemplated in the state-centred approach. This arises at both the sub-national—such as the issue of the recognition of indigenous forms of government in aboriginal societies[26]—and supranational levels—where attention has focused on the task of 'translating' state-based constitutional ideas to 'postnational' bodies such as the EU.[27] However, the most pressing challenge comes from economic globalization, which has led to 'the formation of a transnational system of power which lies in good part outside the formal interstate system.'[28] Accordingly, any discussion of states' constitutional authority now has to take account of the disciplining effects of the global economy, and the power networks formed by transnational corporations.

One of the most significant political phenomena of the past twenty-five years has been the spread of the ideas and practices of economic neoliberalism which stressed the virtues of the free market and the vices of big government. Neoliberalism first found political expression in the Thatcher and Reagan 'revolutions' of the 1980s, but attained global status in the 1990s through the reach of the 'Washington consensus' which promoted policies of:

> . . . liberalization, privatization, minimizing economic regulation, rolling back welfare, reducing expenditure on public goods, tightening fiscal discipline, favouring free flows of capital, strict controls on organized labor, tax reductions, and unrestricted currency repatriation.[29]

The result of these changes in public policy has been the achievement of neoliberalism's main objective, namely 'a global economy, characterized by global production and global markets for goods, services and finance.'[30] While, for

---

[25] B Ackerman, 'The Rise of World Constitutionalism' (1997) 83 *Virginia Law Review* 771, 772.

[26] See P Havemann (ed), *Indigenous Peoples' Rights in Australia, Canada and New Zealand* (Auckland, Oxford University Press, 1999).

[27] See N Walker, 'Postnational Constitutionalism and the Problem of Translation' in JHH Weiler and M Wind (eds), *European Constitutionalism Beyond the State* (Cambridge, Cambridge University Press, 2003) 27.

[28] S Sassen, 'The State and Globalization' in R Bruce Hall and TJ Biersteker (eds), *The Emergence of Private Authority in Global Governance* (Cambridge, Cambridge University Press, 2002) 91, 109.

[29] R Falk, *Predatory Globalization: A Critique* (Oxford, Polity Press, 1999) 2.

[30] J Jenson and B de Sousa Santos, 'Introduction: Case Studies and Common Trends in Globalizations' in J Jenson and B de Sousa Santos (eds), *Globalizing Institutions: Case Studies in Social Regulation and Innovation* (Aldershot, Ashgate, 2000) 9, 16.

some, neoliberalism's zenith has passed,[31] its legacy in the form of the global economy is still highly influential in shaping the terms of political debate, not least in revising ideas of the state as the principal repository of political power.

As a result of deregulation and privatisation, the active and interventionist state that informed the postwar Keynesian consensus has been significantly reshaped. In many areas of traditional public policy, from school meals and refuse collection to prisons and air traffic control, the state has moved from being provider to enabler. Instead, private bodies, including primarily corporations, are increasingly performing these functions, sometimes in partnership with public agencies, at other times (particularly in developing countries) bypassing the state completely. In either case, this generally involves the reorientation of the principles guiding the delivery of these services, emphasising market-related ideas such as value for money, rather than traditional concerns of the public interest. Furthermore, any account of the extent of state power must take notice of the obligations that states accept in signing up to the global economy. For example, while constructed and administered by states, the anti-protectionism policing mechanisms put in place by the WTO to ensure fidelity to the principles of free trade, narrow the range of the permissible policy options available to states.[32]

An important corollary of these developments is the rise of new forms of political authority which do not fit readily within the template of the nation state. While the state's capacity to exercise political power may be relatively diminished, this does not lead to the disappearance of politics, but rather its reconfiguration. Crucial to understanding this changing landscape of governance is the emergence of 'private or quasi-private regimes and circuits of power, both formal and informal, surrounding and criss-crossing the state in a new web of complex relationships.'[33] For example, international commercial arbitration has become the predominant means of settling transnational commercial disputes.[34] International business associations often operate as 'self-regulatory associations' setting norms and standards across a wide range of industries and professions.[35] International financial markets assign credit ratings to states with a view to influencing their policy decisions.[36]

---

[31] D Drache, 'The Return of the Public Domain after the Triumph of Markets: Revisiting the Most Basic of Fundamentals' in D Drache (ed), *The Market or the Public Domain? Global Governance and the Asymmetry of Power* (London, Routledge, 2001) 37, 46–48.

[32] See JH Jackson, *The World Trading System: Law and Policy of International Economic Relations*, 2nd edn (Cambridge, MA, MIT Press, 1997).

[33] P Cerny, 'Globalization and the Disarticulation of Political Power: Towards a New Middle Ages' in H Goverde, P Cerny, M Haugaard and HH Lentner (eds), *Power in Contemporary Politics: Theories, Practices, Globalizations* (London, Sage, 2000) 170, 177.

[34] S Sassen, *Losing Control? Sovereignty in an Age of Globalization* (New York, Columbia University Press, 1996) 15–16.

[35] AC Cutler, 'Private International Regimes and Interfirm Cooperation' in Hall and Biersteker (eds), above n 28, 23 at 29.

[36] Sassen, above n 34, at 42.

One of the most significant aspects of the rise of these alternative forms of political authority is the enhancement of the power of multinational corporations (MNCs). In the context of the global economy, the idea that MNCs are simply economic entities is unsustainable. Rather, they are major political actors capable of setting the agenda for debates over public policy, of mobilising and constraining political constituencies, and of generating normative regimes that govern key areas of social life.[37] With regard to the latter point, Claire Cutler discusses how international firms have co-operated to create 'private international regimes' which provide 'an integrated complex of formal and informal institutions that is a source of governance'[38] within particular industries. While not replacing, but often interacting with the state, these regimes are important in explaining the rules and procedures applying, for example, to 'the regulation of the internet, the international minerals industry, the regulation of intellectual property, the insurance industry, and the maritime transport industry.'[39]

The diffusion of political authority in the context of the global economy has led to concerns about the ability of constitutionalism to operate as a check on political power if it speaks only to the state. Moreover, there is a growing awareness—perhaps fuelled by recent examples of corporate corruption and wrongdoing—that private power, as much as public power, has the capacity to oppress.[40] Accordingly, the issue of private power has become an increasingly central preoccupation of contemporary constitutional debates. A number of commentators have proposed updating rights constitutionalism in response to these empirical developments to overcome the criticism that its default position has been to protect the private sphere.[41] Two ways in particular have been canvassed to subject all forms of political power to constitutional scrutiny. The first extends the *reach* of classical negative constitutional rights to private actors, so that they have to take account of obligations, for example, to respect freedom of expression or basic due process rights. The second broadens the *scope* of constitutional protection to impose positive obligations on the state and also to protect rights against encroachment from any source. Sometimes this is to be achieved by reinterpreting existing texts, giving a more expansive reading to provisions that limit constitutional application to the state, so that, for example, they reach non-state actors performing public functions. At other times, this is to be achieved by adding innovative terms to new constitutions, for example,

---

[37] See S Veitch, 'Legal Right and Political Amnesia' in K Nuotio (ed), *Europe in Search of 'Meaning and Purpose'* (Helsinki, Forum Iuris, 2004) 89, 103.

[38] Above n 35, at 29 (quoting AC Cutler, V Haufler, and T Porter, 'Private Authority and International Affairs' in AC Cutler, V Haufler and T Porter (eds), *Private Authority and International Affairs* (Albany, NY, SUNY Press, 1999) 13).

[39] *Ibid* at 30.

[40] See J Bakan, *The Corporation: The Pathological Pursuit of Profit and Power* (New York, Free Press, 2004).

[41] See, eg, A Clapham, *Human Rights in the Private Sphere* (Oxford, Oxford University Press, 1993) 151.

that they should have (some) horizontal application, or protect social and economic rights.

Locating our discussion of rights constitutionalism in the wider processes of globalization addresses the question—so far neglected in the literature—of the connections between them. It has been argued that the very nature of the modern constitutional state, operating under the liberal legalist rule of law with its emphasis on rights and individual autonomy, provided the permissive structure for the rise of transnational neoliberalism.[42] And this is a point made not only by critics of globalization: the World Bank, for example, has also stressed how clear and enforceable property rights provide the necessary infrastructure for the global economy.[43] Thus, the idea that the Washington consensus evolved out of, and in many ways is consistent with, the values of liberal legalism raises the key issue of whether constitutional rights can operate as a counter-hegemonic restraint on private power.

GLOBALIZATION AND THE EPISTEMOLOGICAL CHALLENGE OF LEGAL PLURALISM

At an empirical level, the challenge of private power focuses debate on the boundaries of constitutional law and scholarship in an age of globalization. Much of this is to be welcomed, not least in reassessing the utility of key dichotomies in liberal thought, including that between public and private. However, there is one boundary which remains largely immune to this process of rethinking, namely the epistemological one. Globalization also challenges core elements of received legal and constitutional knowledge, and heralds the 'passing' of the 'inexorable linkage of law with sovereignty and the state.'[44] In the context of significant sites of non-state authority in the global economy, the state is often no longer able to command, while the commands of other bodies are at times more authoritative. Theories of law whose test of legal order is satisfied solely by the formal pedigree of a rule in official processes 'just do not fit the modern facts.'[45]

One important development that doubts any necessary connection between the state and law is the emergence of new forms of law attendant on changing global business practices. A leading example is the 'movement towards a relatively uniform global contract and commercial law'[46] through the global

---

[42] Santos, for example, argues that '[f]ree elections and free markets were always seen as the two sides of the same coin: the collective good to be achieved by utilitarian individuals engaged in competitive exchange with minimal state interference': B de Sousa Santos, *Toward a New Legal Common Sense* (London, Butterworths, 2002) 315.

[43] World Bank, *World Development Report 1996—From Plan to Market* (Oxford, Oxford University Press, 1996).

[44] N MacCormick, 'Beyond the Sovereign State' (1993) 56 *Modern Law Review* 1, 1.

[45] Twining, above n 3, at 51.

[46] M Shapiro, 'The Globalization of Law' (1993) 1 *Global Legal Studies Journal* 37, 38.

organisation of business practices. The relative unimportance of the state is underscored by the claim that this 'system of private lawmaking' can successfully exist in the absence of a 'transnational court or transnational sovereign to resolve disputes.'[47] Others highlight how the legal profession can no longer be principally regarded in national terms, but is taking on a 'transnational' character as lawyers employ an increasingly homogeneous set of practices in servicing global business.[48] What is important here is that the primary reference point in explaining these global forms of law is not the nation-state, but the global economy.

These arguments undermine the link between legal and political sovereignty that is at the heart of the liberal legalist conception of law.[49] In the context of the global economy, the increasing pressure on the state's capacity to exercise political power undermines claims that the state is 'the exclusive legal-political form of power'[50] in society. Moreover, these developments highlight the legal bases of other forms of social power, thus decoupling law from the state.[51] Harry Arthurs develops this point to argue that even constitutional law can be generated outside the state,[52] and addresses the argument that in placing limits on the policy options available to states, the WTO agreements should be regarded as the 'constitution of the world economy.'[53] While he agrees that the global economy necessitates a broader constitutional focus than the traditional state-centred approach, he contends that we also have to adjust our focus outwards to see how these formal regimes are 'complemented, modified or displaced, by private processes of negotiations, legislation, regulation, adjudication and administration.'[54] On this account constitutional law is also found in the activities of large multinational corporations.[55]

These developments highlight the claims of the paradigm of legal pluralism, which questions whether 'the equation between nation, state and law'[56] alone provides the test for legal order. While legal pluralist scholarship predates contemporary globalization discourse, it has existed at the margins of legal study, seen as concerned with the 'exotic or pathological.'[57] However, the challenge of globalization calls for a timely re-examination of legal pluralism's contention to

---

[47] *Ibid.*

[48] HW Arthurs and R Kreklewich, 'Law, Legal Institutions and the Legal Profession in the New Economy' (1996) 34 *Osgoode Hall Law Journal* 1, 50–55.

[49] See K Jayasuriya, 'Globalization, Sovereignty, and the Rule of Law: From Political to Economic Constitutionalism' (2001) 8 *Constellations* 442.

[50] Santos, above n 42, at 70.

[51] *Ibid.*

[52] HW Arthurs, 'Constitutionalizing Neo-Conservatism and Regional Economic Integration: TINA x 2' in TJ Courchene (ed), *Room to Manoeuvre? Globalization and Policy Convergence* (Montreal and Kingston, McGill-Queen's University Press, 1999) 17.

[53] *Ibid* at 27.

[54] *Ibid* at 31.

[55] *Ibid* at 31 and 37–41.

[56] Santos, above note 42, at 86.

[57] M-M Kleinhans and RA Macdonald, 'What is a Critical Legal Pluralism?' (1997) 12 *Canadian Journal of Law and Society* 25, 30.

provide a more plausible knowledge of law. The core charge of legal pluralism is that the liberal legalist paradigm rests on a fundamental misdescription, and that the reduction of law to state law is empirically unsustainable: instead, it posits multiple sources of law. These include laws made in the family, in the workplace, in indigenous societies, among neighbours, which contribute to the legal orderings of these settings while lacking the imprimatur of the state. Legal pluralism further charges that not only can we find law beyond the state, but that formal state law fails to exhibit the special characteristics claimed on its behalf: in particular, it is often incoherent and instrumentally ineffective.

The claims of legal pluralism are particularly important given that proposals to reform rights constitutionalism generally take for granted the key tenets of liberal legalism: it is assumed that the relation between rights constitutionalism and private power, and the ability of the former to constrain the latter, turns on the outcome of normative constitutional debate over how rights should be interpreted, or the values they should embody. This can be seen as a sub-paradigmatic response,[58] with private power presenting a challenge *within* rather than *to* rights constitutionalism, and one that can be resolved using existing resources. We can contrast this with the legal pluralist call to engage debate at the paradigmatic level, which requires us to 'reconsider . . . the assumptions and intellectual structures upon which our analysis and actions are based.'[59] Thus, the key challenge of legal pluralism is whether the tools and concepts associated with state-centred approaches to law are adequate to theorising and responding to the issue of private power. In other words, the paradigmatic debate of modern law makes the adequacy of our existing legal and constitutional knowledge a central component of the inquiry into the relation between rights constitutionalism and private political power.

A NEW DYNAMIC: RIGHTS CONSTITUTIONALISM, GLOBALIZATION AND LEGAL PLURALISM

The challenges of globalization suggest that contemporary debates on constitutionalism must confront the argument that ours is a time of paradigmatic transition. Globalization and legal pluralism combine to challenge some of the key tenets of rights constitutionalism within the liberal legalist paradigm. They both decentre the nation state as the primary level of analysis and alter our perception of who the key constitutional actors are, removing courts and lawyers from any preordained position. Linked to the foregoing, they both undermine the link between law and national culture and history: global modes of governance are seen as developing their own logic, while according to legal pluralism the state is no longer determinative of the existence or character of law. Furthermore,

---

[58] Santos, above n 42, at 173.
[59] HW Arthurs, *Without the Law: Administrative Justice and Legal Pluralism in Nineteenth-Century England* (Toronto and Buffalo, University of Toronto Press, 1985) 1.

each questions the notion of law as command: globalization questions where sovereignty resides, while legal pluralism emphasises the indistinct nature of the commands that the state seeks to give. In short, they combine to undermine the orthodoxy that constitutional study is concerned solely with a national document enforced by formal procedures before state courts.

Instead, an alternative intellectual framework is proposed, grounded in *a new dynamic between rights constitutionalism, globalization and legal pluralism*. This dynamic reveals that the empirical challenge of globalization and the epistemological challenge of legal pluralism necessitate a rethinking of constitutional law. This dynamic ushers in an epistemological crisis of liberal legalism. It highlights the lack of fit between the descriptive assumptions of rights constitutionalism, and the empirical world unveiled by globalization and legal pluralism. This underscores the inadequacy of the state-centred account of law in an age of transnational private power. Furthermore, it problematises the liberal legalist assumptions that constitutional doctrine can be remade into a coherent whole which once reordered acts in a linear manner to secure its objectives. This leads to the conclusion that rights constitutionalism does not deliver what it promises as an instrument of social engineering, casting significant doubt on its effectiveness to restrain private power.

The dynamic further reveals the high political stakes of this epistemological crisis. It shows that rather than being an autonomous discourse, rights constitutionalism is a site of struggle between hegemonic and counterhegemonic forces. The key to understanding this struggle is to acknowledge fully the rhetorical dimension of legal discourse, that where we state 'law is *x*,' we are involved in *the politics of definition of law*. The prize here is to present as an analytical postulate what is actually a political claim,[60] for example, that law is identified exclusively with the state. The politics of definition that prevail thus privilege certain modes of inquiry as commonsensical. On this view, epistemological foundations do not provide a neutral backdrop within which constitutional debates take place, but are themselves an important factor affecting our understanding of the relation between rights constitutionalism and private power. The liberal legalist politics of definition of rights constitutionalism are grounded in the central distinction in liberal theory between the state—which alone is regarded as exercising potentially oppressive political power—and the naturally free realm of civil society. This distinction justifies the historical constitutionalist concern with public power, and has served hegemonic interests well in the past, for example, by treating powerful actors such as corporations as private legal persons, entitled to the benefit, but not required to bear the burden, of constitutional rights.[61] Moreover, they continue to inform modern

---

[60] See Santos, above n 42, at 90.
[61] See M Horwitz, 'Santa Clara Revisited: The Development of Corporate Theory' in WJ Samuels and AS Miller, *Corporations and Society: Power and Responsibility* (New York, Greenwood Press, 1987) 13.

practice which the available evidence suggests is still seen in terms of processing claims of negative freedoms against the state.[62]

It is at the level of the politics of definition under conditions of globalization that the empirical and epistemological challenges come together. For all rights constitutionalism's apparent success, the paradigmatic crisis highlighted by the dynamic brings the issue of the politics of definition to the fore. This is perhaps most evident in the attempts to respond to the empirical challenge of private power by strengthening rights constitutionalism's negative and positive controls. Where these proposals have been acted upon, the jurisprudential record shows that in practice rights constitutionalism acts as a sword and shield for hegemonic values, while exposing its instrumental limits as a counterhegemonic sword. In this way, the prevailing politics of definition lend powerful symbolic support to the idea that private power is not as serious a political concern as public power, while directing the constitutional agenda away from the question of how private power may be more efficaciously held to account. However, the inability of rights constitutionalism as currently conceived to respond to the empirical challenge of globalization shows that the liberal legalist politics of definition cannot hold under the pressure of the dynamic. This underlines the need for a new politics of definition if we wish to hold private power to constitutional account.

The book is organised into three parts. Part I lays out the grounds of the paradigmatic challenge to state-centred views of politics and law by outlining the reconfiguration of political power effected by globalization. The remainder of the book considers the appropriate response to the challenge of paradigmatic transition. In Part II, I argue that this response should be grounded in the paradigm of legal pluralism, which better captures the operation and empirical reality of law. In Part III, I outline the basis of a legal pluralist theory of constitutionalism, which can provide us with a better understanding of the relation between rights constitutionalism and private power.

In the remainder of Part I, I set out how globalization provides the context for the contemporary study of rights constitutionalism. In chapter two, I argue that, as a consequence of economic globalization, we are witnessing a significant change in the location of political authority, to the advantage of private, particularly corporate, power. I consider the principal ways in which this is manifested, first by outlining the nature and reach of the Washington consensus and how this has recast the role of the state. I elaborate the extent of global corporate political power, drawing on both quantitative and qualitative arguments, to show how corporations influence state policy apparatuses and have come to resemble states themselves. I outline the impact which these changes have had on constitutional discourse in moving the issue of private power to the centre of debate, and discuss the ensuing proposals for reorienting constitution-

---

[62] Hirschl, above n 9, at ch 4.

alism by extending the application of negative rights, and deepening the scope of positive rights. I conclude by querying whether this normative approach is an adequate response to the challenges of the paradigmatic transition.

In Part II, I argue that the descriptive basis of liberal legal and constitutional theory ill fits our age, and that instead the paradigm of legal pluralism accords better with the empirical record. In chapter three, I outline the terms of the paradigmatic debate between liberal legalism and legal pluralism. For liberal legalism, law is exclusively state law, tends towards system and order, and its commands are the primary tools of social engineering. Legal pluralism, in contrast, questions the necessary state provenance of law, and doubts claims for its coherence and instrumentality. Here, I develop the theoretical basis of legal pluralism's challenge to liberal legalism, from which I interrogate the latter's epistemological assumptions in chapters four and five. I outline first external legal pluralism, which sees the world in terms of a multiplicity of interacting (official and unofficial) legal systems and second, internal legal pluralism, which emphasises the asymmetrical and disordering nature of legal relations. In the following two chapters, I test whether liberal legalism or legal pluralism offers the more plausible description of constitutional adjudication.

In chapter four, I consider Ronald Dworkin's theory of 'law as integrity.' Dworkin's position is important, given his thesis that constitutional law is primarily an interpretive exercise, which properly executed, can provide the right answer in hard cases. However, I contend, with reference to jurisprudence on affirmative action, obscenity and hate speech, that reading his theory against the insights of internal legal pluralism highlights some generic problems of the argument from coherence. First, that the abstract nature of constitutional doctrine can produce contrary results when applying the same theory of interpretation, and secondly, that adjudication is not best characterised as the search for coherent principle, but is in practice subject to a series of disordering influences. Chapter five examines whether there is any necessary link between winning the normative argument in court, and translating its assumed social benefits into practice. I present case-studies in three classic fields of constitutional litigation, namely racial equality, abortion and freedom of expression. I argue that in each case the empirical record suggests that the command of constitutional law is muted by the workings of external legal pluralism, and that the assumed importance of courts' rulings, both in direct and indirect terms, is overstated. I reach the interim conclusion that normative theories significantly overestimate the capacity of constitutional adjudication to reorder doctrine and society.

In Part III, I consider the implications of the argument that liberal legalism rest on unsure epistemological foundations for the relationship between rights constitutionalism and private power. In chapter six, I discuss the nature of the politics of definition, and show how the key issue becomes what consequences follow from certain definitions taking hold in the legal, and broader, imaginations. I contrast the prevailing state-centred politics of definition, rooted in classical liberal political theory, with that advanced by the 'new constitutionalism' which draws attention to the constitutional dimension of economic globalization. I show how, on the key issue of rights constitutionalism's counterhegemonic potential, the former operates to protect private power, while the latter seeks to open its exercise to greater account and scrutiny. This reveals that the major importance of rights constitutionalism lies not at the instrumental level of adjudication, but at the symbolic level of how its prevailing politics of definition consolidate or disturb hegemonic interests.

Chapter seven addresses this question by exploring the consequences of the prevailing politics of definition in terms of the issue of rights constitutionalism's engagement with private power. I focus on two strands of the comparative jurisprudence, drawn from the North American and European constitutional experiences respectively, which seek to hold private power to greater constitutional account. The first, the Application to State Institutions (or ASI) model, retains the formal idea that constitutions only apply to the state, but expands the situations where the state can be said to be acting, for example, where non-state bodies are carrying out public functions. The second, the Application to Law (or LAW) model, extends the nature of constitutional obligations beyond the traditional negative limits on government, for example, requiring states to ensure that the positive law does not enable private parties to disregard fundamental rights. My argument is that when we consider how these doctrinal positions have been employed in actual adjudication, this reflects a politics of definition where the state-civil society divide is still strong, and which reveals the limits of rights constitutionalism operating in a counterhegemonic mode.

I conclude by outlining the beginnings of a legal pluralist constitutionalism. I argue that the key to moving to a counterhegemonic constitutional discourse lies in abandoning narrow conceptions of constitutionalism in terms of the adjudication of rights, but instead broadening the terms of debate by opening up the meaning of constitutionalism to debate and scrutiny. Drawing on some recent theoretical and practical developments, I discuss how we might move to an alternative constitutional discourse which symbolises the plural sources of constitutional law, and promotes broader forms of political accountability.

2

Globalization and the Reconfiguration of Political Power

GLOBALIZATION PRESENTS TWO fundamental challenges to rights constitutionalism. First, it highlights a gap between the powers the state is traditionally said to possess, and those which it can now more plausibly be said to
have. This challenges the core idea of liberal political theory that the state is the
exclusive, or even primary, location of politics. Secondly, it highlights a further
gap between our dominant paradigm of law and the empirical workings of law.
This challenges the core idea of liberal legal theory that the state is the exclusive,
or even primary, source of law.

The emergence of the global economy provides the context for these
challenges. In particular, the ascendancy of the Washington consensus has led
to a reappraisal of the role of the state, as redistributive economic management
has given way to greater reliance on the market and private enterprise.[1] These
economic changes also have an important 'political dimension'[2] leading to
the claim that economic liberalisation has provoked a 'transformation [of]
sovereignty.'[3] The success of the modern state was predicated on 'its ability to
promote economic well-being, to maintain physical security and to foster a
distinctive cultural identity of its citizens.'[4] However, it is this notion of sovereignty, conceived in terms of the state's capacity to exercise political power,
which is seen as increasingly under threat in the globalizing world.

The contention that the state is no longer the principal container of politics
has important implications for rights constitutionalism. If constitutional law is
concerned with how political power is constituted,[5] and if constitutional rights

---

[1] See TL Ilgen, 'Reconfigured Sovereignty in the Age of Globalization' in TL Ilgen (ed),
Reconfigured Sovereignty: Multi-Layered Governance in the Global Age (Aldershot, Ashgate, 2003)
6, 6.

[2] M Kahler and DA Lake, 'Globalization and Governance' in M Kahler and DA Lake,
Governance in a Global Economy: Political Authority in Transition (Princeton and Oxford,
Princeton University Press, 2003) 1, 4.

[3] S Sassen, *Losing Control? Sovereignty in an Age of Globalization* (New York, Columbia
University Press, 1996) 14.

[4] M Loughlin, *Sword and Scales: An Examination of the Relationship Between Law and Politics*
(Oxford and Portland, OR, Hart Publishing, 2000) 145.

[5] See D Castiglione, 'The Political Theory of the Constitution' (1996) 44 *Political Studies* 417,
421–22.

are concerned with protecting the autonomy of the individual,[6] then the fact of significant sites of private power questions the relevance of an approach that focuses on the state alone. In this chapter, I set out the case that globalization is effecting a shift of authority from the state to the actors and institutions of the global economy. I outline first, with reference to the implementation of neo-liberal economic and political reforms, the changing role, and relative decline, of the state. I then discuss the rise in the power of large corporations, and show how these are influencing and in some cases supplanting the political functions of the state. I conclude that this reshaping of political power threatens the orthodoxy that 'economic as opposed to political sites do not provide generative contexts for constitutional discourse.'[7]

THE WASHINGTON CONSENSUS AND THE CHANGING ROLE OF THE STATE

While globalization studies have rapidly extended to virtually every corner of social science research, this salience can be part of the difficulty of engaging with the subject.[8] The wide range of fields covered by globalization—whether economics, politics, culture, or others—and the diversity of arguments this raises, poses the question of whether globalization is an empty 'buzzword'. However, this need not lead us to abandon the study of globalization, but instead to be clear as to what we understand by globalization, and our purposes in employing the term. Here, I focus on contemporary changes in global political economy associated with the rise of the ideas and practices known in shorthand as the Washington consensus. This is not to say that economic developments are the only facet of globalization,[9] or that globalization only dates from the past ten to fifteen years.[10] Rather, my argument is that the broader acceptance and implementation of neoliberal ideas from the 1990s onwards should be seen as the major factor contributing to the reconfiguration of political power, and as such is the aspect of globalization that requires the most urgent attention of constitutional discourse.

Perhaps the only point of agreement in the globalization literature is that the term itself is 'an essentially contested concept.'[11] David Held et al identify three

[6] See R Dworkin, *A Matter of Principle* (Cambridge, MA, Harvard University Press, 1978) ch 8.
[7] N Walker, 'The EU and the WTO: Constitutionalism in a New Key' in G de Búrca and J Scott (eds), *The EU and the WTO: Legal and Constitutional Issues* (Oxford and Portland, OR, Hart Publishing, 2001) 31, 37, fn 17.
[8] S Strange, *The Retreat of the State* (Cambridge, Cambridge University Press, 1997) xii.
[9] See JH Mittelman, 'Globalization: Captors and Captives' in JH Mittelman and N Othman (eds), *Capturing Globalization* (London, Routledge, 2001) 1, 12.
[10] See, eg, SE Merry, 'Globalizations Past: From Lahaina to London in the 1820s' in J Jenson and B de Sousa Santos (eds), *Globalizing Institutions: Case Studies in Social Regulation and Innovation* (Aldershot, Ashgate, 2000) 81.
[11] W Grant, 'Globalization, Big Business and the Blair Government' (2000) CSGR Working Paper No 58/00, Centre for the Study of Globalization and Regionalisation, University of Warwick.

broad schools of thought on economic globalization[12]: the hyperglobalists, for whom the world is now a 'borderless' single market where nation-states are becoming obsolete[13]; sceptics, who emphasise the continuing importance and power of nation-states,[14] and who cast current economic phenomena more as 'regionalisation' or 'internationalisation'; and transformationalists, who regard globalization as the source of radical societal changes, which are circumscribing, but not eliminating, state sovereignty in an increasingly interconnected world.[15] In particular, they argue that 'the notion of the nation-state as a self-governing, autonomous unit appears to be more a normative claim than a descriptive statement.'[16] The position I adopt is closest to that of the transformationalists, that as a result of wide-ranging social and economic processes, we are witnessing a qualitative change in societal organisation and functioning.

The nature of these changes is articulated by Anthony Giddens as 'the intensification of world-wide social relations which link distant localities in such a way that local happenings are shaped by events occurring many miles away and vice versa.'[17] Boaventura de Sousa Santos distinguishes two forms of global interconnection: '*globalized localism*' which is 'the process by which a given local phenomenon is successfully globalized'—for example, the global spread of US popular culture—and '*localized globalism*' which connotes 'the specific impact of transnational practices and imperatives on local conditions that are thereby destructured and restructured in order to respond to transnational imperatives'[18]—such as the emergence of free trade areas. If globalization is the transnational extension and habituation of local ideas and practices, which ideas and practices are taking on this global character?

One of the dominant features of globalization was the ascendancy in the 1990s of the Washington consensus, which represented 'a tacit but powerful agreement'[19] among political, business and academic elites on neoliberal economic and political reform. This consensus sought to supplant Keynesian ideas based on the imperative of state intervention with neo-classical economic ideas of the minimal state and the deregulated market. Having developed first in the UK and US in the 1980s, neoliberal policies such as fiscal constraint, free trade, reduced welfare spending and lower taxation, were soon endorsed by governments across the industrialised world,[20] in the transitional economies of Latin

---

[12] D Held, A McGrew, D Goldblatt and J Perraton, *Global Transformations: Politics, Economics and Culture* (Cambridge, Polity Press, 1999) 3–10.

[13] *Ibid* at 3.

[14] *Ibid* at 5.

[15] *Ibid* at 8.

[16] *Ibid*.

[17] A Giddens, *The Consequences of Modernity* (Stanford, CA, Stanford University Press, 1990) 64.

[18] B de Sousa Santos, *Toward a New Legal Common Sense* (London, Butterworths, 2002) 179.

[19] H Arthurs, 'The Re-constitution of the Public Domain' in D Drache (ed), *The Market or the Public Domain? Global Governance and the Asymmetry of Power* (London, Routledge, 2001) 85, 85.

[20] D Slater and F Tonkiss, *Market Society: Markets and Modern Social Theory* (Oxford, Polity Press, 2001) 137.

America and Central and Eastern Europe,[21] and also in the developing world.[22] Accordingly, by the end of the 1990s, one could identify a worldwide shift 'away from an emphasis on state economic management and service provision, to an ethos of "privatism" in the provisioning and regulation of social and economic life.'[23]

For some, the global reach of a 'neoliberal economic consensus'[24] is exaggerated,[25] while others suggest that its scope is more thinly conceived than is often thought.[26] Indeed, contemporary critical scholarship argues against regarding neoliberalism as the inevitable form of economic globalization,[27] and is beginning to imagine what a post-Washington consensus world may resemble.[28] However, it is compatible to resist the idea of the Washington consensus as irreversible, but hold that it continues to provide the baselines for political debate. For example, any constituency that seeks to readjust the balance between the state and the market has to contend with 'the desire of powerful economic actors for low taxes, open markets and acquiescent labour.'[29] Perhaps the most important artefact of the Washington consensus—and which in many ways remains the default position against which counter proposals have to vie—is a qualitative shift in perception over the role of the state.

This is manifested in a three-fold diffusion of state power: first, by 'shrinking the state,'[30] whether by limiting the policy levers it can deploy to influence macroeconomic policy—eg, by handing over to central banks the power to fix interest rates—or by 'hollowing out' the state of its former functions. The acceleration in the latter process in recent years has been marked: whereas privatisation was initially visited on utilities[31] and ancillary services in the public sector, it has more recently been extended to what might once have been seen as core public services such as social security,[32] law and order[33] and air traffic

---

[21] See A Przeworski et al, *Sustainable Democracy* (Cambridge, Cambridge University Press, 1995) ch 5.

[22] MS Grindle, 'Ready or Not: The Developing World and Globalization' in JS Nye and JD Donahue (eds), *Governance in a Globalizing World* (Washington, Brookings Institution Press, 2000) ch 8.

[23] Slater and Tonkiss, above n 20, at 137.

[24] Santos, above n 18, at 314.

[25] See PA Hall and D Soskice, *Varieties of Capitalism: the Institutional Foundations of Comparative Advantage* (London and New York, Oxford University Press, 2001) 56–60.

[26] See M Rhodes and B van Apeldoorn, 'Capital unbound? The Transformation of European Corporate Governance' (1998) 5 *Journal of European Public Policy* 406.

[27] R Falk, *Predatory Globalization: A Critique* (Oxford, Polity Press, 1999) 2.

[28] See, eg, Drache (ed), above n 19.

[29] Arthurs, above n 19, at 106

[30] H Feigenbaum, J Henig and C Hamett, *Shrinking the State: The Political Underpinnings of Privatization* (Cambridge, Cambridge University Press, 1998) 2.

[31] See, eg, C Graham and T Prosser, '"Rolling Back the Frontiers"? The Privatisation of State Enterprises' in C Graham and T Prosser (eds), *Waiving the Rules: The Constitution Under Thatcherism* (Milton Keynes, Open University Press, 1988) ch 5.

[32] See N Harris, *Social Security Law in Context* (Oxford, Oxford University Press, 2000) 9.

[33] One report states that as of September 2001, there were '142,521 beds in 181 facilities under contract or construction as private secure adult facilities in US, UK, and Australia': http://www.ucc.uconn.edu/~logan/

control.[34] As a result, private corporations are now frequently the immediate means of delivering services to the public.

Secondly, the shift of functions from public to private hands, also seeks to reorient our view of the political nature of these functions. Public policy now often engages with issues such as the provision of pensions, or the building of prisons, or investment in air traffic control, not in the political vocabulary of the equitable allocation of resources, but rather in the 'technical' vocabulary of efficiency and effectiveness.[35] This underlines that privatisation is not simply a transfer of control from a minister to a CEO: it also involves downgrading the public interest in guiding the delivery of these services.[36] As David Kennedy puts it, this '[t]echnocratic governance, a displacement of public by private, of political alignments by economic rivalries [has] shrivelled the range of the politically contestable.'[37] The corollary is that those functions remaining in state hands are also to be carried out according to market principles.[38] Thus, political power is not only diffused, but narrowed, further restricting the scope for the interventionist state.

The third, and most significant, development affecting the state is the emergence of the global economy. The successful pursuit of economic liberalisation, allied to technological innovations, has led to an intensification of global economic integration. There is now considerable evidence that domestic economies are more intertwined with and open to each other than at any previous stage of history, as indicated for example by the unprecedented scale of currency transfers[39] or foreign investment.[40] Saskia Sassen captures the resultant relocation of political decision-making as a 'new geography of power' whose key actors and sites include global capital markets, transnational legal firms, new forms for regulating global business such as international commercial arbitration, and electronic economic activity.[41] The global economy also affects decisions made by states, whose interests are now ever more closely linked to the operation of global market forces. For example, global financial markets not only render

---

[34] See Department of Transport, *Transport Act 2000: Public/Private Partnership for National Air Traffic Services Ltd* (Report to Parliament, March 2001): http://www.aviation.dft.gov.uk/nats/pr0103/index.htm.

[35] See Slater and Tonkiss, above n 20, at 138–43.

[36] For a discussion of these concerns in the context of air traffic control in the UK, see House of Commons, Transport, Local Government and the Regions Committee, 1999/2000, Third Report, HC—35, *The Proposed Public-Private Partnership for National Air Traffic Services Ltd* (paras 20–37): http://www.publications.parliament.uk/pa/cm199900/cmselect/cmenvtra/35/3507.htm#a8

[37] D Kennedy, 'The Forgotten Politics of International Governance' [2001] *European Human Rights Law Review* 117, 120.

[38] See M Freedland, 'Public Law and Private Finance—Placing the Private Finance Initiative in a Public Law Frame' [1998] *Public Law* 288 and C Harlow and R Rawlings, *Law and Administration*, 2nd edn (London, Butterworths, 1997) 133–38.

[39] Held et al, above n 12, at 208.

[40] D Held and A McGrew, *The Global Transformations Reader: An Introduction to the Globalization Debate*, 2nd edn (Cambridge, Polity Press, 2003) 25.

[41] Sassen, above n 3, at 1 and 5–6.

national economies vulnerable to large-scale currency speculation,[42] but in assigning credit ratings to states with a view to influencing inward investment, also potentially inhibit their choice of action across 'all areas of policy, not just macro-economic policy.'[43]

In these ways, the global economy undermines the idea that political power resides exclusively, or even primarily, with the state; however, this does not mean that the state has ceased to be important. For one thing, the state remains necessary in providing the infrastructure for global capitalism.[44] Rather, globalization requires us to rethink our view of the state, and its relation to the exercise of political power. It is not the case that globalization makes states the simple tool of neoliberalism, but that as the former 'transforms the conditions under which wealth is created and distributed, it simultaneously transforms the context in which, and the instruments through which, state power and authority is exercised.'[45] Sassen suggests that this should not lead to the conclusion that sovereignty has not been eroded, but rather that it has been transformed and relocated in 'a multiplicity of institutional arenas.'[46] My argument is that the principal corollary of a reconfigured state is the elevation of multinational corporations as major political actors on the global stage.

GLOBAL CORPORATE POWER?

Multinational corporations (MNCs) are regarded by many as the driving force behind the global economy.[47] However, debate ranges over the scale and reach of corporate power. The sceptical objection covers two points: first, through an analysis of economic data, that MNC activity is largely nationally based, and that at most we are witnessing a period of internationalisation not globalization,[48] and secondly, that while nation-states may be complicit in any rise of corporate power, they possess the upper hand in terms of their power to regulate corporate activity.[49] It is therefore important to look at the evidence. I will argue

---

[42] Held et al, above n 12, at 228.

[43] C Leys, *Market-Driven Politics: Neoliberal Democracy and the Public Interest* (London, Verso, 2001) 22: 'Even matters that might once have seemed purely the province of politics, such as professional training and qualifications, or the protection of the national language, can turn out to be of concern to "the market", not to mention matters as vital to investors as proposals to tighten the regulation of money markets or to impose new obligations on the managers of pension funds (*ibid*).'

[44] There is an interesting contrast between the 'deregulatory' rhetoric of neoliberalism, and its reliance on the state to survive and flourish. It is often noted that the development of global capitalism is far from the spontaneous outburst of activity as envisaged by classical liberal theorists such as Hayek, but rather an organised process, where, in order for the state not to intervene in the economy, it has to intervene in the economy (see Santos, above n 18, at 412).

[45] Held et al, above n 12, at 281–82.

[46] Above n 3, at 30.

[47] See Held and McGrew, above n 40, at 26.

[48] See Held et al, above n 12, at 261.

[49] See P Hirst and G Thompson, *Globalization in Question: The International Economy and the Possibilities of Governance* (Cambridge, Polity Press, 1996) 98.

that MNCs now exert global influence in terms of their *modi operandi*, and that the material changes wrought by globalization have resulted in 'a complex inter-relationship between corporate and state power' which 'enhances the global power of corporate capital.'[50]

Quantitative Analyses of Corporate Power

Globalization-sceptics, like Paul Hirst and Grahame Thompson, ground their case in the observation that corporations remain organised at a national level. In support, they cite evidence such as data on the (relatively low) proportion of cross-border economic activity, the national composition of boards of directors, and the extent to which activities such as research and development, production and sales are still municipally-based (and also the location of assets and profits). They conclude that claims as to the unique globalizing character of the present epoch are overstated.[51] Hyperglobalists, like Kenichi Ohmae, on the other hand, portray a world of 'footloose' corporations, detached from any sense of national domicile, able and willing to locate and produce anywhere.[52] It is unnecessary to adopt the latter position to disagree with the sceptics' position that there is no serious agglomeration of corporate power as a result of contemporary economic processes.[53]

The case that we are experiencing a significant augmentation in corporate power relies on a number of indicators which highlight the increasingly global nature of MNC activity. Leslie Sklair here makes a helpful distinction between international and globalizing corporations: the former have a strong national base allied to a number of foreign subsidiaries, while the latter are 'denational-izing from their domestic origin' and are embracing 'genuinely global strategies of operation.'[54] His argument is that those who eschew the recent vintage of globalization conflate internationalisation with globalization, and thereby fail to see the significance of contemporary phenomena for the constellation of economic power. This case is supported by analyses which highlight the increas-ingly transnational mode of organising production and distribution[55] which now make global corporate networks a reality.[56] For example, the car industry has moved from attempts to resist US expansion by promoting 'national cham-pions' in the postwar period to the present situation where firms sell 40 per cent of car production abroad.[57] While such networks can be found at other stages

---

[50] Held et al, above n 12, at 281.
[51] See *ibid* at 261.
[52] *Ibid.*
[53] *Ibid* at 269–70.
[54] L Sklair, *The Transnational Capitalist Class* (Oxford, Blackwell, 2001) 48.
[55] See Held et al, above n 12 at 255, and JH Mittelman, 'The Dynamics of Globalization' in JH Mittleman (ed), *Globalization: Critical Reflections* (Boulder, CO, Lynne Rienner, 1996) 1, 6–7.
[56] See Held et al, above n 12 at 259–70.
[57] *Ibid* at 263.

of human history, it is claimed that the present globalizing era is 'greater in scope, reach and intensity,' not least because of the technological innovations of the digital age which further compress business time and space.[58]

Sklair provides some empirical support for the globalizing thesis. Combining analysis of the *Fortune* Global 500 companies,[59] with interviews with corporate executives, he shows how these companies no longer perceive themselves as 'national companies operating abroad,' but as 'globalising corporations.'[60] For example, Mitsui, originally founded in Japan, stated in its 1996 annual report that its main goal was to expand 'its presence and scope as a global enterprise.'[61] Sklair notes that the two 'megatrends' that were central to Mitsui's activities were the globalization of market principles, and 'the advanced global information network society' that is rendering national boundaries more and more obsolete: in response, it has changed its traditional role of distributing products and services, and is increasingly 'a global entrepreneur'.[62] He also finds considerable indications of globalizing organisation vis-à-vis utility companies,[63] which, given their historic attachment to national economies, he regards as an important indicator of the global economy.[64] His conclusions are that corporations feel compelled to globalize to succeed in the new economy, and to satisfy a 'shareholder-driven growth imperative.'[65]

Research has shown how these structural changes have gone hand in hand with a greater reach and intensity[66] of corporate activity. Some studies highlight

---

[58] S Gill, 'Globalization, Democratization, and the Politics of Indifference' in Mittelman (ed), above n 55, 205 at 209.

[59] Taking the 1996 list as his base, Sklair's analysis of the economic indicators confirms the scale of the corporate sector as per the OECD and IPS data: in 1996, the revenues of the Global 500 companies amounted to $US11 trillion, with combined assets of $US32 trillion: above n 54, at 39.

[60] *Ibid* at 47–80. Referring, for example, to Hirst and Thompson (above n 49), Sklair notes that those sceptical about the existence of genuinely global processes tend to reach their conclusions 'on the basis of aggregate data on such indicators as the proportion of total economic activity that crosses state borders, the lack of foreign members of boards of directors, comparisons with previous periods in history, and national economic systems' (Sklair, *ibid* at 47). While not discounting the potential usefulness of these indicators, Sklair argues (at 35) that an analysis based on the Global 500 has the advantages of concentrating on: '(a) actual corporations rather than aggregate financial flows, (b) the actual business of these corporations . . . and, (c) size and relationship to the globalizing of corporations.'

[61] Quoted in *The Transnational Capitalist Class*, at 52.

[62] *Ibid*.

[63] *Ibid* at 65–67. For example, in his analysis of Edison International (formerly Southern California Edison), he notes that this company has altered its mode of operation as a consequence of its likely reduced share of the Californian market in light of deregulation, and has made a number of overseas acquisitions, including First Hydro in north Wales. However, Sklair argues (*ibid* at 65) that '[i]t is difficult to see how First Hydro could in any way be considered a unit abroad of Edison International.' Similarly, in the field of telecommunications, he suggests that changes in the activities of AT&T are characteristic of the process of globalisation. He places this company on a 'continuum' where in the 1970s it could be seen as a national concern with units operating abroad, whereas in the 1990s, he notes (*ibid* at 66) it 'reflected the corporate consensus that most major corporations were attempting to globalize.'

[64] *Ibid* at 40.

[65] *Ibid* at 73.

[66] Held et al, above n 12, at 245.

the global nature of corporate activity by adverting to levels of foreign direct Investment. For example, UNCTAD's *World Investment Reports*[67] in the late 1990s reveal that the extent of global corporate investment had 'reached record levels'[68] such that MNC activity could be detected not just in the industrialised west, but in the former Warsaw Pact and throughout the developing world (and significantly in Latin America and East Asia). For Held et al, this data suggests that in the 1990s, 'few economies were outside the reach of MNC activity and global production networks.'[69] Stilpon Nestor, former head of corporate affairs at the OECD, attests to the tighter nexus between corporate activity and individuals, commenting that 'the role of the private sector corporation as an engine of economic development and job creation has been vested with a new urgency and importance in the last two decades.'[70]

Other studies emphasise the greater intensity of corporate activity since the 1990s. For example, new productive investment doubled from the 1980s to the early 1990s,[71] and the number of interfirm agreements rose from 1700 in 1990 to 4600 by 1995.[72] Others cast this greater intensity in more dramatic terms. In its 1999 analysis of the world's leading 200 corporations,[73] the Washington-based think-tank, the Institute for Policy Studies, shows that 51 of the world's largest economies (measured in terms of corporate sales against GDP) are corporations. As a direct comparison, it suggests that General Motors, Royal Dutch/Shell and Sony are bigger than Denmark, Venezuela and Pakistan respectively.[74] For some though, these comparisons are inapposite and taken together with the other indicia outlined above, do not make the case for increased global corporate power.[75] It is therefore necessary to supplement these more quantitative analyses with a qualitative assessment of global corporate power.

Qualitative Analyses of Corporate Power

The qualitative objection to theses of globalizing corporate power rests in an assertion of the continuing vitality of state sovereignty. On this account, states

[67] UNCTAD, *World Investment Report 1996: Investment, Trade and International Policy Arrangements* (New York, United Nations, 1996); UNCTAD, *World Investment Report 1997: Transnational Corporations, Market Structure and Competition Policy* (New York, United Nations, 1997); UNCTAD, *World Investment Report 1998: Trends and Development, Overview* (New York, United Nations, 1998): discussed in Held et al, above n 12, at 243–45.

[68] Held et al, above n 12, at 243.

[69] *Ibid* at 244.

[70] S Nestor, 'International Efforts to Improve Corporate Governance: Why and How' (Paris, OECD, 2001).

[71] Held et al, above n 12, at 246, referring to UNCTAD, *World Investment Report 1996*, above n 67, at 16.

[72] Held et al, *ibid* at 247, referring to UNCTAD, *World Investment Report 1997*, above n 67, at 5–6.

[73] S Anderson and J Cavanagh, *The Top 200: The Rise of Corporate Global Power* (Washington, Institute for Policy Studies, 1999): http://www.ips-dc.org/reports/top200text.htm.

[74] Furthermore, 'the Top 200 corporations' combined sales are bigger than the combined economies of all countries minus the biggest 10' (*ibid*).

[75] See, eg, M Wolf, 'Sleep Walking with the Enemy' *Financial Times*, 16 May 2001: http://news.ft.com/ft/gx.cgi/ftc?pagename=View&c=Art&cid=FT3FVM66SMC&live=true

exercise sovereign power in a vertical relationship with their subjects, including corporations. However, it is problematical to conceive of them as either completely separate from, or subordinate to, the state. For example, on the one hand, police responses to anti-globalization demonstrations in Seattle and Genoa seem to demonstrate the continuing reality and presence of state power. However, although the means of organised violence remains (principally) in state hands, the threat of police and military force operates to prevent the world economy destabilising, and so also works to shore up corporate interests.[76] Rather, there is a more complex relationship between states and MNCs, sometimes one of co-operation,[77] at others one of competition,[78] but which in the context of the global economy is best characterised by a significant augmentation in the power of MNCs vis-à-vis nation states. This is manifested in three principal ways: through influencing state political processes, through taking over the role of the state, and through the institutional framework of the global economy.

The State-Corporate Nexus

The state-corporate nexus emphasises the close relations between states and corporations, and the extent to which the latter are implicated in policy making and execution. A growing body of social science literature has highlighted the institutional links between corporations and government. In the age of the global economy, it would be surprising if the views and decisions of the CEOs of multinationals did not have a significance beyond the boardroom. However, it is equally important to emphasise the more formal ways in which corporations are 'increasingly international political actors.'[79] For example, it is now commonplace for transnational firms to have their own 'embassies' and representatives prosecuting their interests, in major centres of political power, such as Washington[80] or Brussels.[81] Also, corporations are mobilising as a political group. David Korten recounts how since the early 1970s, US-based transnational corporations have formed organisations such as the Business Roundtable,[82] which consists of business leaders, including the CEOs of an important cross section of the Fortune 500,[83] and which conduct 'aggressive

---

[76] R W Cox, 'A Perspective on Globalization' in Mittelman (ed) above n 55, 21 at 23.

[77] See Sklair, above n 54, at 84.

[78] As Leys notes, most states, particularly in the run up to elections, still see the reduction of unemployment as a political priority, which might seem to contradict their general support for neoliberalism: above n 43, at 26.

[79] W Grant, *Business and Politics in Britain* (Basingstoke, Macmillan, 1993, rev edn) 85.

[80] DC Korten, *When Corporations Rule the World* (San Francisco, Berrett-Koehler, 1995) 143.

[81] Above n 79, at 85.

[82] Korten, above n 80, at 142–45.

[83] *Ibid* at 144.

campaigns' to promote their interests in the political process.[84] Similar organisations exist in Canada[85] and the UK.[86]

The most visible link between states and corporations is probably the practice of business donations to political parties. In the US, it is estimated that in the 2000 presidential elections, corporate donations to campaigns through official political action committees totalled around $259.8 million, before including the 'soft money' which is given overwhelmingly from the corporate sector.[87] Constitutional law tends to deal with this issue in terms of capping expenditure in the aim of securing greater electoral equality. However, there is little in the constitutional literature about how corporate donations do impact on the policy-making process. In this regard, research such as Thomas Ferguson's into the dollars-votes connection in the US adds to our practical knowledge of constitutional law. Ferguson suggests that there is a link between corporate financial support and the direction of public policy. In an extensive analysis of US electoral history, he argues that 'political changes are usually—but not always—intimately involved with shifts in the balance of power among . . . large investors.'[88] One of the consequences of this increasingly close relationship is the blurring of business and governmental personnel.[89] While the cash-politics nexus may historically have been associated primarily with the US—not an insignificant phenomenon given the scale of US capital and political

---

[84] *Ibid* at 145.

[85] See T Clarke, *Silent Coup: Confronting the Big Business Takeover of Canada* (Toronto, James Lorimer & Co, 1997) 20.

[86] See J Boswell and J Peters, *Capitalism in Contention: Business Leaders and Political Economy in Modern Britain* (Cambridge, Cambridge University Press, 1997) 179.

[87] http://www.fec.gov/press/press2001/053101pacfund/053101pacfund.html. See T Ferguson, *The Golden Rule: The Investment Theory of Party Competition and the Logic of Money-Driven Political Systems* (Chicago and London, University of Chicago Press, 1995) 351. Ferguson estimates that just over a third of monies donated in Senate races, and a quarter to House campaigns, come from PACs; as far as Presidential elections are concerned, Ferguson argues that the role of PACs is 'insignificant' as the vast majority of campaign finance comes directly from individual and corporate donations.

[88] *Ibid* at 87. Ferguson discusses the 1992 election of Bill Clinton in this context, noting (*ibid* at 297) that from the start, the Clinton campaign had strong business support in his own state of Arkansas, including Tyson Foods, Murphy Oil, Wal-Mart, Beverley Enterprises, 'and the investment banking and oil interests associated with the Stephens family.' Other businesses also lent their support, including the investment house, Goldman, Sachs. Ferguson suggests (*ibid* at 298) that the interests of the businesses for Clinton differed only marginally from those which had supported the previous Bush administration: 'Together with the myriad of Washington lobbyists for US and foreign multinationals who contributed heavily to the campaign . . . these interests virtually guaranteed what in any case rapidly became obvious: that the Clinton campaign accepted free trade and an open world economy as its fundamental strategic premise.' For Ferguson (*ibid* at 275), the success of business in securing their agenda in the Clinton presidency was revealed in the economic plan announced in February 1993, which saw 'President Clinton reverse candidate Clinton's priority of economic growth over deficit reduction.'

[89] Ferguson, for example, refers (*ibid* at 275–76) to Bill Clinton's appointment of Robert Rudin, an executive with Goldman, Sachs, to head his National Economic Council, and Lawrence Summers as treasury undersecretary for international affairs, as symptomatic of 'an economic team that looked like Wall Street.'

power—concerns over the link between big money and politics have grown in other G7 countries, including Italy, Japan, France, Germany and the UK.[90]

The Corporate-State Nexus

The corporate-state nexus speaks to how, at the national level, corporations are bypassing states as the direct provider of legislative and executive functions. The argument that corporations exhibit state-like characteristics has been made historically, for example, by highlighting how entities like the British East India Company circulated its own currency and possessed a distinct military capability,[91] or by showing how nineteenth century common law doctrines regarded the corporation as 'a body politic.'[92] We can update this to the present age by showing that in many areas of social life, decisions of multinational companies are the direct source of political decisions affecting citizens' daily lives, and not their national governments. Some approach this by focusing on the scale of corporate power as revealed through its abuse,[93] whether by the commission of corporate crimes,[94] health and safety failings,[95] or environmental exploitation,[96] each of which would be a major scandal if carried out by agents of the state. Others document that where the state no longer does or can act as functionary, corporations have acquired 'quasi-governmental'[97] or 'quasi-state'[98] roles. Noreena Hertz, for example, has shown how corporations are increasingly taking on the role of the state themselves:

> In Nigeria, for example, Shell spent $[US]52 million in 1999 on a social investment programme, building schools, hospitals, roads and bridges, supplying electricity and water to areas that the government effectively abandoned in the early 1980s. In fact, the company now employs more development specialists than the government.[99]

In other cases, corporations are assuming traditional state functions as 'welfare providers and social engineers, environmentalists and mediators.'[100]

The idea that corporations are major political actors is being accepted within the corporate world through the discourse of corporate social responsibility

---

[90] *Ibid* at 352.

[91] Held et al, above n 12, at 239.

[92] A Fraser, 'The Corporation as a Body Politic' (1983) 57 *Telos* 6 at 7.

[93] See generally, MB Clinard, *Corporate Corruption: The Abuse of Power* (New York, Praeger, 1990) ch 1.

[94] See, eg, P Gabrosky and A Sutton (eds), *Stains on a White Collar: Fourteen studies in Corporate Crime or Corporate Harm* (Sydney, Federation Press, 1989).

[95] Clinard, above n 93, at 91.

[96] *Ibid* at 44–47.

[97] D Litvin, *Empires of Profit: Commerce, Conquest and Corporate Responsibility* (New York, Texere, 2003) 269.

[98] N Hertz, *The Silent Takeover: Global Capitalism and the Death of Democracy* (London, Heinemann, 2001) 186.

[99] *Ibid* at 173.

[100] *Ibid* at 172.

(CSR). Sometimes framed as corporate citizenship,[101] this goes beyond the 'minimal' requirements of corporate citizenship, ie, compliance with state company law, and also focuses on 'a complex relationship of interlocking rights and responsibilities [between a corporation and its communities].'[102] Instead of purely economic concerns, this discourse speaks in terms of human rights and environmental standards which have generally been seen as applicable solely to states. This thinking is reflected, for example, in the preamble to the OECD Principles of Corporate Governance, which explains that part of their rationale is that 'factors such as business ethics and corporate awareness of environmental and societal interests of the communities in which they operate can also have an impact on the reputation and long-term success of a company.'[103] While some doubt the motives behind CSR,[104] these developments are emblematic of how, when corporations effectively act like states, this will raise questions over their political accountability.

The Constitutional Framework of the Global Economy

The third way in which MNCs' influence over nation-states is made concrete is the establishment of supranational institutions designed by states to police the global economy. One of the paradoxes of the present age is the extent to which states have created the machinery for limiting their capacity to intervene in economic affairs. The most significant development in this regard is the coming into force of the World Trade Organization (WTO) in 1995, characterised by Held et al as an 'intensification of global economic surveillance.'[105] The WTO represents three important differences from the General Agreement on Tariffs and Trade (GATT) established at Bretton Woods, from which it developed: first, it expands the list of measures included in the GATT agreements;[106] secondly, it contemplates trade now as a global system, rather than simply as agreements between nation-states; and thirdly, it effected an important shift in the guiding criteria for global trade policy, prioritising commercial over other policy concerns.[107] In short, the WTO attempts to set down the 'constitutional structure' of the contemporary world trading system.[108]

[101] See M McIntosh, D Leipziger, K Jones and G Coleman, *Corporate Citizenship: Successful Strategies for Responsible Companies* (London, Financial Times, 1998).

[102] *Ibid* at xxi.

[103] OECD Directorate for Financial, Fiscal and Enterprise Affairs (Ad Hoc Task Force on Corporate Governance), *OECD Principles of Corporate Governance* (Paris, OECD, 1999).

[104] See, eg, Hertz, above n 98, at 176–84.

[105] Held et al, above n 12, at 426.

[106] These now include trade in services, trade related intellectual property measures, trade related investment measures and trade in agricultural goods: see JH Jackson, *The World Trading System: Law and Policy of International Economic Relations*, 2nd edn (Cambridge, MA, MIT Press, 1997) 305–17.

[107] L Wallach, 'The World Trade Organization's Five Year Record: Seattle in Context' in E Goldsmith and J Mander (eds), *The Case Against the Global Economy and For a Turn Towards Localization* (London, Earthscan, 2001) 175 at 177–78.

[108] Jackson, above n 106, at 11.

At the heart of the WTO agreements is a powerful dispute settlement process, which has been described as the 'linchpin' of the whole trading system.[109] Although initiated by states as WTO members, claims under this process are often brought on behalf of MNCs,[110] and in practice have been an important outlet for the exercise of corporate political power. The WTO Dispute Settlement Body (DSB), generally regarded as more comprehensive in scope than the previous GATT procedures,[111] hears complaints from member states over alleged 'infringement of the obligations' under any of the WTO agreements,[112] principally that states have erected tariff or non-tariff barriers to the liberalisation of trade. If the DSB finds a state has acted inconsistently with WTO agreements, the primary form of redress is for that member to bring its national law into compliance,[113] or face having to pay compensation[114] or withdrawal of WTO concessions.[115] As such, the WTO can be differentiated from other international agreements in terms of its potentially coercive powers of enforcement. The DSB has not been shy to use these powers: for example, it has ruled that an EU decision to ban US beef injected with (potential carcinogenic) artificial hormones,[116] Canadian attempts to give tax advantages to domestically produced magazines,[117] and the US federal law that required imported shrimp to be caught by methods which protected sea turtles,[118] all illegally restricted free trade as set down in the WTO agreements, and ordered the parties concerned to amend their laws or face further sanctions. In this way, the WTO and its mechanisms effectively open themselves to act as a proxy for the exercise of corporate power.[119]

Global Corporate Power in Practice

How have MNCs' extensive resources of political power been utilised in practice? This is not a simple case of translating will into might—MNCs, like other political actors, exist in a mediated world of contradictions, unintended and

---

[109] *Ibid* at 124.

[110] Many actions are raised by the US, where, given its leading role in forging the global economy, symbiosis between state and corporate interests is most pronounced. For example, the challenge to the EU ban on beef which had been treated with artificial hormones (WT/DS 26 and 28), Wallach argues, was brought 'by the US at the behest of its agribusiness and pharmaceutical interests' (above n 107, at 179).

[111] Jackson, above n 106, at 125.

[112] Art 3, para 8 of the *Understanding on Rules and Procedures Governing the Settlement of Disputes* (being Annex 2 to the *Agreement Establishing the World Trade Organization*): http://ww.wto.org/english/docs_e/legal_e/28-dsu.wpf.

[113] *Ibid*, Art 22, para 1.

[114] *Ibid*, Art 3, para 7.

[115] *Ibid*, Art 22, para 2.

[116] WT/DS 26.

[117] WT/DS 31.

[118] WT/DS 58.

[119] Eg, in the shrimp-turtle case, the main losers under the US Endangered Species Act were the large industrial fishing concerns, who had to bear the cost of adapting boats to meet these standards (small fishing vessels themselves pose relatively little threat to ocean life such as turtles).

unforeseen consequences. However, the important point is that in the global economy, public policy becomes amenable to MNC pressure. In some cases, this takes a more direct form: for example, a joint report by the European Bank for Reconstruction and Development and the World Bank Institute measuring governance and corruption in the transition economies of the former Soviet bloc,[120] found that 'state capture' in the form of buying laws and policies, was prevalent on the part of transnational corporations in order to secure greater market liberalisation.[121] In the developed world, though, the relationship between states and MNCs is often better expressed by the notion of 'regulatory competition' whereby states compete for MNC investment by offering more attractive regulatory regimes.[122] While this does not necessarily lead to the lowest common denominator prevailing in terms of regulatory regimes, it does mean that states no longer have the final say, as there is always the possibility of a lower standard being adopted elsewhere, a contingency which MNCs exploit by sustaining their assault on (to them) unfavourable regulations.[123]

In a number of important areas, it is clear that MNCs have been successful in reorienting regulatory regimes to their interests. Take, for example, foreign direct investment (FDI). This is very much driven by the interests of MNCs, as it lowers costs and raises profits. However, attracting FDI has also become a central plank of states' policies, through both identifying FDI with economic development and a fear of losing out to other states in the global economy. Accordingly, states have offered a raft of subsidies and inducements to MNCs in the hope of gaining investment.[124] The priority given to winning FDI fuels other important aspects of the corporate agenda: states perceive taxation policy to be a key incentive (or disincentive) to investment, and have reduced both corporation tax and the higher rates of income tax.[125] As well as being of direct

[120] JS Hellman, G Jones, D Kaufman and M Schankerman, *Measuring Governance, Corruption, and State Capture: How Firms and Bureaucrats Shape the Business Environment in Transition Economies* (Washington, EDRB and the World Bank Institute, 2000).

[121] See J Hellman, G Jones and D Kaufman, 'Seize the State, Seize the Day: An Empirical Analysis of State Capture and Corruption in Transition' (paper presented to the World Bank's Annual Conference on Development Economics) http://papers.ssrn.com/sol3/papers.cfm?abstractid= 240555 last accessed Nov 04.

[122] See generally WW Bratton and JA McCahery, 'Regulatory Competition as Regulatory Capture: The Case of Corporate Law in the United States of America' in WW Bratton, J McCahery, S Picciotto, and C Scott (eds), *International Regulatory Competition and Coordination: Perspectives on Economic Regulation in Europe and the United States* (Oxford, Clarendon Press, 1996) 207, 210–17.

[123] Inequality of resources, working in favour of MNCs, is one of the structural features of the global trade regime: eg, George and Wilding note that the poorer members of the WTO from industrially developing countries, have relatively little capacity to influence its processes, as the costs of maintaining a mission at the WTO headquarters, and hiring an international law firm to represent their interests, are so high that they generally are unable to afford them: V George and P Wilding, *Globalization and Human Welfare* (Basingstoke, Palgrave, 2002) 85.

[124] Held et al, above n 12, at 259.

[125] Leys, above n 43, at 25. As Leys observes (*ibid*), in the day-to-day battles of regulatory competition, MNCs generally maintain the upper hand through their financial and technical resources, often in the form of a battery of international corporate lawyers, and so they can wear out 'the usually poorly resourced and frequently amateur public opposition.'

benefit to MNCs on their profit and loss sheets, such policies also support their longer term objectives: for example, increasing the share of revenue from indirect taxation shifts the burden of social security more onto employees.[126] For some, these developments are indicative of a general change from a welfare to a competition state,[127] where the discourse of public policy is conducted less in terms of ameliorating the disruptive consequences of market capitalism and more with 'sustaining and sharpening competitiveness.'[128]

We can find further evidence for the promotion of MNCs' political interests if we adopt a sectoral outlook. Public health is perhaps the leading example of how all three of MNCs' resources of political power reorder its provision to serve corporate interests. First, we can see the influence of the corporate agenda on the public policy process—both indirectly, through the general neoliberal thrust to cut public sector functions and costs,[129] and directly, through the lobbying by the private sector.[130] Whatever the source of the impetus, the result, in the developed economies of the west, has been the widespread opening of health services to market forces, for example, through the adoption of mechanisms like the internal market.[131] Secondly, particularly in the developing world, corporations are becoming the direct source of healthcare for many people, whether by setting up clinics, or running Aids education campaigns.[132] Thirdly, where state reforms have not satisfied corporations' wishes, the WTO framework has provided a further outlet to broaden their influence. For example, the WTO secretariat has argued (in effect on behalf of US healthcare companies seeking to remove the remaining barriers to their full entry to the UK health system) that the General Agreement on Trade and Services (GATS) should extend to health services.[133] Taken together, these actions by MNCs contribute to regarding healthcare in terms of commodification, rather than a universally available public good. We can therefore state that in the globalizing age, corporations can,

---

[126]   See George and Wilding, above n 123, at 58.

[127]   *Ibid* at 61, quoting P Cerny, 'Paradoxes of the Competition State: The Dynamics of Political Globalization' (1997) 32 *Government and Opposition* 251.

[128]   George and Wilding, *ibid* at 61. Compare Hall and Soskice (above n 25) who argue that, contrary to conventional wisdom, business groups have played a key role in the development of welfare states, as 'social policies can improve the operation of labor markets, notably from the perspective of the firm' (*ibid* at 50). However, this point is compatible with the analysis presented in the text, confirming the influence of corporations in the development of public policy. The key question then becomes how this corporate influence affects the context of social policy, and as Hall and Soskice themselves state, '[v]irtually all liberal market economies are accompanied by "liberal" welfare states, whose emphasis on means-testing and low levels of benefits reinforce the fluid labor markets that firms use to manage their relations with labor' (*ibid* at 50/1).

[129]   *Ibid* at 64.

[130]   Leys, above n 43, at 207–08.

[131]   George and Wilding, above n 123, at 63.

[132]   Hertz, above n 98, at 171. As Hertz observes, companies' activities here are not necessarily motivated by compassion, but by how rampant disease in the relatively inexpensive labour markets can affect their profit: '[e]ach employee infected by HIV costs a mining company approximately £10,000 a year once AIDS develops.'

[133]   Leys, above n 43, at 209.

and do, exercise political power on a breadth and scale that renders the idea that they are subordinate to the state's sovereign power increasingly untenable.

THE CHALLENGE FOR RIGHTS CONSTITUTIONALISM

To many schooled in traditional approaches to legal scholarship, it may appear counter-intuitive that a monograph on constitutionalism should open with a discussion of empirical developments in global political economy. Constitutional law, as every student is taught in the first week of law classes, is concerned with the establishment and regulation of the institutions of the state.[134] This entrenches a knowledge of constitutional law which, with a few exceptions,[135] has directed constitutional study away from concerns with private power. This constitutional knowledge reflects the sheer historical weight of the state-centred paradigm,[136] but also the functional consideration that regulating the private sphere is the role of legislative politics rather than constitutional law, and the related pragmatic concern that courts and adjudication may not be conducive to placing effective limits on private power.[137]

However, to the extent that analyses of economic globalization require us to rethink the nature and location of political authority, we can see this knowledge of constitutional law increasingly engaging with the economic realm. Two developments in particular have resulted in (some) constitutional lawyers no longer treating private power as a peripheral issue: first, the extent to which, as a result of the reconfiguration of the state, private actors are now deeply involved in the performance of traditional state functions,[138] and secondly, political concerns over the exercise of private power, and the extent to which this threatens rights constitutionalism's goals of protecting freedom and autonomy.[139] These developments challenge constitutions' ability to 'constitute' in the sense of structuring and regulating the exercise of political power, if they speak only to the institutions of the nation-state. Accordingly, and also reflecting the growing salience of charters of rights in processing political controversies, the constitutional agenda is now moving beyond its traditional boundaries in the nation-state, and is considering how rights constitutionalism can operate as a check on private power.

---

[134] See, eg, AW Bradley and KD Ewing, *Constitutional and Administrative Law*, 13th edn (Harlow, Pearson, 2003) at 3: '[C]onstitutional law concerns the relationship between the individual and the state, seen from a particular viewpoint, namely the notion of law.'

[135] See AS Miller, *The Modern Corporate State: Private Government and the American Constitution* (Westport, CT, Greenwood Press, 1976).

[136] See J Tully, *Strange Multiplicity: Constitutionalism in an Age of Diversity* (Cambridge, Cambridge University Press, 1995) 67–69. See also W Sadurski, 'Liberalism and Constitutionalism' in M Wyrzkowski (ed), *Constitutional Cultures* (Warsaw, Institute of Public Affairs, 2000) 137, 137.

[137] See PW Hogg, 'The Dolphin Delivery Case: The Application of the Charter to Private Action' (1987) 51 *Saskatchewan Law Review* 273, 279.

[138] See J Freeman, 'The Private Role in Public Governance' (2000) 75 *New York University Law Review* 543.

[139] See T Evans, *The Politics of Human Rights: A Global Perspective* (London, Pluto, 2001) ch 3.

Two ways have been proposed as a means of updating rights constitutionalism to respond to the empirical challenge of private power in the global economy. The first seeks to extend the reach of constitutional provisions limiting state action, such as freedom of expression or due process rights, so that they also limit private actors. This generally takes the form of an interpretive argument, and seeks to establish that on a proper reading of provisions on constitutional application, a more extensive range of actions becomes subject to constitutional review. This expansive turn is a reaction to the formalistic approach which applies rights only in the strict vertical relationship between individuals and state institutions. This argument takes a variety of forms, for example that the private actor has been licensed by the state, or that it is performing a governmental function. Accordingly, this opens up the prospect of applying constitutional rights to relations between private parties.

If the first reform seeks to expand the reach of classical negative rights, the second is characterised by an attempt to strengthen positive constitutional protection. This responds to the challenge to constitutionalism's ability to promote freedom and autonomy, by seeking to broaden the scope of constitutional rights. This tends to be expressed in more instrumental terms, and takes seriously the dangers from private power by proposing a thicker conception of constitutional liberty and equality. In practical terms, this emphasises the need for greater positive controls, whether by expanding the set of constitutionally protected rights to include social and economic rights such as the right to health, education and housing, or to place an obligation on the state to act to remedy breaches of constitutional law perpetrated by private actors.

While these proposed reforms move away in part from a state-centred knowledge of constitutional law by addressing the issue of private power, in other important ways they remain firmly within established constitutional epistemology. Debate is joined at how constitutional texts should be interpreted and what values they should promote. It is assumed that what is important is, first, winning the interpretive argument, reflecting the idea that constitutional discourse can be made into a coherent body of normative commands, and, secondly, setting these commands to the correct instrumental coordinates, so that they will act on their subjects to achieve the desired social outcome. As such, these reforms suggest that the issue of private power can be dealt with by adapting our existing constitutional knowledge.

However, making private power a central feature of the constitutional debate raises the stakes more than seems to be realised. In particular, the proposed reforms underestimate how the empirical challenge of economic globalization reveals the extent of the epistemological crisis facing rights constitutionalism. This crisis is provoked by opening up three fundamental assumptions of our received constitutional knowledge to scrutiny. First, the empirical fact of extensive private power raises the general question of the adequacy of the (persistent) view that state law is the exclusive form of legal normativity. Secondly, locating our discussion in the paradigmatic debate of law brings the assumptions underlying the interpretive and instrumental approaches into play, problematising the idea that autonomy can be promoted by enforcing rights before courts. Thirdly, making private power a key element of the debate makes us ask why it was previously excluded, focusing attention on the politics at work in defining constitutionalism in state-centred terms.

The pressing issue for rights constitutionalism in the context of globalization is not simply how to reform constitutional doctrine to deal with the empirical challenge of private power, but rather to confront the implications of the epistemological crisis which the latter provokes and lays bare. This makes the central question for contemporary constitutional scholarship whether existing epistemological structures can deliver any meaningful counterhegemonic engagement with private power. It is therefore important to be clear as to the nature of the epistemological crisis of constitutional law provoked by globalization. Accordingly, we turn now to the terms of the paradigmatic debate of modern law between liberal legalism and legal pluralism.

Part II: Rights Constitutionalism and the Challenge of Legal Pluralism

3

The Paradigmatic Debate: Liberal Legalism and Legal Pluralism

FOR MOST LAWYERS, the question of law never arises—according to the dominant paradigm of liberal legalism, law is exclusively state law, made by legislatures or pronounced by courts. Moreover, it is simply assumed that law is a coherent system of norms that operates directly on society as a tool of social engineering. This paradigm is so deeply ingrained in the legal imagination that to claim, for example, that law exists outside the state, will appear counter-intuitive to many. However, in recent times, there has been renewed interest in the paradigm of legal pluralism, and its account of the multiple forms of state and non-state laws operating in society. Legal pluralism presents three challenges to the dominant knowledge of law: first, to the centralist notion that law only emanates from the state; secondly, to monist ideas of the systematic coherence and singularity of law; and thirdly, to the positivist view that we can trace a legal order as something 'out there' apart from the agents who created it. These challenges set the terms for the paradigmatic debate of modern law.

A number of leading writers contend that an age of globalization makes the claims of legal pluralism a central concern for legal theory.[1] Breaking the link between legal and national culture opens to question how we should conceptualise legal phenomena in contemporary times. Accordingly, the paradigmatic debate asks whether liberal legalism or legal pluralism provides the more helpful intellectual framework for constitutional scholarship, both in terms of comprehension and prescription, for responding to the challenges of globalization. In this chapter I elaborate the terms of the paradigmatic debate, and outline the fundamental challenges of legal pluralism to the epistemological foundations of rights constitutionalism. I first locate liberal legalism in the key doctrine of liberal legal and political theory: the rule of law. I then outline the different phases of legal pluralist scholarship to highlight its historical counter-narrative to the assertion that the state alone provides the test for legal order. I next consider how the principal theoretical explanations for legal pluralism undermine the special characteristics claimed on behalf of rights constitutionalism. In this

---

[1] See B de Sousa Santos, *Toward a New Legal Common Sense* (London, Butterworths, 2002) 92; W Twining, *Globalisation and Legal Theory* (London, Butterworths, 2000) 233; and G Teubner, ' "Global Bukowina": Legal Pluralism in the World Society' in G Teubner (ed), *Global Law Without a State* (Gateshead, Athenaeum Press, 1997) 3.

regard, I distinguish between *external legal pluralism*—which emphasises rights constitutionalism's limited instrumental effectiveness through its interaction with other legal orders—and *internal legal pluralism*—which emphasises how constitutional doctrine, as with all legal orders, tends to be marked by relative disorder. To the extent that the legal pluralist challenges can be sustained, this makes the adequacy of the assumption that rights constitutionalism can operate as a counteregemonic restraint on private power a central part of our inquiry.

LIBERAL LEGALISM

The globalization of rights constitutionalism is more than a globalization of institutional form, but for scholarship also a globalization of method. This method is located in 'an ideal of the autonomy of law' which 'highlights law's adjudicative nature and control functions and therefore its rule orientation and conceptual nature.'[2] This normative methodology rests on a shared set of epistemological assumptions, which we can locate firmly within the dominant paradigm of law in western thought, namely liberal legalism. As this methodology is generally uncritically accepted, the legal knowledge on which it is based tends to be assumed, rather than explained and justified. However, in the globalizing age, the shortcomings of these assumptions are becoming ever more apparent. Accordingly, to clarify the terms of the paradigmatic debate, it is important first to explore and render explicit the epistemological foundations of rights constitutionalism.

Liberal legalism is the dominant paradigm in western legal thought, and informs the popular imagination, as well as the bulk of legal scholarship and practice. In this view, law is formal state law, where the most important actors are lawyers and legislators, and which finds its 'epitome' in 'the court of law and the trial according to law.'[3] It is perhaps most widely regarded as having a normative orientation, which Scott Veitch captures as 'an ethical attitude to how humans do or ought to relate to each other when it comes to their legal relations in community.'[4] This ethical attitude is informed by the need for legal controversies 'to be conducted in accordance with predetermined rules of considerable generality and clarity' (legalism) which seek to promote the moral value of 'independence, or, rather, independence in interdependence, independence in community'[5] (liberalism). It is important to see how liberalism entails legalism (although the converse does not apply): if we wish to protect autonomy, it is

---

[2]   M Loughlin, *Public Law and Political Theory* (Oxford, Clarendon Press, 1992) 60.

[3]   S Veitch, *Moral Conflict and Legal Reasoning* (Oxford and Portland, OR, Hart Publishing, 1999) 137, quoting JN Shklar, *Legalism: Law, Morals and Political Trials* (Cambridge, MA, Harvard University Press, 1986) 1.

[4]   *Ibid* at 139.

[5]   *Ibid* at 138, quoting N MacCormick, 'The Ethics of Legalism' (1989) 2 *Ratio Juris* 184 at 184 and 188.

important to have in place a coherent set of systematically enforceable rules. This account of liberal legalism does not just exist in the mind of legal theorists, but finds practical expression in the globalization of rights constitutionalism. Here, entrenched rights are regarded as necessary to protect individual freedom, while the process of constitutional review provides clear ground rules so that individuals can effectively plan their conduct.[6]

The doctrine of the rule of law is fundamental to constituting liberal legalism as a distinct paradigm. If we regard paradigms as providing a community of scholars with 'model problems and solutions'[7] in a particular field, then the model problem of liberal legalism has been,[8] and continues to be,[9] the search for the criteria of valid law. Paul Craig[10] outlines three different schools of thought on the rule of law: the formal conception, which focuses on whether laws have been passed according to the 'correct legal manner';[11] the substantive conception where the key to a valid law is how it fits with 'the best theory of justice';[12] and the 'middle way' which explains its procedural requirements as a 'principle of institutional morality'[13] which can, on occasion, justify (some) substantive limits on government action.[14] This analysis might seem to undermine the claim that these different positions come together within a single paradigm. However, underlying this ostensible disagreement is a series of assumptions which, once articulated, shows that this disagreement is internal to a common epistemological framework.

First, what binds together all liberal legalist approaches to the rule of law, and reflecting their roots in the Enlightenment project of modernity, is that the test of a valid law is the extent to which it promotes individual autonomy.[15] For example, the formal version requires the protection of rights to exercise self-governance with respect to the community, so that laws which fail the test of validity would include those restricting the political rights of citizens to participate fully in the political process.[16] More substantive versions envisage

---

[6] TRS Allan, *Constitutional Justice: A Liberal Theory of the Rule of Law* (Oxford, Oxford University Press, 2001) 17.

[7] Loughlin, above n 2, at 31, quoting T Kuhn, *The Structure of Scientific Revolutions*, 2nd edn (Chicago, University of Chicago Press, 1970) viii.

[8] AC Hutchinson and P Monahan, 'Democracy and the Rule of Law' in AC Hutchinson and P Monahan (eds), *The Rule of Law: Ideal or Ideology* (Toronto, Carswell, 1987) 122.

[9] See, eg, D Dyzenhaus (ed), *Recrafting the Rule of Law: The Limits of Legal Order* (Oxford and Portland, OR, Hart Publishing, 1999).

[10] 'Formal and Substantive Conceptions of the Rule of Law: An Analytical Framework' [1997] *Public Law* 467.

[11] *Ibid* at 469.

[12] *Ibid* at 477.

[13] *Ibid* at 485.

[14] As Craig notes (*ibid* at 486), the difficulty that middle-way theorists confront is that while they explain the rule of law as a 'principle of institutional morality' in terms of the need to constrain excesses of government power, there is no obvious means of limiting the substantive aspect of this conception of the rule of law so as not to include, eg, arguments based in respect for human rights, also within this principle.

[15] Veitch, above n 3, 140.

[16] See Allan, above n 6.

invalidating laws which unreasonably interfere with the civil rights to enjoyment of the private sphere,[17] or economic rights to the enjoyment of private property.[18] While they might draw the line in different places, what unites these positions is that the question of the appropriate extent of individual autonomy in liberal societies provides the framework for placing limits on the scope of legality.

Secondly, while the rule of law is generally understood as a normative theory, it is important to see that underlying these disparate viewpoints of law is a shared set of descriptive assumptions as to how law promotes individual autonomy in practice. We can approach what this view of law consists of by considering Dicey's famous exposition on this theme, which remains among 'the most influential'[19] versions in the academy. For Dicey, the rule of law had three elements: 1) that no punishment can be imposed 'except for a distinct breach of the law in the ordinary legal manner before the ordinary courts;' 2) that every person 'is subject to the ordinary law;' 3) that rights find their source in 'judicial decisions determining the rights of private persons . . . brought before the courts.'[20] While some leading scholars have found the connection between these three elements ambiguous[21] or obscure,[22] Harry Arthurs suggests that two common themes run through each formulation, namely a 'double emphasis' on 'the exclusive legitimacy of [ordinary] law' and the 'adjudicative monopoly of the 'ordinary courts of the land." '[23]

Viewing the rule of law in this way thickens the epistemological basis of liberal legalism. First, Dicey's distinction between the ordinary law of the ordinary courts, and the pronouncements of 'persons in authority,'[24] shows that the rule of law confers legitimacy on the exercise of some forms of power by converting them into the exercise of law. The latter clearly includes the law handed down by the state's official courts, but within Dicey's constitutional framework, where an Act of Parliament constituted the highest legal norm, it must also include statute law as well.[25] This touches on the uneasy relationship between parliamentary sovereignty and the rule of law in Dicey's account, with the

---

[17] See R Dworkin, *Freedom's Law* (Cambridge, MA, Harvard University Press, 1996).

[18] See R Epstein, *Takings: Private Property and the Power of Eminent Domain* (Cambridge, MA, Harvard University Press, 1995).

[19] J Shklar, 'Political Theory and the Rule of Law' in Hutchinson and Monahan (eds), above n 8, 1 at 5. David Dyzenhaus endorses Dicey's continuing centrality '[i]n the public law model of England and in those legal orders which follow the English model': D Dyzenhaus, 'Recrafting the Rule of Law' in Dyzenhaus (ed), above n 9, 1 at 10.

[20] AV Dicey, *Introduction to the Study of the Law of the Constitution*, 10th edn (London, Macmillan, 1959) at 202–03.

[21] Loughlin, above n 2, at 144.

[22] O Hood Phillips, 'Dicey's *Law of the Constitution*: A Personal View' [1985] *Public Law* 587 at 591.

[23] HW Arthurs, 'Rethinking Administrative Law: A Slightly Dicey Business' (1979) 17 *Osgoode Hall Law Journal* 1 at 6 (quoting Dicey, above n 20 at 188).

[24] *Ibid*.

[25] As Arthurs notes, the reference to the 'ordinary law' must also include at least some statutes, as they are 'rules which will be enforced by the courts': *ibid* at 9.

latter at least being seen as a political precept constraining the former, now upgraded by some modern interpreters as a juridical principle.[26] However, even if the rule of law as the ordinary law of the courts, makes defeasible some statute law,[27] this can be seen as a 'disagreement about the way in which we identify legal norms,'[28] while agreeing that whatever counts as a valid law has, of necessity, its exclusive provenance in the state. Thus, the first core feature of liberal legalist epistemology is that law is formal.

Secondly, the special legitimacy of state law rests to some extent in its possessing unique attributes which promote individual autonomy in practice. Dicey's prescription that no person should be 'lawfully made to suffer in body or goods' except for a clear breach of the ordinary law, ascribes to the latter the special character of setting clear and consistent rules in contrast with a 'wide, arbitrary, or discretionary power of constraint.'[29] This is the basis of the rule-based paradigm, ie, 'the modernist view of law [as] a system of interrelating and non-contradicting rules,'[30] and informs traditional approaches to legal scholarship in terms of exposition, clarification and ordering.[31] Thus, the second core feature of liberal legalist epistemology is that law is coherent. Third, it is crucial to see how the liberal legalist emphasis on protecting individual rights is premised on a view about the effectiveness of law. Arthurs reminds us that Dicey's argument that the ordinary courts are the best means of securing individual freedom is not just a prescriptive claim, but was also Dicey's description of the historical record in England, ie, that to have cases decided by the 'ordinary courts' will lead to the protection of individuals' private rights.[32] This generally implicit assumption that law acts in a direct, instrumental manner continues to underpin debates on the rule of law, where the prize, according to Christine Sypnowich, is to devise a formulation which will 'check . . . political ventures, and . . . restrict the means we deploy to further our ends.'[33] Thus, the third core feature of liberal legalist epistemology is that law is an effective means of protecting individual rights.

These assumptions of the exclusive or universal legitimacy, internal coherence, and effectiveness or instrumentality of state law underpin and explain the prevailing form of normative constitutional scholarship. It is simply taken as read that constitutional law is concerned with the interpretation and application

[26] See Loughlin, above n 2, at 209/10.

[27] See Allan, above n 6, at 231–42.

[28] Craig, above n 10, at 487.

[29] Above n 20, at 188.

[30] G Samuel, *The Foundations of Legal Reasoning* (Antwerp, Maklu, 1994) 129.

[31] See, eg, AWB Simpson, 'The Rise and Fall of the Legal Treatise: Legal Principles and the Forms of Legal Literature' (1981) 48 *University of Chicago Law Review* 632.

[32] Arthurs notes that the attempt to excuse Dicey's descriptive errors in this regard by casting his version as solely a prescriptive account of the Rule of Law, was a later rationalisation, and that Dicey himself understood his work to as equally descriptive: above n 23, at 7.

[33] C Sypnowich, 'Utopia and the Rule of Law' in Dyzenhaus (ed), above n 9, 178 at 178. These instrumental assumptions are confirmed by her casting (*ibid*) the question 'at the heart of the rule of law' as: 'Why should we follow legal procedures which might constrain our pursuit of justice?'

of the official law establishing and limiting the organs of the state. Further, if state law is a systematic whole, then the task of the scholar is to establish the meaning of constitutional norms, by developing a systematic and coherent theory of interpretation, which distinguishes constitutional reasoning from contingent political argument. Moreover, if state constitutional law is the instrumental means of social engineering, then the task of the scholar is to engage in normative debate over how justice can best be served. Whether these assumptions are justified in practice will be explored in the following two chapters. For the present, though, we turn to consider the nature of the challenge to the liberal legalist paradigm from its principal rival: legal pluralism.

LEGAL PLURALISM

The past forty years have witnessed a 'renaissance'[34] of legal pluralist scholarship. Although itself characterised by considerable pluralism,[35] its basic mission has been to demonstrate 'that state of affairs, for any social field, in which behaviour pursuant to more than one legal order occurs.'[36] This idea of the multiplicity of law had been relatively marginalised by the mainstream canon, partly as a result of the 'exotic' nature of legal pluralist studies,[37] and partly through the repeated assertion that 'real' law is found in courts, contracts and statutes.[38] However, due in no small part to the paradigmatic crisis of modernity provoked by globalization, there is now a concerted attempt to reclaim a pluralist knowledge of law which, it is claimed, better fits the 'empiricism, particularism, indeterminacy and disorder' of our times.[39] The challenge of legal pluralism is important for our inquiry as it undermines all three core elements of liberal legalist epistemology. For legal pluralism, law is not found solely in the processes of the state, and is neither internally coherent nor externally instrumental: it accordingly questions whether rights constitutionalism, operating within the liberal legalist rule of law, even in adapted form, can achieve its objectives of protecting freedom and autonomy in an age of globalization. It should be emphasised that what we are discussing here is legal pluralism's

---

[34] M-M Kleinhans and RA Macdonald, 'What is a Critical Legal Pluralism?' (1997) 12 *Canadian Journal of Law and Society* 25, 29.

[35] See RL Kidder, 'Justice and Power in Studies of Legal Pluralism' in BG Garth and A Sarat (eds) *Justice and Power in Sociolegal Studies* (Evanston, IL, Northwestern University Press, 1998) 194, 194. See also GR Woodman, 'The Idea of Legal Pluralism' in B Dupret, M Berger and L Al-Zwaini (eds), *Legal Pluralism in the Arab World* (Dordrecht, Kluwer, 1999) 3, 12–17.

[36] J Griffiths, 'What is Legal Pluralism?' (1986) 24 *Journal of Legal Pluralism* 1, 2.

[37] See RA Macdonald, 'Metaphors of Multiplicity: Civil Society, Regimes and Legal Pluralism' (1998) 15 *Arizona Journal of International and Comparative Law* 69, 75.

[38] *Ibid* at 72–73.

[39] *Ibid* at 71.

epistemological challenge to liberal legalism. This point is especially important given the normative overtones of 'pluralism'—however, there is no necessary positive connotation about legal pluralism,[40] and so it is important to disentangle the epistemological and normative claims made on its behalf. Accordingly, I set out here the key epistemological critique advanced by legal pluralism with regard to rights constitutionalism, namely that the latter cannot deliver what it promises to those who are drawn to argue and agitate on its terms.

Legal Pluralism and the Challenge to Legal Centralism

Legal pluralism charges that liberal legalism represents a fundamental misdescription. Its basic, and probably most famous, contention is that the state does not have a monopoly on law. Moreover, it is claimed that the legal pluralist paradigm is the one with the greater historical pedigree.[41] Recent attempts to revive this narrative can be divided into three broad phases: classical legal pluralism, post-colonial legal pluralism, and globalization and legal pluralism. While there are important differences and disagreements within and between these phases,[42] they are united in a common project of mapping the existence of legal phenomena beyond the state. In other words, their objective is to displace the legal centralist default that the state alone can provide the criterion for the existence of legal order.

Classical legal pluralism[43] arose from developments in anthropological research to question the western belief that, prior to the imposition of European law in colonial societies, there was no law and order. Instead, classical legal pluralists, through techniques of ethnographic mapping[44] sought to demonstrate that 'far from being savage anarchies, . . . [precolonial] societies were quite orderly and capable of holding together over time.'[45] The key point was to render contingent the western notion of law by showing that indigenous

---

[40] Santos, above n 1, at 90. I develop this point further in chapter six.

[41] See, eg, Kleinhans and Macdonald, above n 34, at 29 and Santos, above n 1, at 42. For an account of how the civil law of ancient Rome can be characterised in terms of legal pluralism, see GCJJ van den Bergh, 'Legal Pluralism in Roman Law' reproduced in C Varga, *Comparative Legal Cultures* (New York, NYU Press, 1992) 451.

[42] For an overview of some of the principal issues in this debate, see GR Woodman, 'Ideological Combat and Social Observation' (1998) 42 *Journal of Legal Pluralism* 21.

[43] SE Merry, 'Legal Pluralism' (1988) 22 *Law and Society Review* 869, 872. Merry refers to 'classic legal pluralism' as 'the analysis of the intersections of indigenous and European law' in colonial societies. Classic texts under this heading include: MB Hooker, *Legal Pluralism: an Introduction to Colonial and Neocolonial Law* (Oxford, Clarendon Press, 1975); L Pospísil, *Anthropology of Law: A Comparative Theory* (New York, Harper and Row, 1975); S Roberts, *Order and Dispute: An Introduction to Legal Anthropology* (New York, St Martin's Press, 1979); and SF Moore, *Law as Process: An Anthropological Approach* (London, Routledge and Kegan Paul, 1978). For an overview of this period in legal pluralist thought, see J Dalberg-Larsen, *The Unity of Law: An Illusion? On Legal Pluralism in Theory and Practice* (Berlin, Galda and Wilch Verlag, 2000) ch 2.

[44] See Hooker, *ibid*.

[45] Roberts, above n 43, at 12.

'law-like' phenomena pre-dated the colonial state.[46] For example, recent work on the history of colonialism in North America has shown how the aboriginal peoples lived in organised societies,[47] with their own political systems that included, inter alia,

> provisions for behaviour and thoughts related to making a living from the environment, raising children, organizing the exchanges of goods and labor, living in domestic groups and larger communities, and the creative, moral and intellectual aspects of human life.[48]

The point is not that aboriginals had analogical equivalents of western property laws, or that this is what the 'correct' version of legal history should relate,[49] but that to assign the label 'law' to the later arrival of the western variety of legal phenomena is 'no more than a distinction of relative emphasis in the sources of information most readily available, not an ontological divide.'[50]

In the 1970s, research within the law and society movement emphasised that legal pluralism was not just a feature of exotic settings, but was also prevalent in the industrialised west.[51] Scholarship in this post-colonial phase developed legal pluralism by also positing the operation of non-state law throughout modern society, in settings as diverse as business,[52] suburbs,[53] sport,[54] and prisons.[55] As with its classical precursor, this account of law's ubiquity attempted to

---

[46] As Woodman puts it in the context of studies of legal pluralism in Africa, 'the advent of the colonial state was not the beginning of law. It was rather the addition of some new, complicating factors to the existing legal world. There is no ground for claiming that customary law was not or is not a form of law, and that law arrived in Africa only when colonialism arrived.': GR Woodman, 'Legal Pluralism and the Search for Justice' (1996) 40 *Journal of African Law* 152, 157.

[47] C Bell and M Asch, 'Challenging Assumptions: The Impact of Precedent in Aboriginal Rights Litigation' in M Asch (ed), *Aboriginal and Treaty Rights in Canada: Essays on Law, Equality and Respect for Difference* (Vancouver, University of British Columbia Press, 1997) 38, 64–71.

[48] *Ibid* at 67.

[49] We should be careful not to present the discussion as a competition between Western and aboriginal laws, each conceived of in monolithic terms. For one thing, aboriginal societies continue themselves to be marked by plural forms of normative ordering: see N Oman, 'The Role of Recognition in the Delgamuukw Case' in J Oakes, R Riewe, K Kinew and E Maloney (eds), *Sacred Lands: Aboriginal World Views, Claims, and Conflicts* (Edmonton, Canadian Circumpolar Institute, 1998) 243.

[50] Woodman, above n 42, at 43.

[51] For a good overview of this direction in scholarship, see RL Abel (ed), *The Politics of Informal Justice*, Vols. 1 *and* 2 (New York, Academic Press, 1982). (Scholarship in this period emphasises how 'pluralist' should not necessarily be equated with normatively positive. For example, Abel argues that non-state processes, such as Alternative Dispute Resolution (ADR), may in fact undermine rights won in state legal fora which were better able to neutralise disparities in power).

[52] S Macaulay, 'Non-contractual Relations in Business: A Preliminary Study' (1963) 28 *American Sociological Review* 55. (Macaulay's work was 'generally ignored until the mid-1970s' (Merry, above n 43, at 783) when there was an upturn in law and society interest in the ideas of legal pluralism.)

[53] C Greenhouse, 'Nature is to Culture as Praying is to Suing: Legal Pluralism in an American Suburb' (1982) 20 *Journal of Legal Pluralism* 17.

[54] S Macaulay, 'Images of Law in Everyday Life: The Lessons of School, Entertainment, and Spectator Sports' (1987) 21 *Law and Society Review* 185, 204–07.

[55] S Henry, *Private Justice: Towards Integrated Theorizing in the Sociology of Law* (New York, Routledge and Kegan Paul, 1983).

counter centralist views of law by showing how functions traditionally associated with state law, eg, the adjudication of disputes,[56] are also carried out in non-state settings. One prominent example of this scholarship is in the field of industrial relations which emphasises that in the normative regimes which affect workers, state law is often less important than:

> ... [n]orms or rules [which] are generated internally: contracts, collective agreements, arbitral awards, codes of conduct, informal understandings and, above all, customary patterns of behaviour, which though always changing, at any moment plausibly capture what is understood to be 'the law.'[57]

Other studies have underlined the explanatory importance of non-state normative orderings.[58] For example, it is argued that to understand fully the process of collective bargaining—the building block of labour relations in the postwar era[59]—we need to refer to the 'implicit understandings, custom and usage, patterned behaviour, cultural assumptions, power relations and technological imperatives'[60] of day-to-day employment practice.[61]

Feminist scholarship has also underscored the general importance of looking beyond the state, here to gain a more accurate picture of 'women's legal world[s].'[62] While some of this work is carried out under the rubric of the public–private divide[63] rather than legal pluralism, it too rejects a state-centred view of legality. For example, if we consider women's experiences of the workplace, this reveals a continuing gender imbalance in terms of pay, often in the face of state guarantees of equal treatment.[64] This suggests, descriptively, that

---

[56] M Galanter, 'Justice in Many Rooms: Courts, Private Ordering and Indigenous Law' (1981) 19 *Journal of Legal Pluralism* 19.

[57] HW Arthurs 'Understanding Labour Law: The Debate over "Industrial Pluralism"' (1985) 38 *Current Legal Problems* 83, 90. Arthurs suggests that there are in fact three levels of normative regime which must be taken into account to understand labour law. These are, in descending order of importance: the 'indigenous law of the workplace,' special rules of formal state law, such as employment legislation, and last, general rules of state law, which includes constitutional law (*ibid* at 92). He rejects the idea that any gap between formal law and what occurs in practice is a result of imperfections in the former: rather, this is indicative of the limits of state law and the reality that there is a multiplicity of sources for the assemblage of rules that constitute industrial relations (*ibid* at 87).

[58] See, eg, Moore, above n 43, at 59–65.

[59] Arthurs, above n 57, at 83.

[60] HW Arthurs, 'Labour Law without the State' (1996) 46 *University of Toronto Law Journal* 1, 2.

[61] See also, Henry, above n 55, at 121.

[62] A Manji, 'Imagining Women's "Legal World": Towards a Feminist Theory of Legal Pluralism in Africa' (1999) 8 *Social and Legal Studies* 435.

[63] See generally, SB Boyd, 'Challenging the Public/Private Divide: An Overview' in SB Boyd (ed), *Challenging the Public/Private Divide: Feminism, Law and Public Policy* (Toronto, University of Toronto Press, 1997) 3. See also M Thornton (ed), *Public and Private: Feminist Legal Debates* (Melbourne, Oxford University Press, 1995).

[64] 'The rising numbers of women in the labour force reflect entry into industries and occupations that are characterised by low pay, low recognized skill requirements, low productivity, and low prospects for advancement ... Women still earn only 71.8 cents for men's $1.00 when full-time/ full-year workers are studied. Women are also still mainly employed in female job ghettoes, generally working *for* men': SB Boyd, 'Can Law Challenge the Public/Private Divide? Women, Work and Family' (1996) 15 *Windsor Yearbook of Access to Justice* 161, 172 (footnotes omitted).

for the most part, the workplace is organised around norms that women will work, for example, in certain jobs or for certain rates, which disadvantage them in comparison with men. If we look next at the context of the family, perusal of statute and case books will not reveal that in terms of the domestic division of labour, the governing norm is that 'cleaning, cooking, shopping and child care is primarily women's work.'[65] The same can be said for care of elderly or disabled relatives.[66] Similarly, a more sociologically grounded approach uncovers the extent to which domestic violence against women is still regarded as acceptable within some households.[67]

In recent times, an emerging literature on globalization and legal pluralism has sought to demonstrate how a pluralist conception of law explains the emergence of 'inchoate forms of global law, none of which are the creations of states.'[68] For example, Gunther Teubner argues that if we consider how economic agents internalise and apply the binary coding of legal/illegal,[69] this shows that the global *lex mercatoria* should be regarded as a form of law despite the lack of any state imprimatur for this increasingly important 'transnational law of economic transactions.'[70] On this account, a global merchant's law is necessarily fragmented, and consists of '[discourses] of state law, of rules of private justice or regulations of private government' which together form a 'dynamic process of the mutual constitution of action and structures in the global social field.'[71] In this regard, corporations, already identified as major actors in driving the globalizing economy, are also an important and prolific source of non-state law.[72] Thus, corporations have created norms for conducting their business,[73] which take a variety of forms, and include:

> . . . those buried in the interstices of business transactions and the fine print of financial instruments—a phenomenon of domestic as well as global business relations . . . Still others come about through the promulgation by multinational corporations—acting alone or under the umbrella of sectorial agreements—of codes of behaviour in sensitive areas such as corrupt practices, worker rights, and pollution, or technical standards for products and processes.[74]

---

[65] P Armstrong, 'Restructuring Public and Private: Women's Paid and Unpaid Work' in Boyd (ed), above n 63, 37 at 50.

[66] *Ibid.*

[67] Boyd, above n 63, at 7

[68] Teubner, above n 1, at 4.

[69] *Ibid* at 14.

[70] *Ibid* at 3. (See also H-J Mertens, '*Lex Mercatoria*: A Self-applying System Beyond National Law?' in Teubner (ed), above n 1, at 31.)

[71] *Ibid* at 14.

[72] PT Muchlinski, ' "Global Bukowina" Examined: Viewing the Multinational Enterprise as a Transnational Law-making Community' in Teubner (ed), above n 1, at 79. See also J-P Robé, 'Multinational Enterprises: The Constitution of a Pluralistic Legal Order,' in *ibid*, 45. Robé argues (*ibid* at 52) that reference to state law is inadequate even to explain the existence of the 'enterprise' (as represented, eg, by IBM or Toyota), in comparison with the 'corporation' as the former does not exist in positive law, but is only 'a paradigm—an object of reference in continual use.'

[73] Robé, *ibid* at 60.

[74] HW Arthurs and R Kreklewich 'Law, Legal Institutions and the Legal Profession in the New Economy' (1996) 34 *Osgoode Hall Law Journal* 1, 38 (references omitted).

These empirical studies in legal pluralism set up a sharp descriptive disjuncture with liberal legalism. In positing the pervasive existence of law-like phenomena in a variety of social settings, they have performed the important task of unsettling the commonsensical assumptions that law (and so constitutional law) necessarily and exclusively emanates from the state. However, some have questioned whether this empirical method does not itself exhibit some of the methodological flaws of the dominant 'paradigm. Here, we can identify a fourth phase of scholarship, critical legal pluralism, which while being equally dismissive of ideas of legal centralism, also focuses on the positivist and monist challenges to liberal legalism. This suggests that traditional legal pluralism tends to take the characteristics of state law as its primary referent, but seeks to reproduce these in non-state settings. As such, it falls into the trap of treating law as an 'external object of knowledge,'[75] repeating liberal legalism's error of positivism. Moreover, in 'reifying "norm-generating communities"[76] as substitutes for the state,' there is a danger of replacing monist conceptions of state law with equally monist conceptions of non-state law. In place of identifying the test of legal order in terms of traditional state functions such as social control,[77] critical legal pluralism places the legal subject as 'an irreducible site of normativity'[78] at the heart of its account of law. In Santos's terms, this sees the individual not merely as 'law-abiding,' but also 'law-creating,'[79] and so the key question for critical legal pluralists is not what legal order has jurisdiction over a legal subject, but rather becomes: 'Within which legal order does the particular legal subject perceive himself or herself to be acting?'[80]

For present purposes, the importance of this critical turn does not lie in focusing our attention on internal debates in legal pluralism, but by showing that the epistemological challenge to liberal legalism goes not only to state-centred views of law, but to the special characteristics asserted on state law's behalf. We can see the nature of these challenges by elaborating how the counter-arguments to the monist and positivist accounts of law question assumptions of rights constitutionalism's coherence and instrumental effectiveness. In this regard, I now discuss the theoretical bases of external and internal legal pluralism: the former posits multiple interacting sites of law-production and locates any account of rights constitutionalism's counterhegemonic potential in this internormative world, while the latter takes seriously the law-creating capacity of the individual and its disordering effects on any attempt to systematise constitutional doctrine.

---

[75] Kleinhans and Macdonald, above n 34, at 37.

[76] *Ibid* at 35.

[77] Griffiths, above n 36, at 50.

[78] Kleinhans and Macdonald, above n 34, at 43.

[79] *Ibid* at 39 (quoting B de Sousa Santos, 'Three Metaphors for a New Conception of Law: The Frontier, the Baroque and the South' (1995) 29 *Law and Society Review* 569, 573).

[80] *Ibid* at 36.

External Legal Pluralism and the Multiplicity of Law

Legal pluralism charges that state law often fails to realise its objectives in practice.[81] Classical legal pluralism emphasised the resistance of customary practices
to reordering by the formal law, while post-colonial scholarship cast doubt on
the instrumental ambitions of state law, for example, in the context of the
workplace,[82] or the administration of justice.[83] Studies of globalization and
legal pluralism often attest to the relative powerlessness of state law in regulating the global economy.[84] How then do we explain that other sources of law are
seemingly more effective than state law?

Much theoretical work in legal pluralism pays homage[85] to Sally Falk
Moore's conception of semi-autonomous social fields. Writing in 1973, Moore
set out the basis of a social theory which explains both the plurality of law, and
how this qualifies traditional understandings of state law. Moore's motivation
was to explain the evident fact that state law does not operate in the linear
instrumental fashion presumed by most lawyers.[86] She sought to counter the
tendency in mainstream thought towards abstracting law from its social context
by adopting the methods of social anthropology to develop the idea of the semi-
autonomous social field. Such fields are defined by the capacity to 'generate rules
and coerce or induce compliance to them.'[87] The 'interdependent articulation'
among a large number of social fields 'constitutes one of the basic characteristics of complex societies'[88] and forms the basis of Moore's social theory. It is

---

[81] HW Arthurs, *Without the Law: Administrative Justice and Legal Pluralism in Nineteenth-Century England* (Toronto and Buffalo, University of Toronto Press, 1985) 2.

[82] Moore herself provides further corroboration of the limitations of state law in her study of the garment industry in New York state (above n 43, at 59–65). She finds that, for example, with regard to working hours, the most significant norm is not to be found in state law but in the practices of workers and union officials, whereby extra hours are often undertaken at busy times (to pre-empt later slowdowns). Thus, she concludes (*ibid* at 65) that 'many of the pressures to conform to "the law" probably emanate from the several social milieux in which an individual participates. The potentiality of state action is often far less immediate than other pressures and inducements.'

[83] See, eg, MH Lazerson, 'In the Halls of Justice, the Only Justice Is in the Halls' in Abel (ed), above n 51, vol 1, at 119 and SC McGuire and RA Macdonald, 'Small Claims Courts Cant' (1996) 34 *Osgoode Hall Law Journal* 509.

[84] See, eg, Arthurs and Kreklewich, above n 74, at 24 who argue that while 'in principle, contracts are subject to state law' in practice, 'state law may be trumped by private arrangement, of which the standard form contract is the most ubiquitous example.' See also, Robé, above n 72, at 61.

[85] Merry, above n 43, at 878 refers to this as the 'most enduring, generalizable, and widely-used conception of plural legal orders.' See also Griffiths, above n 36, at 29–37.

[86] Above n 43, at 54. She elaborates (*ibid* at 54–55) that her target is the 'social engineering' view of law which rests on 'the assumptions that social arrangements are susceptible to conscious human control, and that the instrument by which this control is to be achieved is law. In such formulations "the law" is a short-hand term for a very complex aggregation of principles, norms, ideas, rules, practices, and the agencies of legislation, administration, adjudication and enforcement, backed by political power and legitimacy. The complex "law", thus condensed into one term, is abstracted from the social context in which it exists, and is spoken of as if it were an entity capable of control-ling that context.'

[87] *Ibid* at 57.

[88] *Ibid* at 58.

important to emphasise that such fields are only *semi*-autonomous, as they are 'set in a larger social matrix'[89] which renders them 'vulnerable to rules and decisions and other forces emanating from the larger world by which [they are] surrounded.'[90] Moore's account thus provides a theoretical challenge to the liberal legalist focus on the state—law is no longer located in the state but in the complex interaction among semi-autonomous social fields of which the state is but one. More important perhaps, it also undermines the notion of state law's instrumentality by highlighting how this is constrained by its social context; here individual thought and action must be found in a web of overlapping state and non-state laws, the importance of each in any situation depending on their precise articulation with each other.

While Moore's theory remains influential in terms of situating law in a broader constellation of social forces that qualifies its operation, in contemporary terms, the work of Boaventura de Sousa Santos is rightly seen as making a 'very significant contribution'[91] to establishing the theoretical basis of legal pluralism. In *Toward a New Legal Common Sense*, Santos advances a theoretical reconstruction of legal pluralism, which moves beyond the anthropological positing of law-like examples, and provides a sociological explanation of the nature of different forms of law and their relationship to each other. His principal explanatory device is the 'structure-agency map' which conceives of modern capitalist society as political, legal and epistemological constellations, producing six basic forms of power, law and knowledge respectively, which, though related to each other, are structurally autonomous.[92] To flesh out these different forms of power, law and knowledge, Santos distinguishes between six structural places—the householdplace, the workplace, the marketplace, the communityplace, the citizenplace, and the worldplace—which are 'the most consolidated clusters of social relations in contemporary capitalist societies.'[93] This framework emphasises the multiple variety of social relations[94]: as the structural places only operate in constellation with each other, their 'developmental dynamics' are partial.[95] Furthermore, each is grounded in a specific contradiction—for example, between employers and employees in the workplace—and so accordingly social actions are 'often informed by different and mutually incongruent logics.'[96]

---

[89] *Ibid* at 56.
[90] *Ibid* at 55.
[91] Above n 1, at 228.
[92] Santos, above n 1, at 371.
[93] *Ibid* at 374.
[94] These are further defined (*ibid* at 373–4) as 'a complex field of interaction having six dimensions: social agency, institutions, developmental and interactional dynamics, power form, legal form, and epistemological form.'
[95] *Ibid* at 377.
[96] *Ibid* at 378.

For Santos, the plurality of law is revealed by showing how six basic forms of law[97] are 'anchored in, constituted by and constitutive of' the six structural places.[98] His objective here is to uncouple law from the state, and (re)couple it with social power.[99] One form of law is, of course, the state (or territorial) law of what he calls the citizenplace, produced by the institutions of the nation-state.[100] Other forms include: the domestic law of the householdplace; the production law of the workplace; the exchange law of the marketplace; the community law of the communityplace; and the systemic law of the worldplace.[101] An understanding of the developmental logic of each structural place concretises the corresponding form of law. For example, domestic law is 'the set of rules, normative standards and dispute settlement mechanisms both resulting from and in the sedimentation of social relations in the householdplace.'[102] This law is highly informal, and as it is almost totally enmeshed in family relations, there is little perception of its autonomy vis-à-vis those relations. Production law,[103] on the other hand, is grounded in the 'the power prerogatives inherent to the ownership of the means of production.'[104] Its form is often changeable, and depends, for example, on the prevailing culture within any particular corporation. While sometimes informal, sometimes not, it differs from domestic law in that its autonomy is more consciously internalised by those subject to it.[105]

The structural places not only explain the nature of different types of law, but more crucially, their relation to each other: '[T]he legal character of social relations of law does not derive from one single form of law, [but] from the different constellations among different forms of law.'[106] In other words, the legal regime within any of the structural places is an articulation between different

---

[97] Santos defines law as 'a body of regularized procedures and normative standards, considered justiciable in a given group, which contribute to the creation and prevention of disputes, as well as to their settlement through an argumentative discourse coupled with the threat of force' (*ibid* at 86). When Santos refers to multiple forms of law, it is this definition which he has expressly in mind. As such, he appears to open himself up to the charge that he is 'essentialising' law (see BZ Tamanaha, 'A Non-Essentialist Version of Legal Pluralism' (2000) 27 *Journal of Law and Society* 296, 302–06) or making 'unnecessary' or 'artificial' distinctions between the legal and non-legal, when 'the indicia of "the legal" are more like a continuum' (Twining, above n 1, at 231). I will deal more fully with Santos's approach to the definition of law in chapter six, where I suggest it is better regarded as rhetorical than stipulative.

[98] *Ibid* at 384. Santos seems to imply that this is not an exclusive list of 'the great variety of legal orders circulating in society.'

[99] *Ibid* at 356.

[100] For Santos, the position that state law is one among a number of legal forms is not a full-scale assault, but rather 'confirms and relativizes it at the same time by integrating [its hegemonic form in a new and broader constellation of laws]' (*ibid* at 354).

[101] *Ibid* at 384–95.

[102] *Ibid* at 385.

[103] 'Production law is the law of the factory, the law of the corporation, the set of regulations and normative standards that rule the everyday life of wage labour relations (both relations of production and relations in production), factory codes, shop floor regulations, codes of conduct for employees and so on' (*ibid* at 388).

[104] *Ibid* at 388.

[105] *Ibid* at 389.

[106] *Ibid* at 415.

forms of law. To return to some of the previously discussed examples, the law affecting women in the householdplace, such as provisions of family law with regard to child care, is constituted by both domestic and state law.[107] Ongoing changes in the nature of employment whereby people are increasingly 'working at home' means that to understand the law of the workplace, we need to examine the emerging dynamic between domestic and production law.[108] Further, we may characterise attempts by aboriginal groups to assert, for example ancient fishing rights,[109] as involving the interface between community law, here being deployed to strengthen 'subaltern, defensive identities,'[110] and state constitutional law. Finally, in the context of economic globalization, we may look at the degree of isomorphism in the marketplace between the exchange law of *lex mercatoria* and state contract law,[111] and also the extent to which the systemic law of the worldplace,[112] under which we might include the Washington consensus, interacts with rules of international law in affecting relations between nation states.

It is crucial to emphasise that this account of diverse interactions between different forms of law—what we will label their internormativity[113]—is both a portrayal of the multiple nature of legal regulation, and an explanation of its limits. The implications of this position are particularly important for legal discourses which focus on the state. For Santos, state law is distinctive in that it alone is officially regarded as law, and as such, it tends to have an inflated sense of its ability to regulate social life.[114] However, the identification of other forms of (less reflexive) law means that the absence of state law does not equate to deregulation, but reregulation. Rather, the social world consists of overlapping, interpenetrating legal orders, the upshot being that '[o]ne mere change in state law may change very little if the other legal orders are in place and manage to re-establish their constellations with state law in new ways.'[115] Thus, for example, although the state criminal laws of many societies proscribe wife-beating and child abuse, the domestic law which permits them in the householdplace is often the stronger norm.[116]

This account has important implications for our interrogation of the relationship between rights constitutionalism and private power. It challenges the idea that the instrumental effectiveness of rights constitutionalism depends on the outcome of normative debate through the following three propositions of external legal pluralism:

---

[107] *Ibid* at 386.
[108] *Ibid* at 389. For Santos, the result of this intensification of the articulation between domestic and production law is a relative uncoupling of each from state law.
[109] See, eg, *R v Sparrow* (1990) 70 DLR (4th) 385.
[110] Santos, above n 1, at 391.
[111] *Ibid*.
[112] *Ibid* at 393.
[113] Santos uses the term 'interlegality': *ibid* at 437.
[114] *Ibid* at 392.
[115] *Ibid* at 395.
[116] *Ibid* at 394.

1. State law is but one of multiple sources of law.
2. The operation of these multiple legal forms is characterised by their inter-normativity, whereby they constantly overlap and interact with each other.
3. In this internormative world, state law has no special status on account of its provenance, and is often the less important normative regime affecting a particular area of social life.

Internal Legal Pluralism and the Incoherence of Law

Internal legal pluralism speaks to the 'diversity of norms, processes and institutions within . . . any particular legal order.'[117] For example, where customary laws are incorporated within the official legal system in the colonial setting, this has been depicted as 'state law pluralism'[118] which consists of 'multiple bodies of law, with multiple sources of legitimacy.'[119] Others have addressed the pluralism inherent in western state law—whether by developing ideas of 'doctrinal legal pluralism,'[120] or by recovering the history of pluralism which had been displaced by the hegemonic narrative of legal centralism.[121] Santos depicts this internal pluralism as a 'quilt of legalities' where the 'state legal thread [is inter-laced] with multiple local legal threads'[122]—for him, this diversity also charac-terises law in the process of globalization.[123]

   This brings us to an important debate within legal pluralism on the relevance of 'state law' or 'doctrinal' pluralism. On one side, John Griffiths strongly argues that pluralism within state law is of little interest to the social scientist,[124] and that highlighting this is to perpetuate the legal centralist obsession with state law that he wishes to debunk.[125] On the other, Gordon Woodman suggests that, on Griffiths's terms, doctrine can equally be regarded as a social fact,

---

[117]   Kleinhans and Macdonald, above n 34, at 32.

[118]   Woodman, above n 46, at 158.

[119]   *Ibid* at 159.

[120]   Roderick Macdonald locates in the work of Lon Fuller an attempt to 'pluralize legal forms by beginning within the frame of official law' (Kleinhans and Macdonald, above n 34, at 30) which showed 'the diversity of norms, processes and institutions within normative systems' (Macdonald, above n 37, at 77).

[121]   See Arthurs, above n 81, at 188.

[122]   Above n 1, at 163.

[123]   *Ibid* at 165: 'Far from being a monolithic phenomenon, it is extremely diverse, combining uni-formity with local differentiation, top-down imposition with bottom-up creation, formal declara-tion with interstitial emergence, boundary maintaining-orientation with boundary-transcending orientation.'

[124]   Above n 36, at 8. He distinguishes here state law pluralism as 'legal pluralism in the weak sense' from legal pluralism in the 'strong' sense, and which is 'the analysis of an empirical state of affairs, namely the coexistence within a social group of legal orders which do not belong to a single "system." Within this framework, Griffiths argues that pluralism within state law 'has only a con-fusing nominal resemblance to legal pluralism as the designation of an empirical state of affairs in society' (*ibid*).

[125]   *Ibid*.

whose investigation assists our perception of social reality.[126] My position is closer to Woodman's, for three principal reasons. First, rather than drawing a sharp definitional divide (which Griffiths warns against in the case of 'law'),[127] we should see external and state law pluralism as part of the same continuum. Secondly, while under a legal pluralist analysis, state law is no longer central, this does not necessarily mean it is unimportant. Indeed, as I will argue later, there are important consequences in the widespread acceptance of the liberal legalist paradigm as 'commonsense'. There is therefore value in testing the key claim made about the internal orientation of state law. Thirdly, and related, to the extent that it undermines the liberal legalist archetype of formal coherence, this exercise is a powerful antidote to a tendency within legal pluralism to replace one monism—that of state law—with another: thus, *pace* Griffiths, applying the insights of legal pluralism to state law can be seen as subversive of the dominant paradigm.

While Santos presents an account of law in which state law is to be seen as 'highly heterogeneous and internally differentiated,'[128] the theoretical explanation of pluralism within state law is most developed in the work of Charles Sampford. Sampford's object of critique is the 'law as system' orthodoxy[129] which he argues permeates the legal academy and informs positivist (eg, Hart), content (eg, Dworkin) and sociological (eg, Luhmann) theories of legal system. For example, the idea of system underpins Dworkin's quest for the principles best justifying existing practice which can be used to develop the 'chain novel' of interpretation. Each finds failings in the others' attempts, and instead proposes a 'better' account of the legal system. Sampford's main argument is that this attempt to theorise in terms of system and order should be abandoned.[130] Instead, he offers a theory based on disorder, which represents an important attempt to show the implications of theories of social pluralism for our understanding of state law.

Sampford's organising idea is the social melée, which begins with an account of the nature of social relations. The latter he divides into power relations,[131] unintended effects[132] and value effect relations[133]: social interaction can never

---

[126] Above n 42, at 35.

[127] Above n 36, at 37.

[128] Above n 1, at 357.

[129] C Sampford, *The Disorder of Law* (Oxford, Blackwell, 1991) 1.

[130] *Ibid* at 149.

[131] Following Dennis Wrong (*Power: Its Forms, Bases and Uses* (Oxford, Blackwell, 2000)), he distinguishes between four forms of the exercise of power—force, manipulation, persuasion and authority—and five reasons for compliance therewith—legitimate authority, coercion, personal authority, inducement and competent authority: *ibid* at 162.

[132] These are divided between 'anticipatory reactions' (*ibid* at 171), where individuals modify their behaviour because they anticipate the reaction of another (even though the other person is unaware of this) and 'unforeseen effects' (*ibid* at 172), where a person expects his or her action to have some outcome, but not that which does in fact result.

[133] 'In this relation, the attitude of one person (the *value-holder*) tends to lead him/her to act in a manner different from the way (s)he would act if (s)he did not hold the value, and another person (the *value-beneficiary* or the *value-sufferer*) is affected in some way by this difference' (*ibid* at 173).

be homogeneous as it is characterised by various mixtures of these relations. Moreover, these relations will often be perceived differently by those at either end of them. For example, power-holders may believe that compliance is due to their legitimate authority whereas power-subjects may perceive themselves to have been coerced—thus Sampford argues that social relations are typically asymmetrical.[134] This attenuates the capacity of individuals and institutions to mobilise others. Institutions are 'a web of mixed relations between different persons with different environments and values'[135] and so they rarely speak with one voice. This internal disorder itself contributes to the general disorder of the social melée which is 'a fluid, constantly changing set of interactions in complex struggle between a large number of groups and institutions.'[136] Thus, Sampford argues that society should be seen as a 'disorganized struggle' where to the extent social peace prevails, this is not attributable to the systematic following of rules within some overarching consensus, but the result of the disorder between institutions.[137] Moreover, this disorder frustrates the capacity for society to be reordered, as it leads to social inertia whereby the interests of some groups become entrenched and difficult to displace.

The key move in providing the basis for a theory of internal legal pluralism is Sampford's linking of the disorder of society to an account of the disorder of state law. He argues that state law is not immune from the disordering forces outlined above, as it is part of the larger web of varied and complex social relations.[138] Accordingly, it is also marked by asymmetry—for example, where the promulgation of rules passes through chains of legal relations between officials and citizens, where at each point, the main protagonists have a different perception of the rule at stake.[139] Asymmetrical legal relations thus further attenuate the instrumentality of state law, as they themselves contribute to the social melée.[140]

This undermines the liberal legalist assumption of coherence given that the central means of effecting instrumental change within mainstream constitutional theory is through the systematic reordering of doctrine. We can deepen the analysis here by locating Sampford's linking of social and legal disorder and incoherence with the emerging school of critical legal pluralism. As discussed above, this emphasises how legal subjects possess a 'transformative capacity,' and are themselves important sources of legal knowledge[141]: as such, they create law, as much as law creates them. This view of the law-creating legal subject further enriches our picture of internormativity—it is not just the case that different forms of law overlap and interact with each other, but that *at the same*

---

[134] *Ibid* at 160.
[135] *Ibid* at 203.
[136] *Ibid* at 203.
[137] *Ibid* at 204.
[138] *Ibid* at 223.
[139] *Ibid* at 225–27.
[140] *Ibid* at 223.
[141] *Ibid* at 38.

time, legal subjects are giving shape to those legal structures which are also part of the constitution of their legal subjectivity.[142] As such, critical legal pluralism argues that '[n]ormative heterogeneity exists both between various normative regimes which inhabit the same intellectual space, and within the regimes them-selves.'[143]

This analysis has important implications for adjudication, and questions the assumption that through reasoned argument we can reconstitute doctrine into a coherent whole as a precursor to effecting social change. Sampford argues that judges must be seen as acting for a variety of reasons in any context: for exam-ple, lower court judges may be motivated in a particular judgment by a genuine belief that they are following legitimate precedent, or the hope of promotion, or to avoid being overturned on appeal, or to avoid criticism by fellow judges or the legal profession in general. Furthermore, he argues that the senior judiciary, to whom some of the previous considerations are inapplicable, will nonetheless be affected in their behaviour by, for example, the anticipated reaction of the executive and legislative branches.[144] It is not that these factors are extraneous to doctrinal argument, but that they are part of the social context in which judges internalise their attitude to the cases before them. Allied to the last point is Sampford's general argument against the possibility of system: while a judge may produce a response to constitutional argument which is coherent to him- or herself, this will be a different coherence from that created in the minds of other judges.[145] This explains the continuing phenomenon of jurisprudential partiality and contradiction that has been well documented first by the realists, and latterly, by the critical legal studies movement.[146] However, it makes a stronger point which distinguishes legal pluralism from these other approaches,[147] namely that even if judges were to be persuaded by the norma-tive constitutional arguments put to them, and wished to act on them in good faith, the centripetal forces of asymmetrical social and legal relations make it highly likely that doctrinal incoherence would still result.

We can accordingly now posit the challenge of internal legal pluralism to the liberal legalist assumption of coherence in the following terms:

1. Society is characterised by disorder, which is the result of asymmetrical social relations which attenuate the capacity of institutions to impose systematic order.

2. Legal relations are but one variety of social relations; as such, (all) forms of law are marked by asymmetry which attenuates their capacity both to attain internal order, and to be a means of reordering society.

---

[142] *Ibid*.

[143] Kleinhans and Macdonald, above n 34, at 39.

[144] Sampford, above n 129, at 229.

[145] *Ibid* at 151.

[146] See D Kennedy, *A Critique of Adjudication (fin de siècle)* (Cambridge, MA, Harvard University Press, 1997) chs 4 and 5.

[147] Kennedy, eg, accepts that 'crits love determinacy, in its place, as much as the next person' (*ibid* at 129).

3. The internal incoherence of law in general, and state legal doctrine in particular, is further attenuated by the agency of legal subjects, including lawyers and judges, who create law as much as they are created by law.

CONCLUSION

My objective in this chapter has been to 'propagate the myth'[148] of legal pluralism, rather than to engage in internal debates over which is the true pluralist position. That is not to suggest that these are the only possible versions of external and internal legal pluralism, or that there are no important differences between various schools of legal pluralist thought. (My own position, which I will defend in Part III, is closer to critical legal pluralism.) Accordingly, I have sought to outline the legal pluralist case that presents the clearest and strongest challenge to liberal legalism, and which focuses attention on the adequacy, or otherwise, of its foundational assumptions. The theoretical accounts of external and internal legal pluralism outlined above direct us to elements of both the traditional and critical schools in this regard. First, that we need to test interpretive approaches to constitutional law against the internal legal pluralist hypothesis that the modalities of adjudication militate against achieving coherence in practice. Secondly, that we should further test instrumental approaches to constitutional law against the external legal pluralist hypothesis that the effectiveness of rights constitutionalism is compromised by its location in a world of internormativity. To the extent that these hypotheses can be substantiated, they pave the way to constructing an alternative knowledge of constitutional law, better suited to understanding the operation of constitutional rights in an age of globalization.

---

[148] See Kleinhans and Macdonald, above n 34, at 29.

4

Internal Legal Pluralism and the Interpretive Question

QUESTIONS OF INTERPRETATION are central to contemporary constitutionalism. Whether the language is English, French, Hindi or Afrikaans, constitutional courts around the world are dealing with similar sorts of questions: When constitutions protect 'freedom of expression,' does this include obscene expression, or racist speech, or commercial advertising? What amounts to 'reasonable limits' on the exercise of constitutional rights that can be 'demonstrably justified in a free and democratic society'? When constitutions state that they apply to 'legislatures' and 'governments', does this include courts or private law actions? Underlying, and informing, conventional responses to these questions is the core liberal legalist assumption that constitutional doctrine's natural condition is systematic coherence. On this view, scholars and judges should concern themselves with elaborating the correct theory of constitutional interpretation.[1] It is important to stress that coherence should not be seen simply as an abstract quality—rather, it is through the reordering of constitutional doctrine into a (different) coherent whole that it is presumed to have instrumental effects in guiding social behaviour.[2] Accordingly, whether or not the argument for coherence can be sustained has important consequences for whether rights constitutionalism can constrain private power.

In this chapter, I test liberal legalist assumptions of coherence against the claims of internal legal pluralism outlined in the previous chapter by discussing Ronald Dworkin's 'law as integrity' thesis. Dworkin's importance lies both in the influence of his work,[3] and his argument that, notwithstanding that doctrine is often characterised by incoherence and that adjudication involves the making of political choices, we can (re)order constitutional law into a coherent normative hierarchy which will determine the right answer to each controversy. As

---

[1] Accompanying the globalization of charters of rights has been the spread of the normative approach to constitutional scholarship: see eg D Beatty, *The Ultimate Rule of Law* (Oxford, Oxford University Press, 2004) (comparative constitutionalism); D Meyerson, *Rights Limited* (Kenwyn, RSA, Juta, 1998) (South Africa); and TRS Allan, *Constitutional Justice: A Liberal Theory of the Rule of Law* (Oxford, Oxford University Press, 2001) (United Kingdom).

[2] See HW Arthurs, *Without the Law: Administrative Justice and Legal Pluralism in Nineteenth-Century England* (Toronto and Buffalo, University of Toronto Press, 1985) 2.

[3] See D Dyzenhaus, 'Recrafting the Rule of Law' in D Dyzenhaus (ed), *Recrafting the Rule of Law: The Limits of Legal Order* (Oxford and Portland, OR, Hart Publishing, 1999) 1, 9.

such, his work enables us to highlight and engage with some of the most pressing general issues raised by the interpretive question. In this regard, I consider whether, if judges follow his theory, this will have the effect of securing doctrinal coherence. I argue, with reference to Dworkin's own explanation of US Fourteenth Amendment jurisprudence, that there is a serious theoretical problem here, as 'law as integrity' is equally capable of supporting contrary positions. I then elaborate how Dworkin's failure to convince is indicative of two general difficulties, which I support with reference to case studies on freedom of expression. First, constitutional theory cannot exclude the scope for doctrinal plurality that inheres in judges' status as law-creating subjects, and secondly, in practice, adjudication is a highly fragmented, variegated and ad hoc activity. I conclude that a close examination of the argument for coherence confirms the insight of internal legal pluralism that jurisprudence is congenitally incoherent and disordered.

RONALD DWORKIN'S LAW AS INTEGRITY

Ronald Dworkin's 'law as integrity' thesis is easily the locus classicus of the argument that, properly interpreted, doctrinal materials can lead us to the right answer, as a matter of law, in every case. Dworkin's constitutional theory is an instantiation of his conception of adjudication as essentially an interpretive function,[4] and promises a methodology where judges' 'own convictions about justice or wise policy are constrained in [their] overall interpretive judgment.'[5] It is important to locate Dworkin's work in the intellectual history of liberal constitutional theory. While he may be the liberal whom critical scholars most often try to knock down,[6] he does not represent some stock position, but is attuned to the more serious shortcomings of liberal legalism. In this regard, Duncan Kennedy has described Dworkin as 'the most legal realist'[7] of liberal thinkers. Kennedy has in mind here Dworkin's response to what he calls the 'liberal dilemma,' ie how to provide a democratic justification for judicial review without lapsing into ad hoc consequentialist arguments.[8] For Kennedy, Dworkin's work represents a significant advance in liberal legalism (over, for example, Hartian positivism) by admitting a political dimension to

---

[4] See R Dworkin, *Law's Empire* (London, Fontana, 1986) 226.

[5] *Ibid* at 380.

[6] See, eg, AC Hutchinson, *It's All in the Game* (Durham, NC, Duke University Press, 2000) 121–36.

[7] D Kennedy, *A Critique of Adjudication (fin de siècle)* (Cambridge, MA, Harvard University Press, 1997) 119.

[8] *Ibid* at 113. Kennedy constructs this dilemma with reference to the Warren court jurisprudence in the US, which placed liberals in the position of now having to justify an institution which they had previously attacked in less enlightened times, for example, during the Lochner substantive due process era. In this context, the liberal project is 'to show that this judicial contribution to the substance of both private and public law is democratically legitimate because it furthers the rule of law, rather than merely legislating judicially' (*ibid*).

adjudication.[9] Dworkin is explicit that judges cannot avoid, and indeed are obliged to invoke, considerations of political theory in deciding cases. For David Dyzenhaus, Dworkin's 'great contribution' to legal theory is to illuminate that 'law is not only about setting clear goals but also about argument as to what those goals should be.'[10] Thus, Dworkin's conception of the law–politics divide does not equate to a distinction between a closed, deductive system on one side, and political argument on the other: for Dworkin, law is argumentative.[11]

Dworkin's interest, and challenge, is that despite his agreement with important elements of the critical stance on liberal legalism and contemporary constitutional theory,[12] he sets himself firmly against the conclusion that law is hopelessly open-ended, or a bare disguise for power politics. While he accepts, given the fact of the political dimension of constitutional interpretation, that 'we should expect to find distinctly liberal or radical or conservative opinions [and] this is exactly what we do find,'[13] he also believes that to the extent law is incoherent, this is because of human failure.[14] The major part of his work deals with how coherence can be restored. Thus, while his law-politics divide is not as formal as some versions of liberal legalism, this divide nonetheless remains in place, and although law is seen as argumentative, only a small class of political argument is capable of crossing over to become legal argument.[15] Accordingly, although constitutional adjudication necessarily involves judges making political choices, he believes he can show which political choices are demanded by the constitution. Thus, the criterion of success which Dworkin sets himself is that if judges follow his theory in constitutional cases, they will purge doctrine of internal legal pluralism.

Law as Integrity and Dworkin's Constitutional Theory

The key to Dworkin's constitutional theory is his account of law as integrity. The basis of this is the 'adjudicative principle of integrity' which requires judges to regard law as written by a single author, here 'the community personified,' and which expresses 'a coherent conception of justice and fairness.'[16] In practical

---

[9] *Ibid* at 120.

[10] Above n 3, at 9.

[11] In this context, Kennedy (above n 7, at 121) regards Dworkin appears as 'the heir . . . and the developer of the legal realist tradition.'

[12] Above n 4, at 360–71.

[13] R Dworkin, *A Matter of Principle* (Cambridge, MA, Harvard University Press, 1978) 164–5 (quoted in Kennedy, above n 7, at 121).

[14] Compare RA Macdonald, 'Metaphors of Multiplicity: Civil Society, Regimes and Legal Pluralism' (1998) 15 *Arizona Journal of International and Comparative Law* 69, 75.

[15] As Loughlin points out (M Loughlin, *Sword and Scales: An Examination of the Relationship Between Law and Politics* (Oxford and Portland, OR, Hart Publishing, 2000) 12), while Dworkin admits a political dimension to adjudication, it is only certain political issues which 'are converted into "questions of justice." '

[16] Above n 4, at 225.

terms, this imposes the twin test of 'fit and justification'[17] on judges deciding legal controversies:

> [Integrity] insists that the law—the rights and duties that flow from past collective decisions and for that reason license or require coercion—contains not only the narrow explicit content of these decisions but also, more broadly, the scheme of principles necessary to justify them.[18]

The requirement of fit, which connects Dworkin to an earlier, more formalist liberal legalism, may be sufficient to dispose of the instant case; however, what distinguishes his own version is the recognition that where there are two or more plausible interpretations, the judge's 'own moral and political convictions are now directly engaged.'[19] However, he or she is not able to choose freely from those convictions, but has to decide which interpretation shows the community's standards, from the perspective of political morality, in the best possible light.[20] Here, the role of principles is crucial:

> Law as integrity asks judges to assume, so far as this is possible, that the law is structured by a coherent set of principles about justice and fairness and procedural due process, and it asks them to enforce these in the fresh cases that come before them, so that each person's situation is fair and just according to the same standards.[21]

Thus, principles are the means whereby adjudication performs its interpretive function: they crystallise the best justification of past decisions, and are the resources judges employ in ensuring coherence within the narrative of law. In this way, Dworkin asserts that law as integrity can provide the 'right answer' in every case: accordingly, he rejects the need to respond to the traditional liberal legalist dilemma of whether judges invent or find the law—for him, we can only understand legal reasoning 'by seeing the sense in which they do both and neither.'[22]

Dworkin's constitutional theory fits within his law as integrity thesis, and posits three practical considerations for deciding constitutional cases. First, here, more so than any area of law, judges must acknowledge its interpretive character, which cannot be satisfied by retreating to the false certainties of historicism or passivism, as the 'question of law . . . is inescapable.'[23] Secondly, judicial political judgments are equally unavoidable; however, these are not unconstrained choices as constitutional theory 'must fit and justify the most basic arrangements of political power in the community.'[24] Thirdly, Dworkin's reading of these arrangements inserts a metaprinciple of equality into the

---

[17] *Ibid* at 255.
[18] *Ibid* at 227.
[19] *Ibid* at 256.
[20] *Ibid* at 256.
[21] *Ibid* at 243.
[22] *Ibid* at 225.
[23] *Ibid* at 371.
[24] *Ibid* at 380.

process. This combines the priority of the egalitarian principle, which instructs the government to treat everyone 'with equal care and concern,'[25] and the policy–principle distinction, which establishes rights as trumps in the realm of principle over how far the legislature can pursue collective policies for the general welfare. This does not impose some specific notion of equality, for example utilitarian or libertarian, on legislatures when they make policy, but instead requires that they respect '*some* plausible conception of equality'[26] which means they must recognise certain rights as circumscribing their policy deliberations.

Thus, for Dworkin the 'crucial interpretive question'[27] is what rights legislatures must respect. He discusses the US Supreme Court's Fourteenth Amendment jurisprudence to show how his method will lead Hercules, his judicial *alter ego*, to the right answer in constitutional cases. Starting from the premise that the constitution guarantees a right against official racial discrimination, he outlines three possible justifications of this right which will aid Hercules in mapping its precise contours. These are: the suspect classifications approach, which views racial prejudice as a special case of the requirement not to treat people differently on some irrational basis; the banned categories approach, which prevents any governmental reliance on racial grounds; and the banned sources approach, which rules out collective decisions which are motivated by prejudice against a particular group.[28] By applying the tests of fit and justification, Hercules can establish which is the best theory of the constitution, and so provide us with the principled basis for prospective adjudication.

Dworkin asks how Hercules would decide and justify the Warren Court's seminal decision in *Brown*.[29] He dismisses the suspect classifications approach because the idea that no special consideration be given to the racially motivated nature of some citizens' preferences no longer reflected Americans' conceptions of racial justice.[30] Dworkin emphasises that his is not an abstract rule-based theory, but a dynamic one which can adapt to changing societal attitudes by endorsing either the banned categories or banned sources approach as 'consistent, in 1954, with ethical attitudes that were widespread in the community.'[31] It is not necessary for Hercules to choose between the two to decide *Brown*; however, it is now clear that the constitutional duty to treat everyone with equal care and concern at least requires a heightened scrutiny of historically rooted forms of discrimination.

Which theory *best* reflects constitutional practice and structure is elaborated in Dworkin's discussion of the Supreme Court's decision in *Bakke*.[32] The issue is crystallised here as UC-Davis Medical School's refusal of a place to Alan

---

[25] *Ibid* at 296.
[26] *Ibid* at 382.
[27] *Ibid*.
[28] *Ibid* at 382–84.
[29] *Brown v Board of Education of Topeka* 347 US 483 (1954).
[30] Above n 4, at 387.
[31] *Ibid* at 388.
[32] *Regents of the University of California v Bakke* 438 US 265 (1978).

Bakke, to which he would have been entitled had he not been white, would certainly fall foul of the banned categories approach, which outlaws any differential treatment on racial grounds; however, this is not necessarily the case under the banned sources approach, where the scheme would be permissible provided it did not covertly discriminate against some other group.[33] While the former approach may fit better with previous decisions, it can only embody a principle against discrimination on account of innate characteristics, which he finds US practice to have firmly rejected.[34] However, for Dworkin, racial discrimination is unjust 'not because people cannot choose their race, but because that discrimination expresses prejudice.'[35] Thus, Hercules would decide *Bakke* employing the banned sources approach as the best available interpretation: on this basis, affirmative action schemes are valid, provided they do not disadvantage groups which have been systematically discriminated against in the past.[36] Bakke's argument that he has been unconstitutionally discriminated against on the grounds of his race is therefore rejected.

Problems with Implementing Law as Integrity

How would judges who wish to be true to law as integrity apply Dworkin's theory in constitutional adjudication? Let us return to the issue of affirmative action, and assume that the banned sources approach is the best account of the constitution. Dworkin claims that if judges adopt this approach, this will restore constitutional jurisprudence to its proper state of integrity as judgments conform to the principle enumerated in *Bakke*. It seems reasonable to assume that Hercules would regard much of the Rehnquist Court's decisions, such as *Croson*[37] and *Adarand*,[38] as falling short of integrity, by invoking the 'colorblind' approach which makes any form of racial categorisation constitutionally

---

[33] Dworkin, above n 4, at 394.

[34] 'Statutes invariably draw lines along natural differences of geography and health and ability: they subsidise workers who have by chance come to work in one industry or even firm rather than another, for example, and restrict licenses to drive or practice medicine to people with certain physical or mental disabilities' (*ibid* at 394–95).

[35] *Ibid* at 395.

[36] *Ibid* at 396.

[37] *City of Richmond v JA Croson Co* 488 US 469 (1989). This case involved a challenge to a Minority Business Utilisation Plan that set aside 30% of dollar amount of contracts to minority businesses. O' Connor J (for the majority) stated that the Constitution required all governmental racial classifications to be subject to strict scrutiny. Accordingly, as the record showed no history of racial discrimination in the awarding of city contracts, the plan was set aside on the basis that less restrictive means were available, and the remedy over-inclusive.

[38] *Adarand Constructors Inc v Peña* 515 US 200 (1995). Here, the Supreme Court heard a challenge to a federal programme of 'subcontractor compensation clauses' (ie, the prime contractor was awarded compensation for hiring subcontractors certified as controlled by 'socially and economically disadvantaged individuals' (*ibid* at 200)). O' Connor J, for the majority, held that any federal, state or local racial classifications must be subjected to strict scrutiny, and remanded the case to the lower court.

suspect. However, it is possible to reconcile Dworkinian reasoning with these results. First, we have to bear in mind the dynamic nature of law as integrity, such that the list of historically prejudiced groups is 'open to revision as social patterns change.'[39] Thus, a judge, trying to be faithful to Hercules's rendition of *Bakke*, would ask: 'does this case involve a group which has been historically subject to discrimination?' A rationalisation of decisions like *Adarand* could be: 'affirmative action was necessary to reverse deep-seated patterns of official discrimination; however, formal equality of blacks before the law has now been achieved, therefore there is no longer any need for special measures advantaging that group.'[40] We may disagree strongly over that judge's reading of the record: but it may be unfair to say that that judge is not faithfully elaborating the practical implications of the constitutional protection of equal concern and respect. Rather, we might conclude that law as integrity, by itself, says nothing to that judge as to how he or she should decide when equality has been achieved, or what period thereafter should elapse, so that we may 'declassify' the suspect nature of some categorisations, or at a more fundamental level, how we would measure the achievement of equality.

Absent race as a suspect classification, the banned sources approach becomes redundant, and affirmative action would likely be decided simply according to the principle that 'discrimination expresses prejudice.'[41] However, as Dworkin himself recognises, it is possible to construct a constitutional argument against affirmative action within the former approach. On this account, there is a general requirement for governments to take into account all citizens' interests, which they violate 'whenever [they ignore] the welfare of some group in [their] calculation of what makes the community as a whole better off.'[42] For example, in *Bakke*, it could be argued that the quota system failed to meet this requirement as it was unable to address its impact upon people in the plaintiff's position.[43] In fact, a mirror of this form of argument—that the general welfare can outweigh attempts to overcome historical prejudice—seems the best characterisation of the Rehnquist Court's approach, which does not say that affirmative action is never constitutional, but that, applying strict scrutiny, it can only pass muster if it is 'narrowly tailored' to further 'compelling governmental interests'[44] so as not to impinge on the general requirements of equal

[39] Dworkin, above n 4, at 396.

[40] Indeed, it can be argued that the notion of restoring minorities to some status quo ante of equality is the best rationalisation of decisions approving of affirmative action.

[41] Dworkin, above n 4, at 395.

[42] *Ibid* at 397.

[43] *Ibid*: 'Davis argues that its quota system plausibly contributes to the general welfare by helping to increase the number of qualified black doctors. Bakke might argue to the contrary that Davis's quota system prevented it from even attending to the impact of its admissions decisions on people in his position.'

[44] See *Adarand*, above n 38, at 202 (per O' Connor J). Cf *Grutter v Bollinger* 539 US 306 (2003) (conjoined with *Gratz v Bollinger* 539 US 244 (2003)), where the Supreme Court, applying the test of strict scrutiny, upheld the University of Michigan's Law School's race-conscious admissions plan as this furthered the compelling state interest of attaining a diverse student body. While

treatment. The task, therefore, for law as integrity, is to show judges when the general requirement should displace the special right. However, we must doubt whether it can with any degree of specificity: although Dworkin thinks that Hercules would repel Bakke's more general argument, he nonetheless concedes that *'reasonable judges might disagree with that part of his overall conclusion.'*[45] Accordingly, law as integrity will not deliver us from finding 'distinctly liberal or radical or conservative opinions'—we should expect as many different types of decisions as there are reasonable disagreements over affirmative action.

THE PROBLEM OF INTERNAL LEGAL PLURALISM

Dworkin's local difficulty in substantiating his law as integrity thesis highlights some generic problems for the constitutional theory project, and which support the case for internal legal pluralism. Whatever his idiosyncrasies, Dworkin is fully engaged with the contemporary constitutional debate, which does not conceive of rights in absolute terms, but accepts that there are concerns of the general welfare which will often justify their limitation. Where such rights do prevail, this is justified on the basis that rights constitutionalism guarantees our democratic infrastructure and our right to be treated with equal concern and respect, and so courts may intervene to correct flaws in democracy when the elected branches ignore these rights.[46] Liberal legalism seeks to provide a further democratic guard: in elaborating when courts may intervene, judges must not supply their own ideology, but are themselves the servants of the community's conception of limited government.[47] Dworkin is thus at the heart of the key issue, as he wrestles with the requirements of democracy, but always as instantiations of constitutional practice and structure, and not the theorist's own politics.[48]

O'Connor J's majority judgment sets out to clarify the holding in *Bakke*, it is questionable that it succeeds in this aim. Scalia J argues in his partial dissent (joined by Thomas J), that the compelling state interest identified by the majority is less the '"educational benefit" that emanates from the fabled "critical mass" of minority students, but rather Michigan's interest in maintaining a "prestige" law school whose normal admissions standards disproportionately exclude blacks and other minorities' (*ibid* at 347). For Scalia J, '[i]f that is a compelling state interest, everything is.' As such, he suggests that the majority judgment 'seems perversely designed to prolong the controversy' (*ibid* at 348) over the constitutionality of racial preferences in public educational institutions.

[45] Above n 4, at 397 (emphasis added).

[46] The *locus classicus* of this position is of course JH Ely, *Democracy and Distrust: A Theory of Judicial Review* (Cambridge, MA, Harvard University Press, 1980). For a discussion of the potential similarities between Ely and Dworkin, despite their ostensible differences, see N Duxbury, *Patterns of American Jurisprudence* (Oxford, Oxford University Press, 1995) 293–94.

[47] See, eg, T Campbell, *The Legal Theory of Ethical Positivism* (Aldershot, Dartmouth, 1996).

[48] See, eg, M Cappelletti, 'The "Mighty Problem" of Judicial Review and the Contribution of Comparative Analysis' (1980) 53 *Southern California Law Review* 409 and D Beatty, *Constitutional Law in Theory and Practice* (Toronto, University of Toronto Press, 1995).

Our discussion of Dworkin's theoretical difficulties suggests two major practical problems for this project, which I will explore in more detail. First, constitutional theorists are on the horns of a dilemma: if their theories are formulated in too general terms, this will invite a choice among competing values, and open up the scope for reasonable judges to disagree about the requirements of the constitution; however, if the theory is so specific as to remove any judicial discretion, then it is nothing more than the bare a priori assertion of the theorist's ideology. In practice, constitutional theorists retreat from the charge of ad hoc consequentialism by showing how their accounts give us a 'single more general requirement for which [constitutional rights] could plausibly be said to be standing in.'[49] My argument is that this generality is unable to satisfy liberal legalism's criterion of coherence as it does not, and indeed cannot, prevent judges from exercising their law-making capacity.

Secondly, it is by no means clear that even more specific theories would inexorably guide judges to the same result[50]: this brings us to the problem that constitutional theories must be tested in the context of actual adjudication. Dworkin suggests that Hercules should abstract himself from practical issues, such as the pressure of the docket, or the need to build alliances and make compromises in order to reach agreement on decisions.[51] Unfortunately for Dworkin, real judges do not have these luxuries. My argument here is that adjudication is better explained in terms of the variety of real pressures and motivations affecting judges—manifested in the form of asymmetrical social and legal relations—rather than as the Herculean search for principle. Thus, not only is constitutional theory unable to furnish judges with the means to elaborate a principled jurisprudence—in practice, they are not much interested in doing so. Accordingly, we should not see internal legal pluralism as human error to be corrected by either a better theory or a better application thereof,[52] but as the expected state of affairs.

---

[49] Meyerson, above n 1, at xxvi.

[50] Dworkin draws a distinction between the academic and practical elaboration of various theories of interpretation (Dworkin, above n 4, at 385). He believes that unlike the suspect classifications and banned sources approaches, the banned categories approach 'needs no distinct practical elaboration, because its academic elaboration is already practical enough' (*ibid*). However, we can see the scope for some practical elaboration in Dworkin's own list of the banned categories which is to include 'race, ethnic background, and perhaps gender' (*ibid* at 384, emphasis added). When is gender to be included? Should sexual orientation be a banned category? Why not social class? These questions cannot be answered by reference to the notion of 'banned categories' alone, but will necessarily involve judicial invocation of, and selection among, competing political values.

[51] *Ibid* at 380–81.

[52] See, eg, D Beatty, 'The Canadian Charter of Rights: Lessons and Laments' in GW Anderson (ed), *Rights and Democracy: Essays in UK-Canadian Constitutionalism* (London, Blackstone, 1999) 3, at 21–27.

Internal Legal Pluralism and Constitutional Theory

The first generic problem raised above is whether constitutional theory, by operating on the general plane, possesses the wherewithal to settle definitively every constitutional controversy. The challenge here is legal pluralism's claim that not only are judges law-creating subjects, but that given their individual make-ups, they will create different laws, and so give a range of doctrinal answers to the same constitutional issue: in other words, can constitutional theory overcome the possibility of internal legal pluralism? Here I agree with Dworkin that 'detail is more illuminating than range,'[53] and consider the debate between Dworkin and David Dyzenhaus as to whether the constitutional principle of equal concern and respect is offended when legislatures regulate pornography. This debate is particularly interesting, not only because each works within liberal legalist methodology to show what is the correct constitutional response, but also because Dyzenhaus's argument is that his is the better Dworkinian interpretation of constitutional equality.

Dworkin's position,[54] applying the tests of fit and value, is that the constitutional protection of freedom of expression prevents the criminalisation of private consumption of materials deemed obscene.[55] He finds that the positive state of US constitutional law is intolerant of restrictions on the content of speech, but also that this is the best justification, since (following Isaiah Berlin) there is no definitive way of choosing the ideal form of society. Rather, we must 'choose among possible combinations of ideals, a coherent set [to define our individual way of life],'[56] and so censorship of pornography cannot be justified since freedom of expression is 'at the core of the choice'[57] democracies have made with regard to a modus vivendi among incommensurable values. Dyzenhaus objects that Dworkin is not being true to the primary constitutional value of equality.[58] For Dyzenhaus, Dworkin's significance lies in his attempt to move away from the priority of negative liberty. On this account, autonomy does not consist solely in a right to non-interference with the private sphere, but in an individual right to equal concern and respect. Making equality 'the organizing principle of liberal political theory'[59] opens up the possibility of restraining expression when this undermines autonomy by perpetuating inequality.

[53] Above n 4, at 397.

[54] R Dworkin, 'Two Concepts of Liberty' in E and A Margalit (eds), *Isaiah Berlin: A Celebration* (Chicago, University of Chicago Press, 1991) 100.

[55] Dworkin's position on pornography seems to have evolved over the years. In *A Matter of Principle* (above n 13), he argues, at 358, that while the right to moral independence 'requires a permissive legal attitude toward the consumption of pornography in private,' he also believes that a 'certain concrete conception of that right nonetheless permits a scheme of restriction.'

[56] Dworkin, above n 54, at 107.

[57] *Ibid.*

[58] D Dyzenhaus 'Pornography and Public Reason' (1994) 7 *Canadian Journal of Law and Jurisprudence* 261.

[59] *Ibid* at 264.

Dyzenhaus argues that this is the case with pornography because it eroticises inequality.

Dyzenhaus takes the example of the Supreme Court of Canada's decision in *R v Butler*,[60] which involved a free speech challenge under the Canadian Charter against a conviction for distributing obscene material.[61] In upholding the conviction, Sopinka J measured the protection to be afforded to Butler's expression in terms of whether it furthered the 'core values' of free speech, which included individual self-fulfilment.[62] In his examination of the 'core values,' he emphasised the centrality of individual self-fulfilment; as pornography was far from this core to the extent that it victimises women and dehumanises their sexuality,[63] it was not a form of expression deserving of constitutional protection. On the other hand, the legislative objective sought to deal with the harm occasioned by pornography towards individual self-fulfilment.[64] Dyzenhaus praises the judgment for recognising that autonomy and equality, properly understood in terms of the background moral principles of freedom of expression, are complementary rather than antagonistic, and for refusing to allow autonomy to trump equality when the latter is under threat from the expression seeking protection.[65]

Dyzenhaus's criticism of Hercules's presumed dissent in *Butler* is that if Dworkin genuinely values equality over liberty, he must drop the commitment to global neutrality which leads to his strong defence of free speech.[66] However, we can imagine a judge faithfully implementing constitutional equality reasoning as follows: 'equal concern and respect means I should not discriminate as to conceptions of the good life; pornography invokes these conceptions, therefore I must not censor it if I am to promote the equal autonomy of all.' In other cases, the same judge may hold that equality does not compromise ideas of the good life so clearly, eg affirmative action. In other words, one could reason from equality to dissent in *Butler* without embracing the absolute position on global neutrality associated with negative liberty.

Dyzenhaus's second criticism is that if Dworkin relies on this argument, then 'the most this would show is that he has a moral position that differs from that of pro-censorship feminists.'[67] I agree with Dyzenhaus that this reduces the force of Dworkin's claims for law as integrity; however, I do not agree that we can instead demonstrate that there is a principled case in favour of censorship which a true Dworkinian would adopt.[68] It is not that Dworkin's is the constitutionally

---

[60] (1992) 89 DLR (4th) 449.

[61] Criminal Code RSC 1985, c C–46, s 163. S 163 (8) defined an obscene publication as 'any publication a dominant characteristic of which is the undue exploitation of sex, or of sex and any one or more of the following subjects, namely, crime, horror, cruelty and violence.'

[62] Above n 60, at 481.

[63] *Ibid* at 484.

[64] *Ibid* at 479.

[65] Above n 58, at 276.

[66] *Ibid* at 262.

[67] *Ibid* at 273.

[68] *Ibid* at 274.

wrong application of equality, merely that it is different. That is also the most that can be said for Dyzenhaus's position as well (in other words, he cannot withstand his own critique of Dworkin). Each presents a perfectly plausible argument from equality, fully justifiable according to the values they find to be the most important underpinnings of constitutional practice, but neither is entitled to say that the other is not being consistent with law as integrity. A more realistic explanation of the differences between them is not that either is flawed in the art of exegesis, but that the general formulation they reason from opens up a number of choices which can only be resolved by more specific reasons which are necessarily more consequentialist in nature[69]—which, of course, is what liberal legalism suggests not only we should, but can, avoid.

   To return this discussion to its broader context, we see here two important protagonists in liberal legal theory grappling with the key contemporary issue of the requirements of constitutional equality for adjudication. If Dworkin and Dyzenhaus are unable to reach any coherent consensus, then we might reasonably ask whether we have any reason to hope for anything better from judges?[70] However, legal pluralism makes a stronger point here than simply highlighting differential levels of judicial ability: rather, the discussion confirms the generic problems of achieving doctrinal coherence. Dyzenhaus's critique, just as much as Dworkin's account, is firmly within the liberal legalist tradition—his ambition is to show how a more general requirement, as an instantiation of equality, if properly applied, can lead judges to correct or better decisions. However, in setting out his argument, he demonstrates that arguments such as his are unable to constrain judges while operating at the level of generality necessary to qualify as constitutional theory. Thus, to the extent there is reasonable disagreement over what equality requires, we should expect to find this in the jurisprudence. Moreover, his only alternative, a more particularist argument, is both ineligible as a constitutional theory given its inability to distinguish judicial and political reasoning, and ipso facto, no help in producing coherence. Accordingly, legal pluralism raises serious theoretical doubts over the assumption that constitutional doctrine can be made into a coherent and systematic whole.

Internal Legal Pluralism and Constitutional Practice

Our discussion of Dworkin and Dyzenhaus highlights the difficulty of normative approaches to constitutional law in overcoming the theoretical objection of internal legal pluralism. It is important, though, also to consider to what extent the practice of adjudication confirms (or otherwise) the inadequacy of liberal legalist epistemological assumptions. Accordingly, I now focus on whether the

---

   [69] In other words, it is one's position on whether the benefits to the individual of being left alone or the benefits to the community (or some traditionally oppressed group within it) are more important which determines how one interprets the demands of equal concern and respect.
   [70] Compare Dworkin, above n 4, at 380.

principled search for coherence is the best explanation of what judges are doing in practice. Dworkin, and other constitutional theorists, might here object that what they are concerned with is what judges *ought* to do, and that the mapping of what *is* the case is the concern of positivist, not normative, legal theory.[71] This, though, is too easy an escape: Dworkin's normative exhortations must surely imply that there is a sufficient basis in practice for his 'ought' to be readily turned into an 'is'. As Frederick Schauer puts it, 'there is an important empirical question whether there are many actual judges who are in fact like Hercules,'[72] with important empirical and normative implications if answered in the negative.[73] Accordingly, it is appropriate for our inquiry to test liberal legalist assumptions against the real world, with real judges subject to real pressures.

The major problem for liberal legalism's attempt to portray adjudication in systematic terms is that judges often (and sharply)[74] disagree with each other.[75] How do we explain this? Is it plausible to maintain, as liberal legalism would have it, that all these judges are engaged in the search for constitutional principle, with only a handful ever succeeding? My argument is that, following Sampford, this is better explained by emphasising the plural forms of judicial behaviour:

> [J]udges do not tend to build systems of any kind . . . Rather they see themselves using (conveniently ill-defined) judicial techniques to deal with the material presented to them during the arguing of cases. Some of these techniques involve authority- and source-based arguments. Some involve content- and principle-based arguments. Some involve consequentialist and pragmatic arguments. Each technique is available, and judicial discretion exists as much in the choice of technique as the different uses to which it is put.[76]

In this regard, we can draw on a number of studies which, taking the empirical record as their focus, show the variety of ways in which judges reach their decisions. Some retain a doctrinal focus, and highlight the variety of interpretive moves open to judges in constitutional cases.[77] Philip Bobbitt, for example,

---

[71] See Dyzenhaus, above n 3, at 2.

[72] F Schauer, 'Incentives, Reputation, and the Inglorious Determinants of Judicial Behaviour' (2000) 68 *University of Cincinnati Law Review* 615, 618.

[73] *Ibid*.

[74] See MV Tushnet, 'Following the Rules Laid Down: A Critique of Interpretivism and Neutral Principles' (1983) 96 *Harvard Law Review* 781.

[75] See, eg, FL Morton, PH Russell and MJ Whitey, 'The Supreme Court of Canada's First One Hundred Charter of Rights Decisions: A Statistical Analysis' (1992) 30 *Osgoode Hall Law Journal* 1, 37. For example, Morton et al catalogue how after 100% unanimity in the first year of adjudication under the Canadian Charter of Rights and Freedoms, the Supreme Court of Canada has now settled to an average of only 60% unanimity.

[76] C Sampford, *The Disorder of Law* (Oxford, Blackwell, 1991) 87. See also Schauer, above n 72, at 625–34.

[77] See, eg, RH Fallon Jr, 'How to Choose a Constitutional Theory' (1999) 87 *California Law Review* 535. Fallon, speaking more to the US academic literature than the judicial record, divides constitutional arguments into a number of sub-categories. He distinguishes (at 538) between 'text-based theories,' whose validity rests on their 'fit' with the constitution, and 'practice-based

distinguishes between (at least) five 'archetypes' of constitutional argument from his reading of US constitutional jurisprudence: historical arguments, textual arguments, structural arguments, prudential arguments and doctrinal arguments.[78] Bobbitt's argument is not just that these are different theories of interpretation, but that they are representative of the *actual* argumentative techniques employed by different judges at different times when deciding constitutional cases.[79] Thus, some judges can employ different techniques in the same case, or between cases.[80] Other explanations of judicial discord step outside the internal doctrinal perspective. This is first associated with the legal realists,[81] who posited a number of 'extra-legal'[82] influences on the disposal of cases. This position has been updated by studies that have sought to show how judges are either horse-traders,[83] or (slightly more loftily) strategists,[84] seeking to advance their own position in the deeply political process of hammering out doctrinal compromise. Others have argued that adjudication is marked by judicial discretion exercised for ideological reasons,[85] which, to the extent judges are informed by different beliefs and philosophies, produces a further source of doctrinal conflict.[86]

theories,' whose claims reside in their consonance with, for example, previous judicial practice. He also identifies a further sub-division between 'substantive' theories of interpretation, which speak to the values that adjudication should promote (here he includes Rawlsian liberalism) and 'formal' or 'methodological' theories of interpretation, such as originalism, which seek an understanding independent of the values of the interpreter.

[78] See P Bobbitt, *Constitutional Fate: Theory of the Constitution* (New York, Oxford University Press, 1982) 7, chs 2–6.

[79] It should be stressed that Bobbitt himself does not draw the sceptical conclusion advanced in this book—rather, he works within the interpretive question, and regards 'the next frontier in American constitutional scholarship' as determining what judges should do when these modalities of interpretation conflict: P Bobbitt, 'Methods of Constitutional Argument' (1989) 23 *University of British Columbia Law Review* 449, 457.

[80] For an account of the different argumentative techniques employed by the Supreme Court of Canada, see S Peck, 'An Analytical Framework for the Application of the Canadian Charter of Rights and Freedoms' (1987) 25 *Osgoode Hall Law Journal* 1. Peck's conclusion (*ibid* at 3) from his survey of Canadian Charter jurisprudence is that 'judges are led to the conclusions they reach as much by their choice of values and their choice of role, that is their choice whether to adopt judicial activism or restraint, as by the doctrine they invoke.'

[81] See Duxbury, above n 46, at 68.

[82] Schauer, above n 72, at 620. Schauer lists (*ibid* at 619) the various '[extra-doctrinal] causal influences on judicial decision-making' identified by the realists as including 'the judge's views about the immediate equities of the case at hand, the judge's less particularistic views about wise public policy, or the judge's array of philosophical, and policy views, an array that is nowadays called "ideology."'

[83] B Woodward and S Armstrong, *The Brethren: Inside the Supreme Court* (New York, Avon Books, 1981).

[84] L Epstein, *The Choices Judges Make* (Washington, CQ Press, 1998).

[85] For a representative sample of this scholarship, see JAG Griffith, 'The Political Constitution' (1979) 42 *Modern Law Review* 1 (United Kingdom); A Stone, *The Birth of Judicial Politics in France* (Oxford, Oxford University Press, 1992) (France); M Mandel, *The Charter of Rights and the Legalization of Politics in Canada*, rev edn (Toronto, Thompson Educational Press, 1994) (Canada); and MV Tushnet, *Red, White and Blue: A Critical Analysis of Constitutional Law* (Cambridge, MA, Harvard University Press, 1988) (United States).

[86] See, eg, J Bakan, B Ryder, D Schneiderman and M Young, 'Developments in Constitutional Law: the 1993–94 Term' (1995) 6 *Supreme Court Law Review* (2d) 67.

It is important not to use the above studies to reduce judging to any one determinant—in particular, it is not necessary to reject liberal legalist notions of coherence by accusing judges of being purely tools in the service of a higher power,[87] or ideologues acting in bad faith.[88] Rather, the point is that even if we accept judges are acting in good faith 'to interpret and deploy legal rules as the argumentative resources . . . for their decisions,'[89] the disordering influences enumerated above show that this does not lead to a coherent rule-based model of adjudication.[90] The strength of these studies is accordingly *cumulative*, and lies in providing us with a range of factors which sit more plausibly with the complexity of adjudication in practice. Thus, sometimes judges will deploy different argumentative styles in the same case (giving contrary results), sometimes their decisions will be affected by tactical concessions in exchanges with their colleagues, and at other times informed by implicit value-choices—or all three at once. The key point here is that identifying this mixture of factors affecting judicial decision-making refutes the idea (necessary for theories such as Dworkin's to succeed) that judges, as a collectivity, are motivated by the search for overarching constitutional principle. The most we can say is that adjudication represents a series of individual searches for principle, the problem here being, as Sampford puts it, that such systems 'are created in the mind of an individual,' and remain there.[91]

In the remainder of this section, I test the argument that a more pluralistic approach is a better explanation of constitutional adjudication by focusing on two pairs of Canadian Supreme Court decisions on freedom of expression. These cases are particularly interesting examples of the tendency noted above towards doctrinal incoherence. In the first pair, *Keegstra*[92] and *Zundel*,[93] the Supreme Court heard appeals against convictions for propagating anti-Semitic views: in the former, by a 4–3 vote, it rejected the appeal, in the latter, again by a 4–3 vote, it struck down the conviction. The second two cases, *Irwin Toy*[94] and *RJR-Macdonald*[95] concerned challenges to statutes restricting the plaintiff companies' rights to advertise their products: both cases were again decided by a single vote,[96] but only one statute passed the constitutional test. In each pair, although there was a certain similarity of subject matter, the impugned provisions were slightly different: *Keegstra* concerned section

---

[87] See, eg, Mandel, above n 85.

[88] Kennedy, above n 7, at 20.

[89] AC Hutchinson, 'The Rule of Law Revisited: Democracy and Courts' in Dyzenhaus (ed), *Recrafting the Rule of Law*, 196 at 212.

[90] *Ibid*: 'It is not so much that judges ignore the rules as that they could not follow the rules even if they were minded to do so.'

[91] Above n 76, at 151.

[92] *R v Keegstra* [1990] 3 SCR 697.

[93] *R v Zundel* (1992) 95 DLR (4th) 202.

[94] *Irwin Toy v Québec* (1989) 58 DLR (4th) 577.

[95] *RJR-MacDonald Inc v Attorney-General of Canada et al* (1995) 127 DLR (4th) 1.

[96] 3–2 in *Irwin Toy*, 5–4 in *RJR-MacDonald*.

319[97] of the Criminal Code criminalising 'hate speech', while *Zundel* involved the section 181[98] offence of spreading false news; the Québec statute[99] in *Irwin Toy* banned advertising aimed at under 13-year-olds, while in *RJR-Macdonald*, the federal statute[100] dealt with tobacco products. Accordingly, these cases provide highly relevant tests for our rival epistemologies: do they confirm a view of adjudication based on the search for principle, or one characterised by relative disorder?

For the liberal legalist view to prevail, we need to be convinced not only that there is a coherence between these judgments—that the Charter properly entails such fine distinctions as to uphold section 319(2) of the Criminal Code, but to strike down section 181,[101] or to ban advertising when it is aimed at children, but not smokers—but also that the judges are attempting to weave these differences into an integrated narrative. In her majority opinion in *Zundel*, McLachlin J (as she then was) sets out to show how this case can be distinguished from *Keegstra*, and so attempts to reconcile both decisions. The main doctrinal issue in these cases was presented as the proximity of the impugned speech to the 'core values' of expression (which had been elaborated in *Irwin Toy* as seeking the truth, participation in the democratic process, and individual self-fulfilment).[102] McLachlin J's argument in *Zundel* was that the activities targeted by section 181 could be seen to lie at the heart of freedom of expression values.[103] Given this proximity to the core values, there has to be a stringent proportionality examination, which section 181 failed as it was overbroad, catching 'virtually all controversial statements of apparent fact.'[104] She distinguishes this judgment from *Keegstra* by contrasting the 'low or negative value' of the hate speech caught by section 319, with the 'broad spectrum' of speech, 'much of which may be argued to have value' affected by section 181.[105] In

---

[97] S 319(2) of the Canadian Criminal Code reads as follows: 'Everyone who, by communicating statements other than in private conversation, wilfully promotes hatred against any identifiable group is guilty of (a) an indictable offence and is liable to imprisonment for two years, or (b) an offence punishable on summary conviction.'

[98] The full text of s 181 is: 'Everyone who wilfully publishes a statement, tale or news that he knows to be false and that causes or is likely to cause injury to a public interest is guilty of an indictable offence and liable to imprisonment for a term not exceeding two years.'

[99] Consumer Protection Act, SQ 1978, c 9.

[100] Tobacco Products Control Act, SC 1988, c 20.

[101] For apparent academic support for this view, see PW Hogg, *Constitutional Law of Canada*, loose-leaf edn (Toronto, Carswell, 1997) 40–23.

[102] Above n 94, at 612. In free speech cases, the Supreme Court has adopted a 'large and liberal' interpretation of expression, which includes all communication short of violence (*ibid* at 607); the major doctrinal work thus centres on whether limitations on speech satisfy the general savings clause in s 1. The test here is presented by the Court in terms of whether the limitation meets the broader tests of rationality and proportionality it has developed since *R v Oakes* (1986) 26 DLR (4th) 200.

[103] Above n 93, at 276. The case was in fact decided on the prior point that s 181 did not embody a pressing and substantial legislative objective, which McLachlin J characterised as dating from the 13th century, with the purpose of protecting the security of the state in the guise of the head of power (*ibid* at 268). (Compare dissenting judgment of Cory and Iacobucci JJ, *ibid* at 227).

[104] *Ibid* at 276.

[105] *Ibid*. She also referred approvingly to Dickson CJC's depiction of s 319(2) objectives in *Keegstra* as being 'important'.

RJR-Macdonald, the majority (again per McLachlin J) pointed to a number of contrasting factors with *Irwin Toy*: for example, only in the former had the legislature resorted to use of the criminal law (as opposed to a regulatory regime), which, as it involved 'a contest between the state and the accused,' was not entitled to a high degree of deference,[106] and also that in the former case the ban was total, but only partial in the latter.[107]

Accordingly, the majorities in both *Zundel* and *RJR-Macdonald* seek to justify the difference between them and *Keegstra* and *Irwin Toy* respectively in terms of coherence (although, if they are correct, we might wonder if an average of barely over .500 is good enough). However, if we look below the surface of these cases, we can dispute that they represent the elaboration of coherent principles. In this regard, I will make two related arguments: first, that if we look more closely at what (basically) the same set of judges say in each pair, these cases are not so readily reconcilable, and secondly, that these contradictory judgments embody a range of disordering influences which militate against coherence in adjudication.

The principal argument against coherence here is that the same arguments that win in *Zundel* and *RJR-Macdonald*, are essentially the same that lose in *Keegstra* and *Irwin Toy*. In other words, there is greater consonance between the respective majorities and dissents of both pairs, than between the actual disposals. Thus, in her dissent in *Keegstra*, McLachlin J regarded section 319(2) with the same opprobrium as she later did section 181 in *Zundel*, and argued that the former 'invokes all of the values upon which section 2(b) of the Charter rests,'[108] leading it to be subjected to a heightened proportionality analysis, which, in her view, it failed. Whereas both Dickson CJC's opinion in *Keegstra*, and Cory and Iacobucci JJ's dissent in *Zundel* placed the speech in question far from the core values of expression. Similarly, in *Irwin Toy*, McIntyre J's dissent characterised the Consumer Protection Act as placing the state in the same antagonistic role[109] later assigned to it with regard to the Tobacco Products Control Act by McLachlin J in *RJR-Macdonald*. In contrast, the *Irwin Toy* majority and *RJR-Macdonald* dissent depicted both statutes as involving the competing rights of different (including vulnerable) groups in society. The argument that what we see in these cases is less an elaboration of principle, but more a clash between two different views on how strictly state restrictions on

---

[106] Above n 95, at 91.

[107] *Ibid* at 100.

[108] Above n 92, at 863/4. Cf *Zundel*, where this is somewhat watered down to the proposition that the sorts of activities which a jury might find contrary to the public interest, and so convict under s 181 'may well relate to the core values protected by [freedom of expression]' (above n 93, at 276).

[109] In his discussion of the Consumer Protection Act, McIntyre J recounted previous examples of state censorship, including the Church's control of the language of worship, and restrictions on the public education of women, in support of his conclusion that: 'Our concern should be to recognize that in this century we have seen whole societies utterly corrupted by the suppression of free expression. We should not lightly take a step in that direction, however slightly' (above n 94, at 636).

expression should be viewed (with each winning out once in both pairs of cases), finds further support if we examine the judicial voting record. In *Keegstra* and *Zundel*, we can identify two groups of three judges, one in favour of, one against, legislative deference, who maintain their broad positions in each case.[110] There is also a certain overlap between the judicial positions taken in the commercial expression and hate speech cases.[111] However, it should also be noted that although these broad positions recur throughout the cases, not all judges can be easily assigned to one camp or the other[112]: the most obvious example being L'Heureux-Dubé J, the only judge to endorse both the *Keegstra* and *Zundel* opinions.

My argument is that a judge's stance between these positions in a particular case reflects his or her resolution of a number of issues which are then expressed as the requirements of the constitutional rule, not the other way around. One such issue is how they conceive of expression. On one view, speech is a linear and transparent medium, whose prime characteristic is its common form, and where the benefits of free expression are seen in terms of quantity; on another, speech is social and relational, which is best understood in terms of its content, and where its benefits are seen in more qualitative terms.[113] If judges rely on the former view, they are likely to be suspicious of all regulation of speech, whereas if they tend towards the latter, the regulation of some types of speech, judged to be socially harmful,[114] will not pose the same constitutional danger. In other words, it is judges' underlying conception of communication which determines their location of an expressive action to the core values of free speech. Related to this is how judges conceive of individuals: as Richard Moon has catalogued, in free speech cases, the court oscillates between seeing people as autonomous agents, to be left alone, and as susceptible to manipulation, thereby needing constitutional protection.[115] How this is resolved leads not only to plural disposals of similar issues, but to the differences in judicial methodology, which ranges between philosophical exploration of the bounds of freedom, and causal

---

[110] In *Keegstra*, Dickson CJC is supported in the majority by Wilson, L'Heureux-Dubé and Gonthier JJ, with McLachlin J's dissent being joined by La Forest and Sopinka JJ. By *Zundel*, Dickson CJC and Wilson J had left the Court, but their positions on the issue are effectively taken up by the co-authors of the dissent, Iacobucci and Cory JJ, with Gonthier J again being in favour of legislative deference.

[111] Eg, McLachlin J argues in favour of striking down the challenged measure in three cases (where she was joined by Sopinka J), or four if we see her taking over McIntyre J's position from *Irwin Toy*. Also, if we see Cory J filling Wilson J's position in the later case in each pairing, there is again a common position held throughout in favour of deference.

[112] Eg, La Forest J votes with the anti-deference stance in *Keegstra* and *Zundel*, but issues a ringing endorsement of legislative deference in *RJR-MacDonald*. Whereas Iacobucci J is in favour of deference in *Zundel*, but votes to strike down the Tobacco Products Control Act.

[113] See J Bakan, *Just Words: Constitutional Rights and Social Wrongs* (Toronto, University of Toronto Press, 1997) ch 4.

[114] Of course, those taking a more content-based view may well disagree on what speech is more socially harmful.

[115] R Moon, 'The Supreme Court of Canada on the Structure of Freedom of Expression Adjudication' (1995) 45 *University of Toronto Law Journal* 419 at 423.

inquiries into the harms caused by restrictions on speech.[116] How judges resolve these issues is of course question-begging, and points us to the role ideological choices,[117] reflecting the judges' (however implicit) views of the proper role of the state and its relation to the individual,[118] play in the exercise of judicial discretion in adjudication.[119]

CONCLUSION

It should be stressed that it is not my purpose in highlighting the choices made by judges which lead to the divisions in the cases under discussion to criticise judges for not being true to the holy grail of principle. Rather, my point is that that such choices are an inescapable part of what judges do, even when they are faithfully trying to follow the rules. These choices may themselves produce individual judicial forms of 'coherence'—such as L'Heureux-Dubé J's (singular) view that *Keegstra* and *Zundel* stand for the same principle—but it is the interaction between these unique systems which makes doctrinal disorder inevitable. The cases under discussion may be atypical—in others there may be less, or more, judicial disagreement—but the issues which they raise are not. They confirm that if we persist in explaining hard cases in liberal legalist terms of the collective judicial search for an overarching constitutional principle, then such cases will continue to create difficulties. However, if we instead adopt the theoretical insights of internal legal pluralism, then explaining the twists and vagaries of adjudication is not so hard after all—it is just its practice that remains exceedingly complex.

---

[116] See, eg, LE Weinrib, 'Hate Promotion in a Free and Democratic Society: *R v Keegstra*' (1991) 36 *McGill Law Journal* 1416, who (at 1418) criticises McLachlin J's judgment in *Keegstra* for relying on causative criteria rather than normative argument about the purposes of the constitutional protection of speech. For present purposes the key issue though is not which approach is constitutionally permitted (and how we would decide this), but that both approaches recur, and indeed are deployed at different times by the same judge. Thus, in *RJR-MacDonald*, McLachlin J refers to the need for the state to demonstrate 'the actual connection between the [legislative] objective and what the law will in fact achieve' (above n 95, at 90), which in the absence of such proof it fails; however, there is also a decidedly normative aspect to her judgment, as when she adheres to the view that protecting commercial speech promotes the purpose of free speech in advancing autonomy by enhancing individuals' choice by giving them information relating to 'price, quality and even health risks associated with different brands' (*ibid* at 102).

[117] See P Macklem, 'Constitutional Ideologies' (1988) 20 *Ottawa Law Review* 117.

[118] Again, here we can see a certain degree of consistency across issues: for example, La Forest J's position in *RJR-MacDonald* in favour of legislative deference on social and economic issues reflects a more social democratic stance in favour of state regulation to correct disparities of social power, which he carries through to other areas of Charter jurisprudence. For example, see his opinion in *Thomson Newspapers Ltd v Canada (Director of Investigation and Research)* [1990] 1 SCR 425 at 534–35. Whereas McLachlin J is often more at home in the classical liberal wing of the court, which insists on a strong protection for the individual's private sphere. Again, this approach runs through her other judgments: see *Committee for the Commonwealth of Canada v Canada* (1991) 77 DLR (4th) 385 at 448.

[119] See Peck, above n 80.

5

External Legal Pluralism and the Instrumental Question

CONSTITUTIONAL SCHOLARSHIP, ESPECIALLY when addressing the interpretive question, can often resemble political philosophy—however, we should avoid regarding it as a purely abstract discourse. Rather, this theoretical activity must be linked to its concrete purposes, namely the social benefits that are thought to accrue from winning the normative argument in constitutional cases. The instrumental assumption of liberal legalism is captured by Stuart Scheingold's classic formulation of the myth of rights:

> The assumption is that litigation can evoke a declaration of rights from courts; that it can, further, be used to assure the realization of those rights; and, finally, that realization is tantamount to meaningful change. The *myth of rights* is, in other words, premised on a direct linking of litigation, rights, and remedies with social change.[1]

Some forms of constitutional scholarship place more emphasis on the instrumental aspect: for example, critical scholars who would not choose a judicially administered charter of rights, nonetheless seek to shift constitutional adjudication towards their preferred political ends.[2] However, instrumental considerations also inform liberal legalist scholars, such as Dworkin, who regards the outcome of constitutional adjudication as of 'capital importance'[3] in protecting individual rights. The pervasive nature of this assumption is also reflected in the level of resources devoted to constitutional litigation by other actors, such as pressure groups[4] and governmental departments.[5]

---

[1] S Scheingold, *The Politics of Rights: Lawyers, Public Policy, and Political Change* (New Haven, Yale University Press, 1974) 5.

[2] Thus, while the strategy of much critical scholarship has been to lay bare the political basis on which constitutional adjudication rests, this is often in service of advocating some other, more enlightened objective, which constitutional rights should promote. For example, Mark Tushnet's response to the 'how would you decide case X?' question, that he would 'make an explicitly political judgment . . . likely to advance the cause of socialism,' can be seen to render explicit the instrumentalist assumption of constitutional scholarship: M Tushnet, 'The Dilemmas of Liberal Constitutionalism' (1981) 42 *Ohio State Law Journal* 411, 424.

[3] R Dworkin, *A Matter of Principle* (Cambridge, MA, Harvard University Press, 1978) 293.

[4] See GN Rosenberg, 'Hollow Hopes and Other Aspirations: a Reply to Feeley and McCann' (1993) 18 *Law and Social Inquiry* 761, 765.

[5] PJ Monahan and M Finkelstein, 'The Charter of Rights and Public Policy in Canada' (1992) 30 *Osgoode Hall Law Journal* 501, 516–22.

In this chapter, I test liberal legalist assumptions of instrumentalism against the claims of external legal pluralism with reference to case studies focusing on constitutional litigation in race relations, abortion and freedom of expression. These areas represent some high profile issues where campaigners have sought to effect social change through constitutional law, and are also where considerable social scientific research has now been conducted on the impact of this litigation. My argument is that the available evidence supports Santos's account of the social world as a site of internormativity, which necessarily constrains the effectiveness of state constitutional law. At best, claims about the direct effects of adjudication are exaggerated, and at worst, constitutional law is often not even indirectly effective, but indeed counterproductive. Accordingly, I conclude that the persistence of a constitutional epistemology based in the command theory of law is not justified by the empirical record.

RACE AND CIVIL RIGHTS

We begin our interrogation of constitutional adjudication's instrumentality by considering the issue of race and equality under the US Bill of Rights. In particular, the focus will be on the Warren Court's Fourteenth Amendment jurisprudence, which has now attained iconic status in terms of constitutional law's capacity to effect progressive social change. The Warren Court's pro-civil rights judgments, beginning with *Brown v Board of Education*,[6] have been described as amounting to nothing less than 'a social revolution,' or as the very least, as the principal force behind 'great changes' to American society.[7] This perception of the Court's significance has sustained a prolonged debate on the constitutional requirements of equality, where one side praises the Court's role as 'an important source of minority or individuals' rights against unjustified public authority,'[8] while the other attacks it for illegitimately engaging in 'social engineering from the bench.'[9]

In examining the impact of Warren era equal rights judgments, we are not holding the Court to the standard of erasing all forms of racial prejudice, thus inviting the inevitable conclusion that it has failed. Rather, the object of scrutiny is the view that certain specified concrete benefits will follow if the Court is persuaded by one side or the other in the constitutional debate. Also, we have to be careful to measure the jurisprudence on its own terms—if, for example, it speaks in terms of desegregating southern schools, then it should be assessed in terms of whether this has been achieved. In these ways, we avoid the charge of caricaturing the Court's record: rather, we are conducting a legitimate inquiry

---

[6] 347 US 483(1954).

[7] A Lewis, 'An Ingenious Structure' *The New York Times Magazine*, 13 September 1987 39, 40.

[8] R Dworkin, *Freedom's Law* (Cambridge, MA, Harvard University Press, 1996) 147.

[9] RH Bork, *The Tempting of America: The Political Seduction of Law* (New York, Free Press, 1990) 84.

into the efficacy of the case law, which takes seriously the intellectual and financial resources spent by the legal and civil rights communities in trying to direct constitutional adjudication to their own ends. A number of quantitative and evaluative studies of civil rights litigation strongly suggest that the Supreme Court did not have any major direct effect in undoing official segregation. Moreover, its principal impact may have been indirect, while there is also evidence of unintended and often counterproductive consequences. In short, the empirical record tells a very different story from the conventional view which assumes constitutional law's instrumentality.

'Top-down' Approaches

There are now a number of studies which challenge the view of the Supreme Court as an important source of minority rights. Gerald Rosenberg's *The Hollow Hope*[10] provides us with a helpful collation of empirical data which he forcefully employs to argue the case that court orders are not self-executing. Rosenberg's target is what he sees as the dominant role of courts as 'powerful, vigorous and potent proponents of change.'[11] The dominant understanding of the Warren Court as the key actor in securing blacks' civil rights is axiomatic of this 'dynamic court' view; however, Rosenberg argues that instead the 'constrained court' model,[12] which emphasises the institutional limitations of the Court to effect change, better reflects the record. Drawing on quantitative data, Rosenberg argues that claims of a direct link between the Warren Court's civil rights jurisprudence and progressive change are found empirically wanting. He undertakes a detailed analysis of the school desegregation cases from 1954–64. This is presented as an appropriate period for isolated assessment of the Court's impact, given both the Court's bold prosecution of desegregation, and the negligible action from Congress and the federal government.[13] Here, the figures show that, for example in the Southern states, where the segregation problem was most acute, there was virtually no change in the percentage of black children attending the same elementary and secondary schools as whites, rising from almost zero in 1954, to only 1.2 per cent ten years later.[14] Rosenberg highlights that once the elected branches of government take up the desegregation case, with the important step being Congress approving the Civil Rights Act 1964, there is a greater intensity of change. In the South, the percentage of blacks in integrated schools rises from 1.2 per cent in 1964 to 32 per cent by 1969 and 91.3 per cent at the end of 1973. In the border states including the District of

---

[10] G Rosenberg, *The Hollow Hope: Can Courts Bring About Social Change?* (Chicago and London, University of Chicago Press, 1991).

[11] *Ibid* at 2.

[12] *Ibid* at 10–21.

[13] *Ibid* at 45 and 49.

[14] *Ibid* at 50.

Columbia, while there was an increase from 39.6 per cent in 1956 to 54.8 per cent by 1964, by 1973 this had risen to 77.3 per cent.[15]

With regard to higher education, Rosenberg again contrasts the Court's firm rejection of the separate but equal doctrine with the continuing fact of segregation, which only begins to change with the passing of the 1964 Act. Here, in the South, we see a change from 4639 blacks attending traditionally white colleges and universities in 1963, to 20,788 in 1966, although this still only amounted to 2.6 per cent of the overall enrolment.[16] In some Southern states, later increases are found, with black enrolment, for example in Alabama and South Carolina, rising from 3.3 per cent and 2.8 per cent in 1970, to 10 per cent and 9 per cent in 1978 respectively. He also finds that while from 1940 the Supreme Court had upheld the voting rights of blacks, for example by 1958, a year after Congress first addressed the issue with civil rights legislation, black voter registration had grown from 5 per cent to 25 per cent. However, the changes after that are more striking: by 1970, five years after the federal Voting Rights Act was enacted in 1965, the percentage of the black population registered to vote was 66.9 per cent.[17]

In contrast to the Court's relative ineffectiveness, Rosenberg argues that the key moment for the civil rights movement was the decision of the Johnson administration to lend its support through the 1964 Act. This provided greater institutional support for implementing change. For example, under the 1964 Civil Rights Act, federal funding of schools was now directly linked to achieving desegregation.[18] Also, the Voting Rights Act, which placed examiners in election districts to monitor devices like literacy tests, led to a more broad-based approach than individual lawsuits to register individual voters.[19] These reforms should also be seen as part of a constellation of factors, including a change of heart by the states' political leadership, and changing social and cultural attitudes which were breaking down racial barriers.[20] Thus, the Court in the 1960s encountered less hostility and opposition from the state politicians, in whose hands the task of implementing desegregation ultimately rested, and also was able to give its orders more weight, for example, by threatening to withhold federal funds from segregationist school boards.[21] Rosenberg's conclusion from this analysis is that given the necessity of executive action, and broader societal

---

[15] *Ibid* at 49. (There are no figures available pre-1956.)

[16] *Ibid* at 56–7.

[17] *Ibid* at 61. Rosenberg also deals with the examples of transportation, accommodations and public places, and housing (*ibid* at 63–70). While in each of these examples, the availability of quantitative data is more problematic than those discussed in the text, he finds that where the Court did speak directly (eg, the state action doctrine effectively immunised private accommodations from coming within the ambit of jurisprudence), the pattern of relative judicial ineffectiveness vis-à-vis the other branches of government is repeated (*ibid* at 64, 67 and 70).

[18] *Ibid* at 47.

[19] *Ibid* at 62.

[20] *Ibid* at 97.

[21] *Ibid* at 100.

receptivity, for social change to occur, 'paradigms based on court efficacy are simply wrong.'[22]

'Bottom-up' Approaches

While Rosenberg gives us a ringing restatement that court orders are not self-executing, some commentators suggest we should be wary of the methodological implications of his approach. Michael McCann charges in particular that by seeking to assign discreet causes to events, Rosenberg himself relies on too instrumental an understanding of causation[23] which exaggerates the potential importance of courts, as well as legislators and administrators, in shaping social conduct.[24] Accordingly, McCann suggests the need to consider 'bottom-up' as well as 'top-down' approaches, which place social struggles at the centre of analysis, and where courts 'play an important, if limited and partial, role in fashioning the different "opportunity structures" and discursive frameworks within which citizens act.'[25] Within this framework, the contribution of courts to social change is also assessed in terms of indirect effects.[26] I agree with McCann that we should be wary of lapsing into an overly instrumental account of social phenomena in our critique of the instrumental assumption in constitutional law; however, with regard to the civil rights issue, we find a strong case that litigation was not very effective even indirectly, and that moreover, it may have had adverse unintended consequences.

Stuart Scheingold's work is perhaps the leading example of the 'bottom-up' approach. Scheingold seeks to carve out a middle way between the myth of rights outlined above, and the view that constitutional adjudication has produced broadly hegemonic results.[27] Instead, he starts from the premise that 'rights in the abstract cannot be thought of as either allies or enemies of progressive tendencies but rather *as an arena for struggle*.'[28] Turning to the desegregation issue, Scheingold argues that it was legislative intervention, not litigation, that was the decisive step.[29] Indeed, if there were any direct effects flowing from *Brown*, it was to harden political will in the south against desegregation, as evidenced by the campaign of 'massive resistance'. Thus, Scheingold finds the claim that *Brown* had an indirect effect, in terms of moral

---

[22] *Ibid* at 105.

[23] M McCann, 'Causal versus Constitutive Explanations (or, On the Difficulty of Being so Positive . . .)' (1996) 21 *Law and Social Inquiry* 457, 460.

[24] M McCann, 'Reform Litigation on Trial' (1993) 18 *Law and Social Inquiry* 715, 730–35.

[25] *Ibid* at 733.

[26] *Ibid* at 732.

[27] Above n 1.

[28] S Scheingold, 'Constitutional Rights and Social Change: Civil Rights in Perspective' in MW McCann and GL Houseman (eds), *Judging the Constitution: Critical Essays in Judicial Lawmaking* (Boston, Scott, Foresman/Little Brown, 1989) 73, 76 (emphasis added).

[29] *Ibid* at 78.

suasion of the key political actors, unsubstantiated. To the extent it had an indirect effect, this was in mobilising political action, first through the civil rights movement, which eventually brought pressure on the legislative and executive branches to act.[30]

The added value of Scheingold's analysis is, that while his overall conclusion remains that the politics of rights have been generally hegemonic, he proffers an explanation as to why *Brown* may have contributed, however contingently, to desegregation. For Scheingold, the key point from the civil rights cases is that adjudication 'cannot neutralize entrenched power,'[31] but 'can only focus attention on accepted values and on departures from those values.'[32] Thus, where the *Brown* decision (indirectly) provoked a crisis, this could be resolved in a progressive manner because US society by the 1960s had 'widely accepted [desegregation] as a just ideal.'[33] However, when the Court provoked crises for race relations on other issues which are still deeply contentious, such as busing or affirmative action, this can be counterproductive for progressive politics as it stimulated those with vested interests to defend them. For example, the expansion then retrenchment of affirmative action jurisprudence can be mapped to the changing economic fortunes of white blue-collar workers, from the bounty of the 1960s to the fiscal downturn of the 1980s.[34] This raises another potential countereffect of court-based strategies, namely that while some blacks will gain from litigation victories, other blacks remain disproportionately represented in the underclass: court-based strategies undermine their ability to escape this both by releasing the sort of backlash discussed above, and through their admission to the middle classes, depoliticising the cohort of dynamic blacks who could best contribute to their liberation.[35] Thus, the limited constitutional victories could have the effect of making the issue of continuing racial inequality less prominent.[36]

Race Relations and Internormativity

My purpose in referring to both top-down and bottom-up analyses of constitutional litigation is not to contribute to the methodological debate which

[30] '[I]t was not the [Warren Court's] decisions themselves but the political mobilization spawned by resistance to the decisions that brought positive results. And not only were these results indirect and unexpected, they were also unwelcome to most civil rights lawyers who resisted politicization' (*ibid* at 80).

[31] *Ibid* at 79–80.

[32] *Ibid* at 81.

[33] *Ibid* at 80.

[34] CJ Nan, 'Adding Salt to the Wound: Affirmative Action and Critical Race Theory' (1993/4) 12 *Law and Inequality* 553, 556.

[35] Scheingold, above n 28, at 82.

[36] Stephen Halpern makes a related point, that as other historically disadvantaged groups took advantage of the limited opportunities for challenging discrimination opened up by the civil rights litigation, this diluted Americans' understanding and response to problems of racial discrimination: SC Halpern, *On the Limits of the Law: The Ironic Legacy of Title VI of the 1964 Civil Rights Act* (Baltimore and London, Johns Hopkins University Press, 1995).

McCann highlights. Rather, my argument is that the *cumulative* message[37] of these studies validates the theoretical stance of external legal pluralism in the concrete setting of constitutional adjudication. To the extent that they underline the limited effect of constitutional law in procuring progressive social change, either directly or indirectly, they confirm that the former does not exist in a binary relationship with the subjects it seeks to command, but is located in a socially mediated world which necessarily attenuates its effectiveness. Thus, these studies show that the field of race relations is marked by internormativity, where, for example, the more powerful legal norms appear to be those emanating from the workplace, whether in opening up scope for black employment in the 1960s,[38] or later resisting attempts to place blacks on a more substantively equal footing. Also, where equality-enhancing measures prevail, this can indicate that other parts of state law, such as executive action, are more effective than constitutional adjudication. Moreover, the most deep-seated influences on conduct may not be attributable to any immediate agency, but are found in 'invisible background norms'[39] of entrenched societal attitudes, which condition how normative relationships are structured and expressed. In other words, the empirical studies of litigation in the field of race and civil rights question the adequacy of a constitutional knowledge based in the linear assumptions of the command model of law. In the remainder of this chapter, I put these assumptions further to the test by considering two other important areas where the instrumental assumption of constitutional law remains strong, viz, abortion and freedom of expression.

ABORTION

Judicial controversies over the constitutionality of statutes criminalising abortion are often where instrumentalist understandings of adjudication are most clearly fixed in the public imagination. It is difficult to think, particularly in North America, of high profile abortion cases without summoning the image of groups of pro-choice and pro-life demonstrators facing each other across the court house steps, each vociferously imploring the judges to grant or withhold the constitutional right to abortion. While this image is undoubtedly emotive, it is important to stress that this reflects the extent to which courts, and rights-based strategies,

---

[37] Both McCann and Rosenberg accept that their different approaches should not be seen as alternatives: see McCann, above n 24, at 743 ('[N]either approach alone is adequate; both provide different but important insights on a host of related issues.') and Rosenberg, above n 4, at 762 ('. . . this is not a question of mutually exclusive approaches . . .').

[38] Rosenberg identifies one of the factors in breaking down racial barriers in the 1960s as the South's attempts to persuade industry to locate there, and its acceptance of peaceful race relations as the price for that relocation (above n 10, at 101).

[39] N Iyer, 'Some Mothers Are Better Than Others: a Re-examination of Maternity Benefits' in SB Boyd (ed), *Challenging the Public/Private Divide: Feminism, Law and Public Policy* (Toronto, University of Toronto Press, 1997) 168, 186.

have come to occupy a central place in the issue of abortion, first in the US,[40] where the constitutional right of women to procure an abortion remains an important focus of public debate.[41] The constitutional prominence of abortion litigation has since been replicated in other jurisdictions including Canada,[42] Germany[43] and states in central and eastern Europe,[44] with the result that some see abortion as the 'showpiece of comparative constitutional law.'[45] Unsurprisingly, this degree of public attention is reflected in scholarly activity seeking to guide the direction of constitutional abortion policy.[46]

The received wisdom is that pro-choice activists have won important victories in a range of jurisdictions. For example, the US Supreme Court's *Roe v Wade*[47] decision in 1973, striking down state laws criminalising abortion in principle, has been hailed as one of the 'most radical decisions'[48] ever issued by that Court. Defending that decision has been a central preoccupation of liberal lawyers,[49] who have applauded the Court in later cases such as *Planned Parenthood of Southeastern Pennsylvania v Casey*,[50] for refusing to reverse *Roe v Wade*, and indeed, in the words of one commentator, for giving it 'a new and better foundation.'[51] Outside the US, the Supreme Court of Canada's ruling in *Morgentaler*[52] that the Canadian Criminal Code dealing with abortion violated the Charter's guarantee of life, liberty and security of the person has been variously described as 'momentous'[53] and a 'landmark case' which 'demonstrates

---

[40] See MA Glendon, *Rights Talk: The Impoverishment of Political Discourse* (New York, Free Press, 1991) 58–60.

[41] See DM O'Brien, *Storm Center: The Supreme Court in American Politics*, 6th edn (New York and London, WW Norton, 2003) ch 1.

[42] J Brodie, SAM Gavigan and J Jenson, *The Politics of Abortion* (Toronto, Oxford University Press, 1992); compare FL Morton, *Morgentaler v Borowoski: Abortion, the Charter and the Courts* (Toronto, McClelland and Steart, 1992).

[43] DP Kommers, *The Constitutional Law of the Federal Republic of Germany*, 2nd edn (Durham, NC and London, Duke University Press, 1997) 335–56.

[44] See W Sadurski, 'Constitutional Courts in the Process of Articulating Constitutional Rights in the Post-Communist States of Central and Eastern Europe (Part II): Personal, Civil and Political Rights and Liberties' EUI Working Paper, LAW 2003/1: http://www.iue.it/PUB/law03-1.pdf 7–12.

[45] GL Neuman, '*Casey* in the Mirror: Abortion, Abuse and the Right to Protection in the United States and Germany' (1995) 43 *American Journal of Comparative Law* 273, 273.

[46] See C Sunstein, *The Partial Constitution* (Cambridge, MA, Harvard University Press, 1993) 270–85.

[47] 410 US 113 (1973).

[48] Rosenberg, above n 10 at 173, quoting JT Noonan Jr, 'Raw Judicial Power' (1973) 22 *National Review* 260, 261.

[49] See, eg, R Dworkin, *Freedom's Law* (above n 8) who, at ch 1 (entitled '*Roe* in Danger'), urged the Court not to reverse its central holding in *Roe v Wade* in the case of *Webster v Reproductive Services* 492 US 490 (1992).

[50] 505 US 833 (1992).

[51] Dworkin, above n 8, at 42. Not all of that judgment's authors would appear to share Dworkin's views. O'Brien notes (above n 41, at 28) that Kennedy J 'would never have joined the plurality in *Casey* to uphold *Roe*' had he envisaged that it would be relied on to strike down the Nebraska partial-birth abortion statute in the later case of *Stenberg v Carhart* 530 US 914 (2000).

[52] *R v Morgentaler* [1988] 1 SCR 30.

[53] LE Weinrib, 'The *Morgentaler* Judgment: Constitutional Rights, Legislative Intention, and Institutional Design' (1992) 42 *University of Toronto Law Journal* 22, 23.

how the Courts can begin to incorporate women's reality within constitutional jurisprudence.'[54] In Germany, the *Bundesverfassungsgerichts* declared federal law criminalising abortion unconstitutional in 1993,[55] thus apparently reversing its previous stance that a positive duty was imposed on the German state to protect the life of the foetus.[56] However, the evidence here also suggests that these court decisions have had much less direct effect than is widely presumed.

Assessing Direct Effects

Taking first the US, empirical data on abortion suggest two conclusions which doubt the direct effectiveness of *Roe v Wade*. First, although it is seen as the moment when abortion ceased to be a crime in principle, there was a significant number of abortions carried out before it was handed down, both outside,[57] and within, the state's abortion laws.[58] Secondly, although the number of legal abortions rose after 1973, this was at no greater rate than the pre-existing trend: thus, while there was an increase by 463,100 from 1969–71, this compares with an increase of 289,600 from 1973–75.[59] Similarly, in Canada, although abortion was only (partially) decriminalised in 1969, it has been estimated that from 1954–1965, between 50,000 and 100,000 abortions were performed, unauthorised by state law.[60] In Germany, while the Constitutional Court had announced its defence of the rights of the foetus in 1975, there was an almost five-fold increase in the number of abortions from the mid-1970s until the late 1980s.[61]

We can best explain this growing sense of dissonance between official pronouncements and actual practice by contrasting state-centred accounts of abortion law with the actual legal regimes which influence women's decisions. The notion that the state is the authoritative source of legal norms pervades discussion on abortion—for example, expressed clearly in the idea that given the absence of legislation of abortion following the *Morgentaler* decision, there was

---

[54] K Mahoney, 'Charter Equality: Has it Delivered?' in GW Anderson (ed), *Rights and Democracy: Essays in UK-Canadian Constitutionalism* (London, Blackstone, 1999) 95, 113.

[55] *Abortion II* case 88 BVerfGE 203, 1993 (see Kommers, above n 43, at 349).

[56] *Abortion I* case 39 BVerfGE 1, 1975 (see Kommers, *ibid* at 336).

[57] Eg, the number of abortions in the 1960s has been estimated at around 1 million *per annum*: KL Karst, *Law's Promise, Law's Expression: Visions of Power in the Politics of Race, Gender, and Religion* (New Haven and London, Yale University Press, 1993) 50.

[58] Rosenberg shows (above n 10, at 180) that the number of legal abortions for 1970, 1971 and 1972 were 193,500, 485,800 and 586,800 respectively.

[59] *Ibid* at 179.

[60] WA Bogart, *Courts and Country: The Limits of Litigation and the Social and Political Life of Canada* (Toronto, Oxford University Press, 1994) 146, fn 80, quoting A Prentice et al, *Canadian Women—A History* (Toronto, Harcourt Brace Jovanovich, 1988) 323.

[61] There was an increase in the number of legal abortions from 17,814 in 1974 to 83,784 in 1988: U Werner, 'The Convergence of Abortion Regulation in Germany and the United States: A Critique of Glendon's Rights Talk Thesis' (1996) 18 *Loyola (LA) International and Comparative Law Journal* 571, 600. For Werner, this shows that the demand for abortion 'proved to be relatively independent from the legal prohibition of abortion' (*ibid* at 601).

a 'legal vacuum'[62] in Canada. However, from a legal pluralist perspective, we can point to at least three important non-state sources which give us a more accurate picture of the law of abortion.

First is what Santos calls the domestic law of the householdplace, which is 'a complex social field in which state and domestic legality engage in a constant process of interaction, negotiation, compromise, conflict, mutual reinforcement, mutual neutralization.'[63] Within this framework, a patriarchal domestic law has historically been an important source of maintaining a conservative view of women's sexuality. From the 1960s onwards though, this form of domestic law has been under increasing pressure in western democracies, resulting in women being less constrained than previously in their choices with regard to lifestyle and reproduction:

> In the generation since the birth control pill became widely available, an alternative model has increasingly reflected social reality: women actively express their sexuality; sex is not tied to marriage, or to motherhood; within marriage, motherhood can be delayed or avoided altogether; motherhood does not necessarily imply marriage. In short, the alternative model claims for women a measure of control over their sexual conduct and maternity that was unimaginable in the 1950s.[64]

Secondly, the medical profession must be seen as important actors whose decisions go some way to giving shape to the prevailing normative regime. Thus, for example, under the pre-*Morgentaler* legislation in Canada, a woman required the consent of a therapeutic abortion committee, composed of at least three doctors, that continuing with pregnancy 'would be likely to endanger her life or health.'[65] Clearly, how doctors interpreted their role would have an important bearing on the availability of abortion. This discretion was confirmed in *Morgentaler* by Dickson CJC, who referred to the findings of the Badgley Report[66] that therapeutic abortion committees acting under the statutory regime at issue established their own guidelines with frequently arbitrary results.[67]

---

[62] J Fudge, 'The Public/Private Distinction: The Possibilities of and the Limits to the Use of Charter Litigation to Further Feminist Struggles' (1987) 25 *Osgoode Hall Law Journal* 485, 542. The notion of a 'legal vacuum' also persists within the sociolegal school, even where their work is designed to show the extent to which state law fails to achieve its goal, or may have unintended consequences: see, eg, Bogart, (above n 60), who writes (*ibid* at 149) of '[t]he absence of any law on abortion' in the post-*Morgentaler* era. It is telling that opposition to this notion remains within the state-centred approach: 'On the contrary, we have abundant law on the subject of abortion—constitutional law that circumscribes the permissible exercise of state power' (Weinrib, above n 53, at 67).

[63] B de Sousa Santos, *Toward a New Legal Common Sense* (London, Butterworths, 2002) 386. Thus, for Santos, the 'problem of discrepancy between law in books and law in action' identified in the text, reflects 'the ongoing process of struggle and negotiation between the state law of the family and domestic law' (*ibid* at 431).

[64] Karst, above n 57, at 52.

[65] Canadian Criminal Code, s 251(4)(c).

[66] Canada, Department of Justice, *Report of the Committee on the Operation of the Abortion Law* (Ottawa, Minister of Supply and Services, 1977).

[67] *Morgentaler*, above n 52, at 68. Dickson CJC, in the same para, went on to note (*ibid* at 69) that '[s]ome committees refuse to approve applications for second abortions unless the patient consents to sterilization, others require psychiatric assessment, and others do not grant approval to married women.'

Rosenberg makes the striking point with regard to the US that following *Roe v Wade*, US hospitals broadly refused to carry out abortions: twelve years after the ruling, only 17 per cent of public hospitals were providing abortion services, the same proportion as the year following the Supreme Court's decision.[68] What made the difference was that other medical professionals, in private clinics, opened for business.

Thirdly, as with race relations, we should include in our explanation of changes in the practice of abortion, the 'invisible background norms' which both shape, and are the product of, broader societal attitudes on matters of sexual politics. Here, we can point to the general liberalisation of social mores associated with the 1960s and 1970s. While marked by both pluralism and fluidity, this trend had taken sufficient hold among elite opinion for it to become more receptive to relaxation of the criminal laws on abortion.[69] Rosenberg also notes that in the years immediately prior to *Roe v Wade*, opinion polls in the US showed considerable decrease in opposition to abortion.[70] Thus we can posit the interim conclusion that although there were significant changes in the abortion laws, writ large, of western states from the 1970s onwards, the most important factors affecting these changes came from non-state sources, and which constitutional adjudication either mirrored, or, at best, enabled to have a limited effect.

Indirect Effects

As with the civil rights litigation, it is necessary to consider the argument that the abortion decisions may have had some indirect progressive effect. In this regard, we can consider two objections to the foregoing: First, that while there may be little evidence of direct change, the litigation energised and politicised the pro-choice campaigners, and lent legitimacy to their arguments. Secondly, that while it may be true that there was no dramatic increase in abortions where courts decriminalised that activity, this did remove real legal barriers of access, particularly to high quality medical services. However, while there may be some support for each statement, the balance of the evidence suggests that the main indirect effect of the abortion cases was to make it more difficult for most women to have an abortion.

Let us take first the question of access—it is undoubtedly the case that in the years since the criminal laws were reformed, the incidence of unsafe, backstreet

---

[68] Rosenberg, above n 10, at 190.

[69] See M Tushnet, *Taking the Constitution Away from the Courts* (Princeton, NJ, Princeton University Press, 1999) 147.

[70] Rosenberg, above n 10, at 236–38. In Canada, a symbolic barometer of public opinion could be the repeated refusals of Canadian juries to convict Henry Morgentaler despite the terms of the Criminal Code: see Bogart, above n 60, at 147.

abortions has significantly decreased.[71] However, the corollary is not that all women now have access to safe abortions by medical professionals. In the US, *Roe v Wade* effectively privatised abortion, with (for profit) private clinics filling the gap left by the reluctant public hospitals, and which by 1985 provided 87 per cent of all abortions.[72] This inserts a further variable into the broader normative regime of abortion, namely the law of the marketplace. In practice, what is most relevant to a woman's ability to obtain an abortion are positive questions of access, which in turn depend on financial wherewithal, rather than the negative question of the constitutionality of criminal restrictions on abortion.

This might not be such a major problem if we could point to legislative action improving access in other ways. However, a second indirect (and unintended by abortion campaigners) consequence was that decisions such as *Roe v Wade* and *Morgentaler* if anything appear to have galvanised opposition to abortion. We can see this expressed both by political elites—for example, by withdrawal of public funds for women seeking an abortion[73]—and by the public at large, varying from organisation of large-scale protest movements, to more direct action, such as picketing, or even bombing, of abortion clinics.[74] To repeat Scheingold's point made in the context of race relations: while constitutional adjudication may be able to provoke a crisis, how this is resolved depends very much on society's willingness to depart from values which are under pressure. Here, as with busing and affirmative action, abortion litigation played contentiously to a divided public, and may have stymied abortion campaigners' efforts by unleashing latent, but deeply-rooted, public hostility. Thus, in a parallel with the civil rights litigation, the abortion decisions may have placed some (particularly urban middle class) women in a better position, but for many, particularly if they lived in more traditional areas,[75] they were in no better position to avail themselves of their now constitutional right to an abortion.

Mary Ann Glendon provides an interesting coda to this discussion, by arguing that the importance assigned by both camps to receiving the courts' blessing for their position contributed to casting the issue as an all-or-nothing clash of rights between pregnant women and foetuses.[76] This leads to an antagonistic, individualistic form of public debate which she argues leads to poor policy: in this regard, she contrasts North America unfavourably with continental Europe where, given a historically less prominent role for courts,[77] there is a more proactive approach focusing, for example, on the need for safe and accessible

---

[71] In British Columbia, for example, it was estimated that between 1946 and 1968 (when the Criminal Code was reformed) abortion-related deaths accounted for approximately 20% of maternal deaths (*ibid* at 160, fn 80).

[72] Rosenberg, above n 10, at 197. The data shows a change from 1973, when 52% of abortions were performed in public hospitals, to 1985, when this had dwindled to 13% (*ibid*).

[73] *Ibid* at 187.

[74] Bogart, above n 60, at 151.

[75] See Rosenberg, above n 10, at 191 and Bogart, above n 60, at 153 and 162.

[76] Above n 40, at 58–59.

[77] Although see Werner (above n 61) for the argument that the differences between the US and German approaches may be narrowing.

procedures, while also providing counselling services.[78] From this we can make the further point that to the extent conducting the abortion debate in terms of rights obviates the possibility of compromise, this actually works to the disadvantage of both pro-choice and pro-life campaigners by reducing the prospects of each of them advancing a substantial portion of their policy agenda.[79]

FREEDOM OF EXPRESSION AND POLITICAL LIBELS

As with abortion, the requirements of freedom of expression have been a recurring theme in constitutional debate across a range of constitutionalist jurisdictions.[80] Robert Post identifies the central question posed by free speech theorists as 'how communication [within society] ought constitutionally to be ordered.'[81] Thus, as with race relations and abortion, we are engaged in normative debate which places a high premium on capturing the instrument of doctrine, whose function is to 'implement the objectives attributed by theory to the Constitution.'[82] Clearly, there are many theories of free speech,[83] and any number of their possible applications. I will therefore narrow my focus to an issue which enables us to see some of the general difficulties besetting the instrumentalist model of promoting free speech through constitutional adjudication. While seeking the truth and the promotion of autonomy both feature prominently in free speech discourse, it is the goal of fostering a rich and vibrant democratic debate which has recently preoccupied courts and scholars.[84] A number of scholars and activists have sought to advance this broad objective by attacking the constitutional validity of libel laws, which, insofar as they protect the reputation of politicians, are argued to have a 'chilling effect', inhibiting the publication of material necessary for healthy democratic debate.[85]

---

[78] MA Glendon, *Abortion and Divorce in Western Law* (Cambridge, MA, Harvard University Press, 1987) ch 1.

[79] Eg, a policy which addressed the interests of both pregnant mothers and foetuses might start from the premise that there is societal approval for *some degree* of abortion provision. Although this is contrary to the absolutist pro-life position, it does not rule out measures such as state provision of counselling or a cooling off period where the interests of the foetus are considered, contrary to the absolutist pro-choice position (*ibid* at 65).

[80] See, eg, R Post, 'Reconciling Theory and Doctrine in First Amendment Jurisprudence' (2000) 88 *California Law Review* 2355; D Schneiderman (ed), *Freedom of Expression and the Charter* (Scarborough, Ont, Thomson, 1991); I Loveland (ed), *Importing the First Amendment: Freedom of Speech and Expression in Britain, Europe and the USA* (Oxford, Hart Publishing, 1998); D Meyerson, *Rights Limited* (Kenywn, RSA, Juta, 1998) 55–176.

[81] *Ibid* at 2355.

[82] *Ibid* at 2355–2356.

[83] See E Barendt, *Freedom of Speech* (Oxford, Clarendon Press, 1985) ch 2.

[84] Post claims that 'the view that the essential objective of the First Amendment is to promote a rich and valuable public debate' has been taken up by some of the US's 'best and most influential constitutional scholars': R Post, 'Managing Deliberation: The Quandary of Democratic Dialogue' (1993) 103 *Ethics* 654, 654.

[85] See A Lewis, '*New York Times v Sullivan* Reconsidered: Time to Return to "The Central Meaning of the First Amendment"' (1983) 83 *Columbia Law Review* 603.

Much activity in this area takes its cue from the US Supreme Court's decision in *New York Times v Sullivan*.[86] In that case, the Court famously held that public officials were constitutionally barred from bringing a defamation action unless they could prove that the statement about their official conduct was made with 'actual malice.' In the US, the case is broadly regarded as a 'landmark' whose central meaning must be defended in the name of press freedom.[87] In this regard, the case has provoked a number of doctrinal issues: what are the requirements of the 'actual malice' test?[88]; who is included under 'public figure'?;[89] and what speech is entitled to the benefit of the *Sullivan* exception?[90] The *Sullivan* case has also been an influential benchmark in other jurisdictions,[91] whether operating as the backdrop to English courts considering extending the qualified privilege defence to public authorities defamed by deliberate lies,[92] or being invoked by the High Court of Australia in providing new constitutional defences to defamation.[93]

My immediate concern is not to engage with these issues in their own terms—rather, I want to highlight a common understanding as to why it would be important to extend the defence against libel to 'all matters in the public domain.'[94] We can posit a three-stage process for achieving the instrumental benefits of free speech: First, policy is translated into positive law, thereby removing the right of politicians to sue personally to protect their reputation. Secondly, the positive law increases the range of speech, in this case through the '[un]blocking of the flow of speech' concerning the conduct of politicians. Thirdly, having used legal instruments to adjust the level of speech in society, a benefit will follow, in present terms 'enabl[ing] voters to make informed decisions about how they [wish] to allocate political power.'[95] What is deemed most crucial is the first stage in determining policy ends because it is assumed stages two and three will follow: the choice here is between promoting a vigorous

---

[86]   376 US 254 (1964).

[87]   Lewis, above n 85, at 603.

[88]   LS Blickenstaff, 'Don't Tip the Scales! The Actual Malice Standard Unjustifiably Eliminates First Amendment Protection for Public Employees' Recklessly False Statements' (1996) 80 *Minnesota Law Review* 911.

[89]   See *Gertz v Robert Welch, Inc* 418 US 323 (1974); *Time, Inc v Firestone* 424 US 448 (1976); *Hutchinson v Proxmire* 443 US 111 (1979); *Dun & Bradstreet v Greenmoss Builders* 472 US 749 (1985); and D Finkelston, 'The Status/Conduct Continuum: Injecting Rhyme and Reason into Contemporary Public Official Defamation Doctrine' (1998) 84 *Virginia Law Review* 871.

[90]   See *Hustler Magazine v Falwell* 485 US 46 (1988) and R Post, 'The Constitutional Concept of Public Discourse: Outrageous Opinion, Democratic Deliberation and *Hustler Magazine v Falwell*' (1990) 103 *Harvard Law Review* 601.

[91]   L Leigh, 'Of Free Speech and Individual Reputation: *New York Times v Sullivan* in Canada and Australia' in Loveland (ed), above n 80, at 51.

[92]   I Loveland, '*City of Chicago v Tribune Co*—in Contexts?' in Loveland (ed), above n 80, at 69.

[93]   *Theophanous v Herald & Weekly Times Ltd* (1994) 182 CLR 104. See S Walker, 'The Impact of the High Court's Free Speech Cases on Defamation Law' (1995) 17 *Sydney Law Review* 43.

[94]   H Kalven Jr, 'The New York Times Case: a Note on "The Central Meaning of the First Amendment"' (1964) *Supreme Court Review* 191 at 221.

[95]   Loveland, above n 92, at 71.

democratic discourse[96] or the traditional aim of libel law in safeguarding reputation.[97]

In the field of libel litigation, we do not have recourse to empirical data as in the previous studies—we are necessarily in a more qualitative realm.[98] What empirical evidence is available appears to confirm that the 'chilling effect' of libel is a real phenomenon in terms of individual decisions taken by editors as to whether to publish.[99] It is not my purpose in this section to dispute this finding—rather, I question whether decisions such as *Sullivan* will result in the invigoration of public debate supposed by their supporters. Again, I should emphasise the narrowness of my target—I am not suggesting that courts or free speech jurisprudence should be expected to deliver the ideal form of democratic discourse. Rather, I focus on the likely impact of persuading courts to deny the protection of libel to political speech: there are strong reasons to doubt any necessary link between the freedom to publish material, that might otherwise have been inhibited, and an increased quality of political debate.

Scholars working within the normative tradition rely on a number of assumptions about how unregulated communication will secure the instrumental ends that they advocate. The first goes to how expression itself operates, and we can highlight here the emphasis on truth and quantity—the more accurate information citizens have about politicians, the richer will be the public debate, and the better they can hold them to account. On this view, speech is essentially linear, a mere conveyance of information, flowing directly into readers for their benefit, when true, to enhance political discussion, or to their detriment, when false, then distorting public discourse.[100] This account can be challenged, by contrasting it with developments in linguistic theory[101] and social science research,[102] which perceive communication to be a more complex and multilayered phenomenon. Under this model, which views expression as a reflexive and dialectical process, language and communication are social constructs. Language does not regulate the social world in a direct linear manner, but is itself a product of, and regulated by, that social world, which accordingly

---

[96] Post, above n 84, at 654.

[97] See E Barendt, 'What is the Point of Libel Law?' (1999) 52 *Current Legal Problems* 110, 112.

[98] In any case, in the civil rights and abortion examples, the empirical data are the starting point for investigation, and not determinative in themselves. What is crucial in each (including the present) case is the interpretation which we apply, and whether we can make the argument that the available (quantitative and qualitative) data favour one conclusion over another (see Rosenberg, above n 10, at 228).

[99] E Barendt, L Lustgarten, K Norrie and H Stephenson, *Libel and the Media: The Chilling Effect* (Oxford, Clarendon Press, 1997).

[100] One of their criticisms of existing doctrine in the US (Leigh, above n 91, at 57) and the UK (Loveland, above n 92, at 71) is that it may lead to the corruptive influence of untrue information entering public discourse.

[101] See, eg, C Taylor, *Human Agency and Language: Philosophical Papers I* (Cambridge, Cambridge University Press, 1985) ch 9. The main positions are set out in R Moon, 'Lifestyle Advertising and Classical Freedom of Expression Doctrine' (1991) 36 *McGill Law Journal* 76, 89–94.

[102] See, eg, C Calvert, 'Awareness of Meaning in Libel Law: An Interdisciplinary Communication and Law Critique' (1996) 16 *Northern Illinois University Law Review* 111, 115.

constrains the range of meanings which listeners and readers attach to what they hear and read.[103] This suggests that libellous statements do not in themselves have a direct effect in bolstering or undermining a public figure's reputation,[104] but that the meaning people attach to them is a more complex process, which depends on a number of social variables. One model posits these as including: 'the pre-publication attitude of the audience towards the plaintiff . . .; the credibility ascribed . . . to the publication . . .; the saliency of the subject matter . . .; and the interpersonal reaction following exposure to the publication.'[105]

If interpretation and context have a central role in ascribing meaning to expression, then considerations of quality not quantity have the more significant bearing on the richness of political discourse. In this regard, legal pluralism suggests that media corporations can no longer be regarded as impartial conveyors of information, but have a key role in the filtering and presenting of data in setting the terms of public debate.[106] This draws on a developed literature in media and communication studies which regards the media as important political actors themselves, who have their own agenda, with powerful means of advancing the same.[107] Focusing on the nature of the resulting normative regime, it has been strongly argued that this is characterised by: the maximisation of profit,[108] lack of serious investigation into established power,[109] and a narrowing of the range of public discourse. In particular, the consonance of dominant media views, and the neo-liberal political agenda, is highlighted,[110] as evidenced, for example, by the almost complete absence of scrutiny of the political activities of corporations (as opposed to providing financial information to investors).[111] This analysis suggests that if, for example, we focus on the US, the years since *Sullivan* have not produced a thorough-going marketplace of ideas—indeed, they are marked by the absence of both media diversity and large-scale citizen participation in democratic processes.[112] This, of course, was not caused directly by the *Sullivan* decision, but it was equally not inhibited by it. Accordingly, we can argue that removing state law sanctions will not by itself

---

[103] Taylor, above n 101, at 231.

[104] See Loveland, above n 92, at 69.

[105] See D McCraw, 'How do Readers Read? Social Science and the Law of Libel' (1991) 41 *Catholic University Law Review* 81, 91.

[106] See J Lichtenberg, 'Foundations and Limits of Freedom of the Press', in J Lichtenberg (ed), *Democracy and the Mass Media* (Cambridge, Cambridge University Press, 1985) 102, 103.

[107] See, eg, M Kahan, *Media as Politics: Theory, Behavior, and Change in America* (Upper Saddle River, NJ, Prentice Hall, 1999) and B Page, *Who Deliberates?: Mass Media in Modern Democracy* (Chicago and London, University of Chicago Press, 1996).

[108] See J Nichols and RW McChesney, *It's the Media, Stupid* (New York, Seven Stories Press, 2000).

[109] See RW McChesney, *Rich Media, Poor Democracy: Communication Politics in Dubious Times* (Urbana and Chicago, University of Illinois Press, 1999) 59–63.

[110] ES Herman and RW McChesney, *The Global Media: the New Missionaries of Global Capitalism* (London, Cassell, 1997).

[111] McChesney, above n 109, at 58.

[112] *Ibid* at 2.

lead to a richer amount of material being made available for public debate—this does nothing to address the very real phenomenon of *private censorship*, where the structural factors listed above combine[113] to inhibit what is released into the public domain.[114]

The conventional constitutional approach to political libels, in assuming the (beneficial) direct effect of court orders on public debate, thus leaves unasked questions about how communication operates, and what are the most important influences on that debate. Yet these questions are central to an accurate knowledge of constitutional adjudication on freedom of expression. The studies referred to above suggest that when we do ask questions about the actual impact of constitutional litigation, we receive answers which cast further doubt on the soundness of the dominant assumption made within normative scholarship about law's instrumentality.

CONCLUSION

In this and the previous chapter, I have subjected the liberal legalist epistemology of constitutional law to critical scrutiny. With regard to the interpretive question, the assumption that constitutional doctrine forms a coherent and autonomous system of rules was found wanting against a theoretically and empirically grounded account of the disordering forces at play in adjudication. With regard to the instrumental question, the assumption that constitutional litigation works as a tool for social engineering could not be sustained in light of case studies that highlight the complexity of the internormative social world. The inability of rights constitutionalism to secure its own agenda, thus indicating the poverty of liberal legalist epistemology, forms the interim conclusion of this book. However, despite the fact that liberal legalism manifestly cannot deliver what it promises, these assumptions continue to inform the globalization of rights constitutionalism. This raises the question of why they persist, and what role they play in shaping the constitutional agenda. In Part III, I consider the implications of these questions for our inquiry into the relation between rights constitutionalism and private power in the globalizing age.

---

[113] Herman and McChesney, above n 110, at 6.
[114] McChesney, above n 109, at 58.

Part III: Constitutional Rights in an Age of Globalization: Towards a Legal Pluralist Theory of Constitutionalism

6

Legal Pluralism and the Politics of Constitutional Definition

L EGAL PLURALISM PROVIDES a powerful counter to our dominant understandings of constitutional law. Its challenge to the liberal legalist assumptions of coherence and effectiveness significantly undermines rights constitutionalism's claims to act as an instrument of social reform. In Part III, I show that legal pluralism's significance goes beyond epistemological critique, and also provides us with a sound explanatory basis of the relationship between rights constitutionalism and private power. A more promising way forward here lies in showing how the 'failures of the instrumental effectiveness of law' can be compensated for by its 'symbolic effectiveness.'[1] On this account, the persistence of rights constitutionalism, despite its inability to deliver what it promises, is explained by its power as a legitimating discourse. In other words, constitutional law's significance is as a site of struggle, rather than as a direct agent for change (or conservation).

Legal pluralism's explanatory strengths rest in showing how the paradigmatic debate brings to the surface a 'politics of definition of law.' According to Santos, any purported 'definition' of law is necessarily a 'complex intertwining of analytical and political claims,' and so in the paradigmatic debate, this insight must not only be fully acknowledged, but also 'conceived as one of the premises of the debate.'[2] This argument places the paradigmatic debate in context: while its outcome may be the supplanting of one form of legal knowledge with another, its primary purpose is to bring to the fore 'the political nature of many barely apparent analytical claims.' Thus, the legal pluralist account of constitutional adjudication rendered above should be seen less as the 'profound questioning of the empirical research in the name of a superior knowledge' but more as 'a story about the precariousness of knowledge.'[3] Accordingly, while legal pluralism highlights the short-comings of statecentred methodologies, this does not mean that state law is unimportant—rather it is important in *different* ways than is imagined by liberal legalism. Grasping how the politics of definition

---

[1] B de Sousa Santos, *Toward a New Legal Common Sense* (London, Butterworths, 2002) 72.
[2] *Ibid* at 90.
[3] B de Sousa Santos, *Toward a New Common Sense: Law, Science and Politics in the Paradigmatic Transition* (New York, Routledge, 1995) 115, 122.

prioritise and legitimate certain forms of inquiry is crucial to understanding how constitutional law does matter.

In this chapter, I focus in detail on what is at stake in the paradigmatic debate. I begin by considering the principal lessons of legal pluralism's epistemological critique: this does not so much invite us to proffer some other overarching 'definition' of law, but rather to focus on the important political purposes which prevailing definitions of law serve. I apply this argument to constitutional law by juxtaposing two competing politics of constitutional definition: classical liberal constitutionalism, whose historical pinnacle is the US Bill of Rights, and scholarship under the rubric of 'new constitutionalism', which looks beyond formal documents and laws to the implicit constitutional dimension of the Washington consensus. I show how each engages differently with private power: the former seeks to protect it from, the latter seeks to open it up to, greater constitutional scrutiny. This leads to the conclusion that rights constitutionalism's hegemonic or counterhegemonic potential does not depend principally on the outcome of normative doctrinal debates. Rather, what is crucial is how the dominant narratives of what is, and is not, a constitution are situated vis-à-vis, and relatively support, broader hegemonic or counterhegemonic discourses.

LEGAL PLURALISM AND THE POLITICS OF DEFINITION

While legal pluralism is a powerful tool in disturbing the epistemological basis of liberal legalism, this only takes us part of the way in outlining its significance for constitutional study. It is therefore important to place the epistemological critique of legal pluralism in context. While this argues that rights constitutionalism is not important in the ways that liberal legalism imagines, this does not mean we should direct our attention exclusively to non-state sources of constitutional law. For one thing, states are, for the present at least, likely to remain the 'central political forms'[4] of the world system. Accordingly, we cannot wish away state constitutional law—rather, the latter's significance in light of the legal pluralist case has to be articulated and confronted. I approach this by considering two of the major objections to legal pluralism—its inability to proffer a satisfactory alternative definition of law, and its diluting of the normative force of 'law'. I argue that both these objections can be countered by seeing how legal pluralism advances a *rhetorical* conception of law.

Analytical and Instrumental Objections to Legal Pluralism

Such is the hold of liberal legalism that to most lawyers 'law' denotes simply state law: any attempt to broaden the category, for example by referring to

---

[4] Santos, above n 1, at 94.

'informal law' or 'non-state law,' is immediately suspect given the presence of the qualifying adjective.[5] This onus to justify abandoning the dominant paradigm is underscored by two substantive objections which go respectively to the analytical and instrumental[6] utility of legal pluralism. The first is that legal pluralist definitions of law which do not take the state as its primary referent are ultimately incoherent. Brian Tamanaha argues that attempts to assert a universal definition of law, which would cover state and non-state settings, rest on a flawed basis.[7] He contrasts the contention that 'law can be conceptualized independent of state law'[8] with legal pluralist definitions of law which show that 'law's conceptual connection to the state cannot be severed.'[9] According to Tamanaha, these generally posit the criteria of law 'by extracting or emulating those elements which appear to be essential to *state law*, then subtracting all trappings of state law.'[10] Tamanaha further argues that legal pluralism's failure to substantiate its core belief that we can move beyond state centred notions of law means that it is of little conceptual use in distinguishing the legal from the non-legal.[11] Thus, legal pluralists have not made out the case that there is something essential about 'law' which justifies collapsing social norms into law[12]; there may well be ' "normative" [or] "rule system" pluralism,'[13] but the question remains over why this should also be labelled 'legal' pluralism.

Allied to this objection to the analytical utility of legal pluralist definitions of law is a second argument, in more instrumental terms, that there is an important value served by restricting use of the term 'law' to those formal acts of the state which accord with the rule of law. In this regard, TRS Allan warns of the dangers of the 'uncritical identification of "law" with any and every assertion of governmental authority' as this would make the citizens and their property 'objects of administration.'[14] While others would draw the line of legality in different places,[15] the idea that 'law' imputes some moral standard to which states

---

[5] See HW Arthurs, *Without the Law: Administrative Justice and Legal Pluralism in Nineteenth-Century England* (Toronto and Buffalo, University of Toronto Press, 1985) 3.

[6] I borrow these headings from Brian Tamanaha, although I employ them in a different manner: see BZ Tamanaha, 'A Non-Essentialist Version of Legal Pluralism' (2000) 27 *Journal of Law and Society* 296, 297.

[7] See BZ Tamanaha, 'The Folly of the "Social Scientific" Concept of Legal Pluralism' (1993) 20 *Journal of Law and Society* 192.

[8] *Ibid* at 201.

[9] *Ibid*.

[10] *Ibid*: 'Thus, the state law model inescapably provides the kernel of the concept of non-state "law."'

[11] Tamanaha, above n 6, at 300–02.

[12] For an example of an approach which implicitly relies on a distinction between social norms and law, see A Etzioni, 'Social Norms: Internalisation, Persuasion and History' (2000) 34 *Law and Society Review* 157, 159–60.

[13] Tamanaha, above n 7, at 199.

[14] TRS Allan, *Constitutional Justice: A Liberal Theory of the Rule of Law* (Oxford, Oxford University Press, 2001) 16.

[15] See D Dyzenhaus, 'Recrafting the Rule of Law' in D Dyzenhaus (ed), *Recrafting the Rule of Law: The Limits of Legal Order* (Oxford and Portland, OR, Hart Publishing, 1999) 1, 9.

should comply remains central in liberal legal theory.[16] A fortiori, this normative delineation of the legal must apply in the non-state setting. For example,
Tamanaha asks the value of regarding domestic relations of the family as a site
of law: for him, not only does this lead to terminological confusion, but brings
a potential political detriment, by suggesting that domestic violence may be
acceptable under the non-state legal regime.[17] On this view, to argue that
conflating what corporations do with the activities of constitutional courts in
adjudicating human rights is to accord a(n unjustified) legitimacy to the former,
while risking undermining the (justified) legitimacy of the latter.

These objections raise important points. The first underscores the difficulty
which legal pluralists necessarily have in 'essentialising' law.[18] At its most
elemental level, legal pluralism is a rebellion against the possibility of an all-
encompassing normative system. Legal pluralists who say that 'law is x' accordingly open themselves up to their own critique, ie, why should we centralise the
meaning of law around a different set of co-ordinates which merely reproduce
the liberal legalist difficulties of giving a comprehensive account of legal phenomena?[19] The second highlights the often uneasy relationship between description and prescription in legal pluralism, of whether we should attach normative
connotations to law purely on account of its state or non-state provenance.

Towards a Rhetorical Conception of Legal Knowledge

These objections take our inquiry forward by showing that the significance of
legal pluralism for contemporary constitutionalism does not principally lie either
in offering an alternative definitive account of law, or in valorising non-state
law in its own terms. They suggest that the more relevant implications of
the paradigmatic debate flow from focusing on its process rather than its
eventual outcomes—on what it entails to challenge dominant methodological

---

[16] See M-M Kleinhans and RA Macdonald, 'What is a Critical Legal Pluralism?' (1997) 12
Canadian Journal of Law and Society 25, 32.

[17] Tamanaha, above n 6, at 304: 'This phraseology should give discomfort to opponents of
domestic violence, for the reason that the term "law" often possesses symbolic connotations of
right.'

[18] Tamanaha, above n 7, at 201: 'The root source of the unbudging barrier subverting all
attempts at formulating a universal scientific or cross-cultural definition of law lies in the goal itself
. . . —that law is a fundamental category which can be identified or described, or an essentialist
notion which can be internally worked on until a pure (de-contextualized) version is produced.
Unsettling as it may be, there is nothing beneath the culturally-generated notion.'

[19] See G Teubner, '"Global Bukowina": Legal Pluralism in the World Society' in G Teubner (ed),
Global Law Without a State (Gateshead, Athenaeum Press, 1997) 3, who (at 13–14) illustrates the
difficulty of assigning a singular function to 'law': '[w]hy should legal pluralism be defined only by
the function of "social control" and not the function of "conflict resolution" as theories of private
justice would suggest? Why could the function of "coordinating behaviour", "accumulation of
power" or "private regulation", which theories of private government would emphasise not be
taken to define legal pluralism? Any why not "discipline and punish" which would tend to include
any mechanism of disciplinary micropower that permeates social life?' (footnotes omitted).

conceptions than what their final replacements might be.[20] My argument is that the key point of the paradigmatic debate does not lie in asking the question 'what is law?' but rather 'why is the answer to the question "what is law" important?' This points to the importance of a rhetorical conception of legal knowledge[21]:

> What is especially characteristic of struggles for law [is] how these disputes about meaning have been framed by disputants as matters of definition . . . What is important is not to 'prove' the 'empirical truth' of [any] definition—itself a problematic exercise that rests on second-order definitions—, but rather to acknowledge the ideology and the objectives that drive the particular perspective chosen.[22]

On this view, the equation of law with state law should be regarded as a 'rhetorical strategy' rather than a 'stipulative definition'.[23] The point is not so much that liberal legalism misdescribes law, by omitting aspects of a more accurate and/or comprehensive definition, but that it misrepresents the nature of the question 'what is law?' by suggesting that this can be answered purely by analytical categorisation. Instead, in John Griffiths's classic formulation, the idea that 'law is and should be the law of the state' should be seen for what it is: as an '*ideology*'.[24] The insight that questions about the meaning of law should be regarded principally in rhetorical terms[25] leads to an important shift in focus: the central issue is now what ends are promoted by propagating state-centred views of law.

A number of writers have illustrated the political interests that have historically been served in the name of state-centred definitions of law. James Tully, for example, discusses John Locke's justification of European colonialism in the seventeenth century.[26] For Locke, European states had reached the stage of historical advancement such that they had 'a common establish'd Law and Judicature'[27]—in contrast, North American aboriginal societies still subsisted

---

[20] As Santos observes, there are in-built limits as to how far an emergent paradigm, such as legal pluralism can go in constructing new knowledge: 'in a paradigmatic transition the emergent paradigm necessarily lacks the appropriate methodology, the empirical research, no matter how epistemologically alert, tends to be conducted according to the method available: those of the dominant paradigm . . . Moreover, because the research programs are formulated within the dominant paradigm, even when they try to break with it, the transgression bears the mark of what it transgresses, and thereby vindicates its presence in unsuspected forms' (above n 3, at 121). This leads Santos to the conclusion that 'the paradigmatic critique cannot, therefore, purport to raise the empirical research as such beyond the limits of the dominant paradigm that has generated it. But it can show those limits' (*ibid*).

[21] *Ibid* at 86–89.

[22] Kleinhans and Macdonald, above n 16, at 33, fn 21. (See also Tamanaha, above n 7, at 300.)

[23] *Ibid*.

[24] J Griffiths, 'What is Legal Pluralism?' (1986) 24 *Journal of Legal Pluralism* 1, 3 (emphasis added and omitted). The full quote is: 'According to what I shall call the ideology of *legal centralism*, law is and should be the law of the state, uniform for all persons, exclusive of all other law, and administered by a single set of state institutions.'

[25] See GR Woodman, 'Ideological Combat and Social Observation' (1998) 42 *Journal of Legal Pluralism* 21, 43.

[26] See J Tully, *Strange Multiplicity: Constitutionalism in an Age of Diversity* (Cambridge, Cambridge University Press, 1995) 71–78.

[27] *Ibid* at 72, quoting J Locke, *Two Treatises of Government*, P Laslett (ed) (Cambridge, Cambridge University Press, 1981) second treatise, s 87.

in the lawless state of nature. Consequently, only Europeans had the power to exercise legal sovereignty, through property rights, over land.[28] In this way, the idea that European societies were uniquely ordered according to law—ultimately identifiable as the positive law of the state—legitimated the appropriation of land, notwithstanding its long-standing occupation by aboriginals, as the exercise of right, not might. The notion that debates about law serve as 'proxies'[29] for broader issues also animates Harry Arthurs' work on the development of English public law in the nineteenth century. Arthurs carefully documents the concerted efforts to centralise administrative law in the ordinary courts,[30] and argues that this 'attack on pluralism'[31] furthered lawyers' professional[32] and political[33] interests, by promoting the idea that the administration should adhere to centralist precepts of the rule of law, for example by observing the rules of natural justice as laid down by the ordinary courts. Santos links the reduction of law to state law to the nineteenth century project of embedding capitalism in western states.[34] Thus, the state appropriated law to itself, and fashioned it as a rational system of universal rules,[35] so that it could be used as a tool for imposing capitalist order on society. Capturing law as formal state law also played an important role in legitimating what was a deeply political act of state intervention on behalf of the capitalist class, by marrying law and capitalism to the idea of rational progress, and branding any other means of societal organisation as irrational. The key was to cast state private law—seen as the essential lubricant for the functioning of capitalism—as not state law at all, and therefore 'disengaged from any political or social content.'[36]

Two important themes emerge from these studies: first, the centralisation of law as state law was not an organic development in human history, but the

---

[28] Tully notes that for Locke, in contrast with aboriginals who were 'commonly without any fixed property on the ground,' the European settlers ('those who are counted the Civiliz'd part of Mankind') 'have multiplied positive laws to determine Property', for 'in governments the Laws regulate the right of property, and the possession of land is determined by positive constitutions' (*ibid* at 72, quoting Locke (*ibid*), ss 27, 38, 30, 50).

[29] See Arthurs, above n 5, at 3.

[30] Eg, by replacing specialised local courts with the general system of county courts: *ibid* at 25–34.

[31] *Ibid* at ch 2.

[32] Arthurs argues (*ibid* at 4) that '[the centralist paradigm] provide[d] a basis for [lawyers'] monopoly over "legal" services and for the economic and psychic rewards of that monopoly.'

[33] Arthurs notes that one of the consequences of the centralist hegemony is that '[f]or most lawyers, administrative law is not the law *of* the administration; it is the law directed *against* the administration, the law by which reviewing judges ensure that the administration does not overreach' (*ibid* at 6, emphasis in original). He links this latter conception of administrative law to the political beliefs of its leading supporter, AV Dicey, whose anti-statist (*ibid* at 197) and anti-collectivist (see HW Arthurs, 'Rethinking Administrative Law: A Slightly Dicey Business' (1979) 17 *Osgoode Hall Law Journal* 1, 10–11) views meant that administrative law in the former sense could never amount to 'law.'

[34] Santos, above n 1, at 40–51.

[35] *Ibid* at 42.

[36] *Ibid* at 45.

result of deliberate acts[37] designed to serve some political objective. Secondly, these acts of will were accompanied by strategies aimed at denying this contingency and thereby suppressing other understandings of law, whether those found in the aboriginal societies of North America, or the local courts of Victorian England. Crucial to this attempt was to portray the equation of law with state law in analytical terms, and to take this method to a reasonable degree of sophistication, fluency in which would be a badge of 'technical' expertise.[38] This strategy succeeded in putting legal pluralists in a double bind: given the exotic nature of their subject, they were perceived as engaging in anthropological, sociological or political, but not analytical, discourse (thus reinforcing the idea that legal discourse concerned purely state law), and in order to engage with the dominant view of law, they had to meet this on analytical terms (thus further masking the political basis of debates about law).[39] The primary significance of legal pluralism therefore lies in demonstrating how the 'commonsensical' acceptance that law is state law disguises that we are engaged here in a politics of definition of law.

The Analytical and Instrumental Objections in Context

This insight places in context the two objections discussed above. First, viewing received definitions of law as the product of human agency reinforces accounts of the law-creating subject: 'there is no *a priori* distinction between normative orders because these normative orders cannot exist outside the creative capacity of their subjects.'[40] This inability to materialise *any* purely analytical means of separating the legal from the non-legal displaces liberal legalism from its seemingly preordained position—rather 'state' becomes just one more qualifying adjective for law, like 'domestic' or 'informal'. Accordingly, given the association of 'law' with 'right, certainty, and power,'[41] we have to ask what are the consequences of making state law the central unit of analysis for constitutional study. Secondly, the implication of the politics of definition is that there is nothing in the label 'law' per se, which gives a norm any necessary positive value. Thus, Tamanaha's concern that labelling family relations 'law' may legitimate domestic violence only makes sense if the purpose of doing so is to valorise all non-state law. However, our purpose could be to highlight the need to confront the problem of domestic violence, by casting it as an exercise of social power which must be addressed. The point is, divorced from the politics of definition,

---

[37] On this point, see Arthurs, above n 5, at 8–9. Santos describes 'the reduction of law to state law' as a 'political fiat' (above n 1, at 90).

[38] For a discussion of the analytical turn in UK public law, see M Loughlin, *Public Law and Political Theory* (Oxford, Clarendon Press, 1992) 13–17.

[39] See Santos, above n 1, at 90.

[40] Kleinhans and Macdonald, above n 16, at 40.

[41] Above n 7, at 205.

there is nothing in the claim that family relations should be regarded as law which has any positive or negative connotation. Thus, we cannot accord a legitimacy to any 'law' purely because of its provenance[42]: this is a necessarily political question, which can only be answered in relation to the purposes served by attaching the label 'law' to some aspect of social life.

The latter point helps us understand the complex relationship between legal pluralism's descriptive and prescriptive claims. While the fact of state or non-state law alone has no normative implications, how we present either of them in a descriptive mode can not only make clearer what prescriptive choices are available, but also must reflect our view of how these choices should be made. Thus, the view of some legal pluralists that state law is not worthy of study,[43] and that non-state orders should be accorded a greater 'symbolic prestige'[44] can be attributed to their 'active antistatist stance.'[45] Others, though, act from different motivations in engaging in legal pluralist scholarship. For example, Tamanaha posits a 'non-essentialist version of legal pluralism,' which takes as its criterion of legality the conventional use of the term 'law'[46] and which he argues enhances our ability to 'describe, understand, study, analyse and evaluate legal phenomena.'[47] Rather than advancing anti-statism, this account contends that legal pluralism should take state law seriously, and that to do so will bring the benefits of clarifying the ways in which state law 'actually *is* involved in maintaining the normative order of society'[48] or how it is used as 'an instrument of power'[49] by elites, serving variously their own and sometimes the general interest. Tamanaha seems to imply that his approach contrasts favourably with the 'significant political impetus' behind essentialist approaches to legal pluralism.[50] However, I draw a different conclusion, namely that all approaches to legal pluralism reflect some 'political impetus'[51] and that Tamanaha shows us that this need not take the anti-statist stance outlined above. Accordingly, for our own inquiry, viewing law in terms of the politics of

[42] Eg, keeping with the example of domestic violence, retaining an exclusive legal focus on the state could be counterproductive in terms of addressing the issue at two levels: first, by suggesting that the issue is dealt with when the state acts (thereby downgrading the legal agency of the perpetrators of domestic violence), particularly if it has enacted a pristine set of criminal laws imposing severe penalties, and second, by casting those instances of domestic violence not caught by state criminal law, being not illegal, as legal, with all the normative connotations involved.

[43] See, eg, Griffiths, above n 24, at 13.

[44] Tamanaha, above n 7, at 205.

[45] Santos, above n 1, at 94.

[46] Above n 6, at 315: 'Under my account, the normative relations within the family will be considered "law" only if the people within that social arena conventionally characterize them in terms of "law."'

[47] *Ibid* at 300.

[48] Above n 7 at 210.

[49] *Ibid* at 211.

[50] *Ibid* at 205.

[51] One could ask here why there is no political impetus in Tamanaha's concern to make explicit how elites use state law to their own ends, or to look to the purposes served by the conventional usage of the term law (and which means, for him, that 'we are [not] trapped in such accounts': above n 6, at 315).

definition shows the importance of making clear how these descriptive and pre-scriptive elements combine in any account of constitutional law.

THE POLITICS OF DEFINITION OF CONSTITUTIONAL LAW

The politics of definition are crucial to understanding the relation between rights constitutionalism and private power. To illustrate this, I develop here the insights of the emerging critical school of legal pluralism discussed in chapter three. Critical legal pluralism takes as its premise that all legal settings are 'shaped by power relations, however overtly or subtly exercised.'[52] On this view, the key question is how legal knowledge, given its role in 'maintain[ing] and creat[ing] realities,'[53] contributes to the legitimation of power.[54] This will partly be a narrative of domination,[55] focusing on how legal subjects are con-strained by hegemonic accounts of law, but also partly one of transformation,[56] identifying ways of imagining law which open up the scope for counter-hegemonic resistance. The extent to which constitutional knowledge unfolds in a hegemonic or counterhegemonic manner requires attention to the symbolic aspect of constitutions.

Constitutions are important 'symbolic artefacts'[57] in disputes over the mean-ing of ideas such as equality, liberty and democracy. Their symbolic effects are manifested in at least three ways: 1) by putting into concrete terms abstract issues of political theory, and so underlining their importance—for example, the sym-bolic linking of marking a ballot paper to the wellbeing of democracy;[58] 2) in 'affirm[ing] the identity of the political society that is made up of those from whom the constitution demands allegiance;'[59] 3) by attaching the label 'consti-tutional' to the resolution of certain political conflicts to mark them out as 'wor-thy of special respect, deference or attention not just in the domain of law but in other contexts as well.'[60] As Ulrich Preuss observes, this label is especially potent

---

[52] H Arthurs, 'Landscape and Memory: Labour Law, Legal Pluralism and Globalization' in T Wilthagen (ed), *Advancing Theory in Labour Law in a Global Context* (Amsterdam, Koninklijke Nederlandse Akademie van Wetenschappen, 1998) 21, 30.

[53] Kleinhans and Macdonald, above n 16, at 38.

[54] RA Macdonald, 'Metaphors of Multiplicity: Civil Society, Regimes and Legal Pluralism' (1998) 15 *Arizona Journal of International and Comparative Law* 69, 78.

[55] As Kleinhans and Macdonald note (above n 16, at 43), there is nothing about emphasising the 'inter and intra-subjective' nature of social life that is necessarily 'radically democratic or necessar-ily egalitarian.'

[56] 'Legal subjects are not wholly determined: they possess a transformative capacity that enables them to produce legal knowledge and to fashion the very structures of law that contribute to constituting their legal subjectivity' (*ibid* at 38).

[57] *Ibid* at 33, fn 21.

[58] J Webber, 'Constitutional Poetry: The Tension Between Symbolic and Functional Aims in Constitutional Reform' (1999) 21 *Sydney Law Review* 260, 271.

[59] R Cotterrell, 'Some Aspects of the Communication of Constitutional Authority' in D Nelken (ed), *Law as Communication* (Aldershot, Dartmouth, 1995) 129, 129.

[60] H Arthurs, 'Constitutional Courage' (2004) 49 *McGill Law Journal* 1, 9.

as the unique claim of modern constitutionalism is its promise of 'a lasting possibility for human progress.'[61] The symbolic power of constitutions accordingly lies in shaping and directing the debates through which political communities reinterpret their past, negotiate their present and plan their future.[62]

What we understand to be constitutional is a central factor in setting the terms of these debates. To demonstrate this, I now contrast two different definitions of constitutionalism: the classical liberal model of the US Constitution, and what has been labelled 'new constitutionalism' which views the processes of economic globalization in constitutional terms. Comparing these models brings two points to the fore. It shows how the different forms of constitutional knowledge which they seek to reproduce direct us to different political agendas, with important consequences for the relation between constitutionalism and private power. Secondly, to the extent the former represents explicit, and the latter tacit, understandings of constitutionalism, it further shows that what is not said to be constitutional also has symbolic effects in suggesting what is, and is not, important by way of constitutional inquiry.

Classical Liberal Constitutionalism

The US Constitution is a useful starting point for unpacking the significance of the politics of definition for constitutional study, given its historical and contemporary relevance. The post-revolutionary settlement of the 1787 Constitution and 1791 Bill of Rights represents the birth of modern understandings of 'constitutionalism',[63] giving the term the more specific meaning accepted today as a codified document protecting individual rights.[64] Moreover, this model of rights constitutionalism has been influential beyond American shores, and has provided the inspiration, in part, for the current round of constitutional globalization.[65] Analysis of the US Constitution from the perspective of the politics of definition brings two important insights. First, it locates the US Constitution in its historical context, and undermines claims that it embodies some 'essence of constitutionalism'[66] showing that from the start,

---

[61] UK Preuss (tr DL Schneider), *Constitutional Revolution: The Link Between Constitutionalism and Progress* (Atlantic Highlands, NJ, Humanities Press, 1995) 37

[62] N Walker, 'Europe's Constitutional Momentum and the Search for Polity Legitimacy' (forthcoming, in I-CON, 2005)

[63] See RC van Caenegem, *An Historical Introduction to Western Constitutional Law* (Cambridge, Cambridge University Press, 1995) 150–51.

[64] See Preuss, above n 61, at 31.

[65] See SM Griffin, *American Constitutionalism: From Theory to Politics* (Princeton, Princeton University Press, 1996) 9.

[66] AE Dick Howard, 'The Essence of Constitutionalism' in KW Thompson and R Ludwokowski (eds), *Constitutionalism and Human Rights: America, Poland and France* (Lanham, MD, University Press of America, 1991) 3. Howard identifies, inter alia, 'limited government' (*ibid* at 19), the '[s]anctity of the individual' (at 21) and the enforcement of the constitution through 'the rule of law' (*ibid* at 23) as 'embryonic' ideas of the late eighteenth century which 'are intrinsic to constitutionalism today' (*ibid* at 30).

the meaning of constitutionalism was the focus of intense political struggle. Secondly, it shows how a classical liberal conception of constitutionalism frames constitutional questions in a manner conducive to the interests of private power.

Given the almost metaphysical status which the US Constitution has acquired,[67] it is important to emphasise that the politics of definition were very much present at the Philadelphia Convention. Jefferson, for example, argued that constitutions should be seen as living documents and so not entrenched to bind future generations,[68] whereas Madison saw constitutions as constraints on government by faction,[69] and so should necessarily be difficult to amend.[70] The events at Philadelphia should also be seen in light of the social climate at the time, with the revolutionary war having awakened a political movement for greater material equality, as manifested, for example in the Shays Rebellion of 1786.[71] In this connection, Russell Galloway has argued that 'the debate over the Constitution . . . was essentially a debate between the defenders of property and defenders of the propertyless.'[72] Whether viewed in terms of high theory or class conflict, the historical context indicates how constitutions were, from the very beginning, sites of contestation between contending political outlooks.[73]

The new constitutional settlement which emerged from this contest contained several key features, which would influence the development of modern constitutional thought and practice: first, the constitution was embodied in a single text; secondly, formally, this text had the status of higher law, binding ordinary law and requiring special procedures to be amended; and thirdly, substantively, the text should guarantee individual rights (at the time, stated in terms of the right to life, liberty and property). While now seen as key elements of liberal democracy, at the time, they were decidedly *anti*democratic in many respects, and designed to protect the propertied class, from what was then seen as the threat of democracy in the form of majority rule.[74] Some of these protections

---

[67] See D Lazare, *The Frozen Republic: How the Constitution is Paralyzing Democracy* (New York, Harcourt Brace, 1996) 1.

[68] See S Holmes, 'Precommitment and the paradox of democracy' in J Elster and R Slagstad (eds), *Constitutionalism and Democracy* (Cambridge, Cambridge University Press, 1988) 195, 202–05. See also Tully, above n 26, at 91–92.

[69] See SL Elkin, 'Madison and After: the American Model of Political Constitution' (1996) 44 *Political Studies* 592, 593.

[70] Griffin, above n 65, at 29–30.

[71] RW Galloway, *Justice for All? The Rich and Poor in Supreme Court History 1790–1990* (Durham, NC, Carolina Academic Press, 1991) 12.

[72] *Ibid* at 14.

[73] At times of US constitutional history, the politics of definition have been to the fore: eg, Bruce Ackerman identifies periods of heightened 'higher lawmaking,' including the foundation of the republic, but also the Reconstruction and New Deal eras: see B Ackerman, *We The People, Volume 1: Foundations* (Cambridge, MA, Harvard University Press, 1991) 40–56. My point of departure from Ackerman is that these periods are only remarkable in terms of the visibility of the politics of definition, which are present and continue throughout US constitutional history.

[74] See J Nedelsky, *Private Property and the Limits of American Constitutionalism: The Madisonian Framework and Its Legacy* (Chicago, University of Chicago Press, 1990) ch 3.

took a specific form, whether in prohibiting states from passing laws 'impairing the obligation of contracts'[75] or protecting property in slaves.[76] However, it is important to see how, more symbolically, hegemonic interests succeeded in capturing the definition of constitutionalism to their ends: this occurs at two related levels.

First, substantive provisions of the US Constitution represent core elements of classical liberal discourse. It has at its root the idea that constitutions should limit government, reflecting the Lockean idea that the state is a necessary evil to protect the freedoms enjoyed by individuals in the state of nature. Furthermore, these freedoms are to be guaranteed to the fullest extent possible through the entrenchment of individual rights. This equates the guarantee of constitutional freedom with the protection of the individual's private sphere, thus reinforcing the classical liberal separation of social life between the state and civil society, with the constitution's role to insulate the latter from interference by the former. Together, these anti-state and individualist elements chimed with the hegemonic interests of the time, and sought to entrench the idea, as Charles Beard put it, 'that the fundamental private rights of property are anterior to government and morally beyond the reach of popular majorities.'[77] Secondly, hegemonic interests were not only served by the substantive definition of constitutionalism, but also by its *conceptual* definition, which emphasises its legal character. This is achieved primarily through the erection of a 'sharp boundary . . . between the Constitution and politics'[78] which presented constitutional argument as a technical discourse, to be conducted by learned experts, ie, lawyers and judges, and therefore not a political discourse.[79] Not only does this justify the practice of judicial review,[80] but it gives constitutional arguments advancing rights claims a special status, so that they did not require to be justified *de novo* in political terms.

Protecting Private Power through the Politics of Definition

A brief excursus into the historical record shows how the hold of classical liberal politics of definition, in three key areas of constitutional adjudication's

[75] US Constitution, Art I, S 10 (see Galloway, above n 71, at 13).

[76] See M Mandel, 'A Brief History of the New Constitutionalism, or "How we changed everything so that everything would remain the same"' (1998) 32 *Israel Law Review* 250, 271.

[77] Galloway, above n 71, at 12, quoting C Beard, *An Economic Analysis of the Constitution of the United States* (1913) 324–325.

[78] Griffin, above n 65, at 16.

[79] *Ibid* at 18: '. . . since constitutional disputes were seen first and foremost as legal disputes, constitutional law became a form of expert knowledge that required legal training. This tended to exclude the public from the development of constitutional meaning, reducing the democratic potential of the constitution.'

[80] Although not expressly part of the original settlement, van Caenegem (above n 63, at 158) notes that judicial review 'was widely advocated in the early years of the republic and some people thought it was implicit in the Constitution'. In any case, it had become a central part of constitutional practice by the late nineteenth century (see Griffin, above n 65, at 90–99).

interface with private power, shaped the form of constitutional argument to favour hegemonic interests. First, where corporations claimed constitutional protection, the Supreme Court has asked whether the statutes under review infringed the area of constitutionally protected freedom.[81] As such, it equated corporations with private individuals,[82] locating both in the free realm of civil society, and so both should receive constitutional protection against interference by the state.[83] Secondly, where the constitutional vires of state legislation restricting the free operation of capital was questioned, the Court focused on whether the former offended the natural rights protected by the Constitution rather than its social necessity.[84] Accordingly, it could hold that due process rights must have a substantive dimension protecting privity of contract.[85] Thirdly, where individuals sought to hold non-state bodies such as corporations to the standards of the Constitution, the Court asked whether the actions of these bodies can be regarded as the actions of the state.[86] This reflects the notion that constitutional rights only limit state power, and further reinforces the idea that corporations, for example, are private bodies, part of civil society, and not centres of political power.

Approaching constitutional argument from a classical liberal politics of definition has served hegemonic interests well over the years, in at least three ways. First, in terms of the direct outcome of adjudication: corporations have enjoyed rights under the First[87] and Fourteenth[88] Amendments, which they have employed to challenge state interference with their property; legislation protecting employees from hazardous working conditions has been struck down as interfering with freedom of contract;[89] and non-state bodies have been generally immunised from subjection to the Constitution's requirements of due process

---

[81] See generally, M Tushnet, 'Corporations and Free Speech' in D Kairys (ed), *The Politics of Law* (New York, Pantheon Books, 1982) 253.

[82] See WJ Samuels 'The Idea of the Corporation as a Person: On the Normative Significance of Judicial Language' in WJ Samuels and AS Miller, *Corporations and Society: Power and Responsibility* (New York, Greenwood Press, 1987) 113.

[83] See M Horwitz, 'Santa Clara Revisited: The Development of Corporate Theory' in Samuels and Miller, *ibid* at 13. Horwitz's recounting (*ibid* at 17) of the terms of the brief filed on behalf of the corporate litigant in the *Santa Clara* case is instructive. There it was submitted that constitutional provisions 'apply . . . to private corporations, not alone because such corporations are "persons" within the meaning of that word, but because *statutes violating their prohibitions in dealing with corporations must necessarily infringe upon the rights of natural persons*. In applying and enforcing these constitutional guaranties, *corporations cannot be separated from the natural persons who compose them.*'

[84] See C Sunstein, 'Lochner's Legacy' (1987) 87 *Columbia Law Review* 873, 876–83.

[85] See LH Tribe, *American Constitutional Law*, 3rd edn (New York, Foundation Press, 2000) at 1343–46.

[86] See L Alexander and P Horton, *Whom does the Constitution Command?* (Westport, CT, Greenwood, 1988).

[87] *First National Bank v Bellotti* 435 US 765 (1978).

[88] *Santa Clara Co v Southern Pacific Railroad* 118 US 394 (1886).

[89] *Lochner v New York* 198 US 45 (1905). For the continuing relevance of substantive due process in constitutional adjudication see DJH Greenwood, 'First Amendment' (1999) *Utah Law Review* 659, 664–65 and S Choudhry, 'The *Lochner* Era and Comparative Constitutionalism' (2004) 2 I–CON 1.

and substantive justice.[90] Secondly, in limiting the possible adverse consequences for private power: for example, even where private action is deemed to be state action, this is seen as exceptional, particular to the facts of the case and resting in the private body's temporary nexus with the state. It does not amount to the idea that the private body represents any constitutional danger in its own right,[91] thus reducing the potential for constitutional argument to be used as a weapon against private power. Thirdly, this delineation of constitutional arguments is presented as the product of an internally ordered, autonomous discourse, rather than an as a political contingency. The result is that while a large number of controversies can be contemplated within the constitutional framework, the framework itself is assumed to be non-problematic[92]: constitutional argument is 'disembodied' from politics, as all protagonists seek to show how their preferred constitutional outcome 'is dictated by some neutral and apolitical principle.'[93] Thus, to the extent this framework remains captured by classical liberal values, those values are put further beyond the reach of their opponents.

It is important to underscore the limited focus of the above analysis. For the present, I am not making any claim beyond that the classical liberal politics of definition underpinning the US Constitution have served as 'a powerful symbol of the idea of individual autonomy in the structure of the American polity.'[94] Moreover, these politics of definition have informed and channelled US public discourse, and worked to the benefit of hegemonic, particularly corporate, interests. However, the implications of this analysis go beyond purely local or historical interest: to the extent that the charters of rights being globalized find their precursor in the US Bill of Rights and also emphasise ideas of individual rights and judicial review, this raises the question of whether their politics of definition facilitate or constrain the development of a counterhegemonic constitutionalism. I address this point at length in the next chapter. First, to illustrate further the nature of the politics of definition, I outline an alternative understanding of constitutionalism which directs us to a very different agenda of constitutional inquiry.

---

[90] See LH Tribe, *American Constitutional Law*, 2nd edn (New York, Foundation Press, 1988) ch 18.

[91] See P Brest, 'State Action and Liberal Theory: A Casenote on *Flagg Brothers v Brooks*' (1982) 130 *University of Pennsylvania Law Review* 1296, 1302.

[92] As Griffin illustrates in his discussion of *Hammer v Dagenhart* 247 US 251 (1918), where the Supreme Court struck down a federal statute prohibiting child labour, there has long been a marked separation in criticism of the Court between the merits of the decision and the broader institutional framework (above n 65, at 88). In the instant case, Griffin notes that while the decision stoked considerable controversy, this did not extend to the institution of judicial review.

[93] LM Seidman and M Tushnet, *Remnants of Belief: Contemporary Constitutional Issues* (New York, Oxford University Press, 1996) 20.

[94] Cotterrell, above n 59, at 146.

'New Constitutionalism'

The US constitutional model, codifying fundamental rights into a single written document, represents the explicit constitution in its highest form. However, legal pluralism teaches us that explicit texts are not the only sources of constitutional norms, and that the tacit constitution is equally important in that regard.[95] With this in mind, I turn now to some recent scholarship under the heading of the 'new constitutionalism.' This speaks to the constitutional character of the Washington consensus and associated neoliberal phenomena, which it is argued has as strong, if not a stronger, bearing on the structuring and regulation of political conduct than texts which self-consciously identify as constitutions. This provides an instructive point of contrast with the classical liberal mode as the politics of definition are to the fore: in this instance, 'constitutionalism' is used as 'a metaphor for the challenges that [global economic governance] presents to the notion of democratic legitimacy.'[96] Moreover, these politics of definition advance a form of constitutional knowledge which problematises, rather than protects, corporate power.

New constitutionalism has been described as 'the quasi-legal restructuring of the state and internationalization of international political forms' which confer 'privileged rights of citizenship and representation on corporate capital.'[97] Stephen Gill, for example, identifies a 'set of political and constitutional changes' which are designed to ' "lock-in" neoliberal reforms with respect to macroeconomic stability, protection of property rights and capital mobility.'[98] He argues that this involves three sets of processes: 'measures to reconfigure state apparatuses' as manifested in treaties such as NAFTA; 'measures to construct and extend liberal capitalist markets,' for example incentives to investment; and 'measures for dealing with the dislocations and contradictions' of global capitalism, including 'targeting the very poorest with real material concessions.'[99] For Gill, these measures should be seen in constitutional terms as they seek to attenuate, sometimes by coercion, sometimes by co-option, the potential democratic challenge to economic liberalisation.[100]

---

[95] See RA Macdonald, 'The Design of Constitutions to Accommodate Linguistic, Cultural and Ethnic Diversity: the Canadian Experiment' in K Kulcsár and D Szabo (eds), *Dual Images: Multiculturalism on Two Sides of the Atlantic* (Budapest, Institute for Political Science of the Hungarian Academy of Sciences, 1996) 52, 58.

[96] C Joerges and I-J Sand, 'Constitutionalism and Transnational Governance' (2000) at 2: www.law.harvard.edu/programs/JeanMonnet/EUatHarvard/Program/Rev2CJ-Harvard_2.rtf last accessed May 02.

[97] D Schneiderman, 'Investment Rules and the New Constitutionalism' (2000) 25 *Law and Social Inquiry* 757, 758.

[98] S Gill, 'New Constitutionalism and the Reconstitution of Capital' (1999) http://www.meijigakuin.ac.jp/~iism/pdf/nenpo_002/Gill.pdf at 1.

[99] S Gill, 'The Constitution of Global Capitalism' (2000) www.theglobalsite.ac.uk at 11–18.

[100] Gill, above n 98, at 2.

David Schneiderman similarly argues that we should conceive of economic globalization in constitutional terms.[101] For him, this arises in two ways: first, in a functional approximation between constitutionalism and the transnational legal rules of the global economy,[102] for example, in precommitting future generations to a neoliberal institutional framework. Secondly, these transnational legal rules can operate as higher law on domestic constitutions, sometimes requiring the latter to amend their internal regime along neoliberal lines.[103] For example, membership of NAFTA has resulted in formal and informal changes in the constitutions of Canada[104] and Mexico,[105] designed to ease restrictions on foreign investment (for example, by neutralising clause 27 of the Mexican Constitution which subjected foreign investment to domestic laws). Underlying both these aspects is 'the language of limits,' and Schneiderman here agrees with Gill that the effect of the new constitutionalism is to remove 'some measure of control over the market'[106] from national politics. Harry Arthurs claims that neoliberal values have now acquired constitutional status in the sense that political positions which accord with the former are deemed legitimate on that count alone, and 'not on the basis of their superior wisdom, equity or cost-effectiveness.'[107] This is manifested, for example, in the tendency of western governments to identify their interests with the liberalisation of the global economy.

Problematising Private Power through the Politics of Definition

This view of the 'new constitutionalism' causes some important shifts of focus from the classical liberal conception,[108] in particular our view of the constitutional significance of private power. For example, corporations, given their role as the prime movers of the global economy, are now regarded not just as sources of law, but as sources of constitutional law. This provokes questions concerning their legitimacy directly, in contrast with the classical liberal account where such questions are only relevant in connection with the state. Thus, for example, under new constitutionalism, it is more difficult for corporations to receive the benefit of constitutional rights, as it is now implausible for them to

---

[101]   Above n 97 at 762–67.

[102]   *Ibid* at 762–63.

[103]   *Ibid* at 764–67.

[104]   D Schneiderman, 'NAFTA's Takings Rule: American Constitutionalism Comes to Canada' (1996) 46 *University of Toronto Law Journal* 499.

[105]   Above, n 97, at 764–67.

[106]   *Ibid* at 764.

[107]   HW Arthurs, 'Constitutionalizing Neo-Conservatism and Regional Economic Integration: TINA x 2' in TJ Courchene (ed), *Room to Manoeuvre? Globalization and Policy Convergence* (Montreal and Kingston, McGill-Queen's University Press, 1999) 17, 27.

[108]   For example, as Gill notes (above n 98, at 10), under 'new constitutionalism' the 'dominant political subject' is the investor (as opposed to the abstract rights-bearing individual of classical liberal constitutionalism).

masquerade as rights-bearing individuals in the free realm of civil society. As Santos has observed, a pluralist concept of law implies an expanded concept of politics, one of the consequences of which is:

> to uncover social relations of power beyond the limits drawn by conventional liberal theory and, accordingly, to uncover unsuspected sources of oppression or of emancipation through law, thereby enlarging the field and radicalizing the content of the democratic process.[109]

We can see this at work in our account of new constitutionalism, which, by emphasising the political consequences of neoliberalism seeks to reorient public discourse on corporate power according to the standards of social justice[110] (in contrast with classical liberal constitutionalism which generally seeks to insulate private power from constitutional scrutiny).

These different approaches to private power underline the symbolic power of the explicit constitution. While the tacit constitution may engage central issues of the appropriate bounds of political power, precisely because it is tacit, these issues are regarded as of secondary importance. For example, the non-designation of a corporate charter as constitutional means that questions such as who exercises corporate power, and by what standards we judge it to be legitimate, are not accorded the same priority as questions over how state power is exercised and legitimated. The objective of the new constitutionalism can then be seen as making the constitutional dimension of neoliberal globalization more explicit, with a view to engendering debate over whether it satisfies standards of procedural or substantive constitutional legitimacy. The contrast with classical liberal constitutionalism is instructive: whereas the latter seeks to put the constitutional framework out of the bounds of political debate, with the effect of further insulating its protection of private power, new constitutionalism puts the framework itself in the spotlight with a view to stimulating debate on the legitimacy of private power. In other words, new constitutionalism gives 'constitution' the political charge which classical liberal constitutionalism seeks to defuse.

CONCLUSION

Elaborating the politics of definition advanced by the two conceptions of constitutionalism outlined above takes forward our inquiry in three important ways. First, it emphasises how the meaning of 'constitution' has been, and continues to be, subject to intense political struggle, putting into perspective the notion of constitutional 'essences.' Secondly, it shows that what we regard as, and as not, constitutional has important consequences on how we approach the question of private power. Thirdly, that the politics of definition do not just

---

[109] Above n 1, at 98.
[110] Gill, above n 98, at 11.

speak to how we frame issues in the abstract, but have concrete implications as to which political values can be successfully prosecuted in practice. Accordingly, a legal pluralist perspective provides us with a richer basis for assessing constitutionalism's counterhegemonic potential than the normative method favoured by liberal legalism.

We can elaborate this by considering the relation between the politics of definition, and the theoretical bases of legal pluralism. Making this connection amplifies the symbolic importance of constitutions, by showing that the key question is what politics of definition take root in the political imagination. We can approach this by exploring some apparent tensions in the legal pluralist position. New constitutionalism seems, on the one hand, to take legal subjectivity seriously by emphasising the multiple interactions which make up individuals' constitutional experiences.[111] Yet, on the other hand, it also appears to insist that there is a reasonably coherent normative hierarchy which conditions how individuals can exercise their law-creating capacities.[112] For that matter, the analysis of the US Constitution also appears to suggest that constitutional jurisprudence has been at various times determinate enough to enable corporations to make significant gains. How can these positions be reconciled?

First, it should be stated that while critical legal pluralism takes individuals' law-creating capacities seriously, this does not reduce to complete subjectivity, such that legal experiences are solely the product of each individual's imagination.[113] Rather, legal subjectivity should be seen in relational terms: '[s]ubjects construct and are constructed by State, society and community through their relations with each other.'[114] These relations can significantly constrain legal subjects, for example when they take the form of '[d]ominant narratives,' imposed 'either directly through the imposition of brute force dressed up in the guise of State officials, or indirectly through the ideology of legitimated state power,' and which subjects then 'recognize and maintain.'[115] This leads to the second point of clarification, that highlighting the internal and external pluralism that attaches to all legal orders does not mean that subjects' experiences of law are hopelessly indeterminate. For example, a theorist such as Sampford,

---

[111] For example, Arthurs argues (above n 107, at 28–29) that to comprehend the full range of constitutional relationships between institutions and individuals, we need to have regard not only to 'formal, juridical arrangements, but also more broadly, . . . the shadow effects, social and cultural implications and symbolic significance of normative regimes which limit our ability to imagine, construct and execute alternative policies.'

[112] Eg, Schneiderman argues that the claim that globalization is marked by an 'irreducible heterogeneity' that 'fails to account adequately for the determinate rules and structures associated with "economic globalization"' (D Schneiderman, 'Constitutional Approaches to Privatization: An Inquiry into the Magnitude of Neoliberal Constitutionalism' (2000) 63 *Law and Contemporary Problems* 83, 83).

[113] See Kleinhans and Macdonald, who argue (above n 16, at 42) that the focus on how legal subjects contribute to the construction of normative orders 'does not necessarily entail the replacement of an objective inquiry by a subjective one.'

[114] Kleinhans and Macdonald, *ibid* at 43.

[115] *Ibid*.

who argues that legal relations are by their nature asymmetrical (and hence work against the possibility of system in law), nonetheless can also hold that the overall legal regime in which individuals find themselves can be relatively stable. This is explained by showing how the disorganising influences which produce social conflict also serve to mute it, the result being 'a *social inertia* in which certain interests tend to become *entrenched* because of the inability of others to dislodge them.'[116] This social inertia can give a determinate framework to social life by embedding dominant interests against attack from their opponents.[117]

It is helpful at this point to return to Santos's account of the structure-agency map of capitalist society. We should recall that for Santos, it is the articulation between different forms of social power, law and knowledge which 'establish the horizon of determination, the outer structural limits of social life.'[118] How these articulations develop is the result of a complex, but attenuated, relationship between structure and agency, which Santos captures through the metaphor that 'structures are solid moments or marks in the flowing currents of practice.'[119] Thus, the prevailing normative hierarchy which shapes individuals' legal experiences is both the work of human agency, but also a potential constraint on human agency, especially when it attains the status of commonsense. When the latter situation prevails, Santos argues this should be seen in terms of 'provisional sedimentations of successfully reiterated courses of action,' 'provisional' because they are 'the context within which determinations and contingencies, constraints and opportunities are played out.'[120] However, although provisional, the prevailing sedimentations have concrete implications in terms of setting the horizon of determination.[121] To connect this with our discussion of constitutionalism: if we seek to understand the 'successfully reiterated courses of action' that inform individuals' experiences of constitutional law, the above analysis confirms the need to look beyond the traditional focus on state charters of rights. Rather, rights constitutionalism is but one factor contributing to the current 'provisional sedimentations' that affect the exercise and distribution of political power: the focus now shifts to what sort of contribution it makes.

---

[116] C Sampford, *The Disorder of Law* (Oxford, Blackwell, 1991) 209. Sampford argues (*ibid* at 211) that given their control over the relations of production, the ' "pre-eminent" class' will have 'greater success in the social melée than the class they "exploit" and classes based on other modes of production. They are more likely to able to set up, take over, hold and limit the actions of institutions so that their interests are furthered rather than challenged.'

[117] For Sampford, whether entrenched interests can be successfully attacked depends on: 'the resources of the attacking/defending party, the resources of those on whose support it can call in such a conflict, the extent and speed of their mobilization, and the power relations in which they can be deployed' (*ibid* at 209).

[118] Above n 1, at 399.

[119] *Ibid* at 354.

[120] *Ibid*.

[121] Santos gives as an example how the hold of 'free trade fundamentalism and hegemonic demands for structural adjustment, stabilization and foreign debt payment' in peripheral societies has the effect there of 'reorganizing all the other structural places, even though the range and the depth of the reorganization may change enormously across social fields' (*ibid* at 400).

If we accept the new constitutionalist argument, those processes identified as the 'constitutionalisation' of neoliberal practices and ideas can be seen to be the current 'provisional sedimentations' at the global level. Casting them in these terms reminds us that they are neither total nor inevitable; nonetheless, they operate in an important 'boundary-setting' mode, placing real constraints on political action. The contribution of constitutional globalization, and its potential to act in a 'path-breaking'[122] mode, thus depends on its articulation with other forms of law and power in making up these provisional sedimentations. The key here is the extent to which the contingent outcome of the constitutional politics of definition contributes to the embedding of certain ideas as common sense in the popular and (perhaps more important) elite imagination. This inquiry focuses at two levels: first, what political arguments prevail in constitutional adjudication, and secondly, how these affect the political arguments that prevail at the broader level of the provisional sedimentations.

We can gain some flavour of the processes involved by returning to the discussion of US constitutionalism. The state action doctrine, in placing a presumptive bar to the constitutional scrutiny of non-state bodies, has led to direct gains by private power in jurisprudential terms. However, the major symbolic importance of adjudication in this context lies in how it embeds classical liberal politics of definition as constitutional orthodoxy—both substantively, that constitutions are about limiting government in the name of individual autonomy, and conceptually, that they are legal discourses and so represent ipso facto the legitimate baselines for political action—and how the hold of these ideas at the level of adjudication plays out at the broader level of public discourse (Santos's horizons of determination) to shape the possibilities of political action. In this regard, it is important to note how (state) constitutional law reflects, but also reinforces the provisional sedimentation of market values (particularly that corporations are not centres of political power to be subjected to direct democratic control), as the framework for American society.[123]

We can now place in context the argument that rights constitutionalism can become a greater force for prosecuting counterhegemonic politics at the global level. To succeed, this has to show that constitutionalism can change the provisional sedimentations by placing effective restraints on hegemonic private power. Nothing in the argument so far outlined says that such a rearticulation is theoretically impossible—both Sampford and Santos, for example, emphasise the contingent nature of prevailing hegemonies, and the possibilities of 'transformative agency'.[124] However, whether such a transformation is likely has to be assessed in the light of real material conditions. To answer this, we now ask what politics of definition inform the globalization of rights constitutionalism, and how these politics of definition condition its engagement with private power.

---

[122] *Ibid*, at 399.

[123] See Elkin, above n 69, at 592.

[124] Santos, above n 1, at 354. See also Sampford, who argues that '[i]f stability is related to the balance of forces mobilized by the parties to [social] conflicts, change results from alterations in that balance' (above n 116, at 210), and Kleinhans and Macdonald, above n 16, at 43.

7

Rights Constitutionalism and the Counterhegemonic Difficulty

IN THIS CHAPTER, I focus directly on the central issue of the relationship between rights constitutionalism and private power. In chapter six, I argued that constitutionalism is best understood as an artefact in the struggle between hegemonic and counterhegemonic forces. This emphasises both the fluidity and contingency of constitutional argument, and that the prize sought is to present the provisional outcome of these struggles as commonsensical, and so privilege some arguments in constitutional terms over others. This approach accordingly places two questions at the centre of our inquiry: what are the politics of definition that accompany the current processes of constitutional globalization? and, how do they affect our capacity to advance counterhegemonic constitutional arguments?

The structure of this chapter is as follows: I first set the discussion in context by showing how constitutional globalization was seen by powerful actors in the global economy as important in providing the conditions for neoliberalism to flourish. This provides the backdrop for considering the argument that a reformulated rights constitutionalism, which strengthens its negative and positive controls, can act as a counterhegemonic constraint on private power. A legal pluralist focus on the politics of definition shows that running through these doctrinal debates are competing views over whether the state promotes or negates individual freedom—in other words, they are situated within the framework of the state–civil society divide. This reveals the limits of trying to remake rights constitutionalism from within: even if doctrine were to be reformulated to reach private actors, it is unlikely that rights constitutionalism could, to any significant extent, be used as a sword for counterhegemonic values. Moreover, it leaves in place a framework which enables, for example, corporations to employ constitutionalism, both as a sword against state attempts to regulate their interests, and as a counterhegemonic shield, reinforcing the idea that the state is the only major centre of political power in society that can oppress individual liberty.

CONSTITUTIONAL GLOBALIZATION IN POLITICAL CONTEXT

We begin our inquiry into the counterhegemonic potential of constitutional globalization by asking why the latter occurred when it did, and whose interests were served by it. In this regard, it is important to locate our discussion in the political context of the late 1980s and 1990s, which, for many states, was a period of transition from previous authoritarian regimes—whether state communism in central and eastern Europe or rule by military junta in Latin America. This time was marked by an intensity of institutional reform, which sought to embed liberal democracy, and so prevent the return to dictatorship.[1] A key aspect of these 'waves of democratization'[2] has been reform of the courts, which have as a result played a prominent role in managing the transition to liberal democracy.[3] One high profile aspect of these reforms has been in the field of criminal justice, directed towards eliminating corruption.[4] However, more important for present purposes has been the increased prestige and activism of constitutional courts in adjudicating individual rights.[5] To understand fully the significance of these rule of law reforms, we have to see how their adoption was perceived by key agents of the global economy to promote neoliberalism.

The first point to make is that these reforms were not spontaneous and unrelated, but often the site of 'high intensity globalization.'[6] For example, Santos links what he calls 'rule of law and judicial programmes' in Latin America to the 'reformist pressure' exerted by 'USAID, the World Bank, the Inter-American Development Bank, the US Justice Department, the Ford Foundation and the European Union (collectively or through some of its members).'[7] Similarly, he notes USAID's investment in 'democracy and rule of law programmes' in central and eastern Europe in the early 1990s.[8] It is perhaps in the developing world where such programmes are most visible,[9] with western governments and global

---

[1] See J Elster, C Offe and UK Preuss (with F Boenker, U Goetting and FW Rueb), *Institutional Design in Post-communist Societies: Rebuilding the Ship at Sea* (Cambridge, Cambridge University Press, 1998) 93.

[2] A Przeworski et al, *Sustainable Democracy* (Cambridge, Cambridge University Press, 1995) 6.

[3] See B de Sousa Santos, *Toward a New Legal Common Sense* (London, Butterworths, 2002) ch 6.

[4] *Ibid* at 317.

[5] The literature on this is vast. For a representative sample, see: D Greenberg, SN Katz, SC Wheatley and MB Oliviero, *Constitutionalism and Democracy: Transitions in the Contemporary World* (New York, Oxford University Press, 1993); H Schwartz, 'The New East European Constitutional Courts' in AE Dick Howard (ed), *Constitution Making in Eastern Europe* (Washington, Johns Hopkins University Press, 1993) ch 6; and CN Tate and T Vallinder (eds), *The Global Expansion of Judicial Power* (New York, New York University Press, 1994).

[6] Santos, above n 3, at 317.

[7] *Ibid* at 326.

[8] *Ibid* at 322.

[9] As Santos notes (*ibid* at 330), in developing countries, these reforms 'are mainly driven by donor countries, international assistance agencies, and international financial institutions' in contrast with the 'semiperipheral countries' of Latin America and central and eastern Europe, where there is often also a strong internal movement for reform.

institutions like the World Bank and International Monetary Fund now taking an active concern in establishing a basic democratic infrastructure.[10]

This renewed interest of the west and international financial agencies in good governance programmes coincided with the awakening of neoliberalism,[11] and it has been suggested that what is novel here is that liberal democratic reforms are seen as necessarily prior to economic liberalisation, not one of its out-comes.[12] This linkage between rule of law reforms and promoting the market economy was made explicit in the World Bank's 1996 World Development Report, *From Plan to Market*.[13] There the World Bank argued that transitional societies must adopt 'a new way of thinking about the entire legal system.'[14] This equates to a vision of the rule of law where 'laws are applied fairly, trans-parently and even-handedly to all'—on this basis, 'individuals can assert and defend their rights; and the state's powers are defined and limited by law.'[15] In specific terms, the hallmarks of a 'dynamic, changing economy'[16] are the creation and allocation of property rights[17] and a constitutional structure which ensures that 'the government will apply the law consistently and will itself abide by certain constraints,[18] refraining from arbitrary intervention and cor-ruption.'[19] Underpinning constitutions and rights are 'competent and reliable courts' which 'provide the foundation on which all enforcement activity . . . ultimately depends.'[20] In this way, what is distinctive about law in market economies is that it 'defines the rules of the game and gives individuals the rights and tools to enforce them.'[21]

An important corollary of this democratisation process has been the bolster-ing of civil society.[22] Regarded as a shorthand term for 'the collection of intermediary groups and voluntary associations that occupy the space between

---

[10] See J Faundez, 'Legal technical assistance' in J Faundez (ed), *Good Government and Law: Legal and Institutional Reform in Developing Countries* (London, Macmillan, 1997) 1, 6–14.

[11] A Leftwich, 'Governance, Democracy and Development in the Third World' (1993) 14 *Third World Quarterly* 605, 606.

[12] *Ibid* at 605.

[13] World Bank, *World Development Report 1996—From Plan to Market* (Oxford, Oxford University Press, 1996).

[14] *Ibid* at 97.

[15] *Ibid* at 87.

[16] *Ibid* at 44.

[17] 'Property rights are at the heart of the incentive structures of market economies . . . In short, fully specified property rights reward effort and good judgment, thereby assisting economic growth and wealth creation' (*ibid* at 48–49).

[18] It is instructive that in its account of these constraints, the World Bank relies on the classical conception of liberal legalism which underpins rights constitutionalism: 'Formal constraints on arbitrary state power in established market economies derive partly from [constitutional law]. These bodies of law ensure that all legislation is consistent with the national constitutions . . . They delineate the rulemaking authority of various state bodies, lay out the procedures for enacting laws . . ., and provide individuals recourse against unlawful or capricious state action' (*ibid* at 94).

[19] *Ibid* at 97.

[20] *Ibid* at 93.

[21] *Ibid* at 87.

[22] N Bermeo, 'Civil Society, Good Government and Neoliberal Reform' in Faundez (ed), above n 10, at 77.

the family and the state,'[23] its strengthening is often seen as central to sustaining democratic transitions, for example, by supporting the establishment of political parties in societies with little tradition of competitive politics.[24] However, its main significance is in contrast with the necessary other of the state which gives it meaning in liberal theory, which emphasises the connection between promoting civil society and the neoliberal economic agenda. In David Held's words, civil society is thus associated with 'the "rolling back of the state"—that is, the freeing of civil society from state domination,'[25] and so becomes 'an essential element of any democratic political order.'[26]

The foregoing provides the context for answering Santos's question: 'what type of state form is both presupposed and produced by the expansion of judicial power?'[27] Santos himself argues that the latter is related to perceived failures of the democratic and welfare state, and that it should therefore be associated with contemporary neoliberal notions of the weak state.[28] For him, this explains, for example, why the 'downsizing of the administrative welfare sector' goes hand in hand with 'the upsizing of the judicial system' as the weak state 'open[s] the space for partial replacement of the political obligation with contractual relations among citizens, corporations, NGOs and the state itself.'[29] This has the further effect of depoliticising the conflict inherent in this transition by casting the issues arising as individual disputes.[30] This analysis, in highlighting that the 'retreat of the state' has been in parallel with these rule of law reforms,[31] suggests that the latter are connected to the rise of the Washington consensus in important ways.

Some supporters of neoliberal globalization make this link explicit by pointing out that what is common to international trade and human rights is that both 'are largely deregulatory—they declare what the State should not do.'[32] On this view, through a series of equations, that rights constitutionalism promotes democracy, and that capitalism is compatible with democracy,[33] the judicial protection of fundamental rights is not seen to present a series of trade-offs between important values, but rather becomes vital to the success of the global economy in neoliberal mode.[34] This faith placed in rights constitutionalism by neoliberal protagonists reflects the hold, in historical and comparative perspec-

---

[23] *Ibid* at 77.

[24] See Przeworski et al, above n 2, at 53–55 and Elster et al, above n 1, at 132–40.

[25] D Held, 'Democracy: From City States to a Cosmopolitan Order?' in D Held (ed), *Prospects for Democracy: North, South, East, West* (London, Polity Press, 1993) 13, 23.

[26] *Ibid* at 24.

[27] Above n 3, at 335.

[28] *Ibid* at 338.

[29] *Ibid.*

[30] *Ibid.*

[31] See Elster et al, above n 1, at 183.

[32] S Charnovitz, 'The Globalization of Economic Human Rights' (1999) 26 *Brooklyn Journal of International Law* 113, 116.

[33] See Santos, above n 3, at 272.

[34] See Charnovitz, above n 32, at 115.

tive, of a classical liberal politics of definition, which has at its base the conceptual and normative divide between the state and civil society. Outlining how this has translated into a constitutional jurisprudence which resonates with key elements of neoliberalism provides the context for considering the argument that rights constitutionalism can be remade in a counterhegemonic manner.

Modern Constitutionalism as Limitations on the State

A comparative approach reveals that constitutional charters of rights are principally concerned with the limitation of governmental action. Sometimes this is made explicit in the text, such as section 32(1) of the Canadian Charter of Rights and Freedoms,[35] which states that it applies only to the federal and provincial legislatures and governments,[36] or the UK Human Rights Act 1998 which restricts its reach to 'public authorities'.[37] Sometimes this is emphasised by constitutional courts, for example, the *Bundesverfassungsgerichts* has said that the 'primary purpose of [the Germans Constitution's] basic rights is to safeguard the liberties of the individual against interferences by public authority.'[38] To this it may be countered that newer forms of constitutionalism, such as those adopted in central and eastern Europe, move beyond an exclusive focus on limiting the state, and also contain positive guarantees.[39] I will return to the counterhegemonic potential of positive obligations on the state below, but for now it is important to note that, in formal terms, they generally enjoy a secondary status to, and cannot be directly enforced in the same way as, negative rights.[40] A

[35] Canadian Charter of Rights and Freedoms, Part I of the Constitution Act 1982, being Sch B of The Canada Act 1982 (UK), c 11.

[36] The full text of s 32 (1) is:

This Charter applies:

(a) to the Parliament and government of Canada in respect of all matters within the authority of Parliament, including all matters relating to the Yukon Territory and Northwest Territory; and

(b) to the legislature and government of each province in respect of all matters within the authority of the legislature of each province.

My point here is historical rather than exegetical, that this wording reflected the intention of the Charter's drafters to restrict its potential application against private bodies, and was deliberately chosen over more ambiguous alternatives, for example, that it 'applied to the Parliament and government of Canada *and to* all matters within the authority of Parliament': JD Whyte, 'Is the Private Sector Affected by the Charter' in L Smith (ed), *Righting the Balance: Canada's New Equality Rights* (Saskatoon, Canadian Human Rights Reporter, 1986) 145, 153 (emphasis added).

[37] Human Rights Act 1998, c 42, s 6.

[38] *Lüth* case (1958) 7 BverfGE 198, translated in DP Kommers, *The Constitutional Jurisprudence of the Federal Republic of Germany*, 2nd edn (Durham, NC, Duke University Press, 1997) 369.

[39] See Elster et al, above n 1, at 86–87.

[40] Eg, as Elster et al note (*ibid* at 87), most of the positive rights guaranteed in the new constitutions in central and eastern Europe 'are not justiciable because they require policy choices by the legislative and executive branches of government. Thus, both the Czech Charter and the Slovak constitutions explicitly stipulate that the positive rights which they grant "may be claimed only within the scope of the laws implementing these provisions."'

comparative perspective shows that while virtually all constitutions enforce negative rights against the state, only some have positive rights, which moreover only become justiciable in limited circumstances, for example, if economic conditions permit.[41] Thus, while accounts of constitutionalism which seek to move beyond the traditional approach—whether of the creole liberal,[42] postliberal[43] or transliberal[44] variety—require a qualifying adjective, the basic model of liberal constitutionalism continues to denote negative limits on state action.[45]

The deeply embedded roots of this central idea, reflecting the classical liberal distrust of the state, and the valorisation of what lies beyond it in the free realm of civil society, is corroborated in the detail of the comparative jurisprudence. Courts have struck out actions brought against private bodies on the grounds that, *ratione personae*, they do not cross the threshold for constitutional application. This has its origins in the US state action doctrine discussed in chapter six. Under this heading, the US Supreme Court has excluded from constitutional review: the decision of an utility company to terminate electrical services, allegedly denying due process;[46] the removal of anti-war protesters seeking to assert First Amendment rights of expression and assembly from a shopping mall;[47] the licensing powers of the state-created Olympic Committee;[48] and courts giving effect to the terms of discriminatory wills.[49] This doctrine has proved influential beyond the US, most strikingly in Canada, and the Supreme Court there has found the Charter inapplicable to: injunctions applying the common law to restrain secondary picketing;[50] the introduction of mandatory retirement schemes by a publicly funded hospital;[51] and court orders making provision for custody under statutory divorce laws.[52] The removal of private action from constitutional scrutiny has also characterised the approach of courts outside North America: the South African Constitutional Court held in

---

[41] See, eg, M Mandel, 'Legal Politics Italian Style' in Tate and Vallinder, above n 5, at 261.

[42] S Woolman and D Davis, 'The Last Laugh: *Du Plessis v De Klerk*: Classical Liberalism, Creole Liberalism and the Application of Fundamental Rights Under the Interim and Final Constitutions' (1996) 12 *South African Journal of Human Rights* 361, 361–62.

[43] KE Klare, 'Legal Culture and Transformative Constitutionalism' (1998) 14 *South African Journal of Human Rights* 146, 151.

[44] Elster et al, above n 1, at 82.

[45] A symbolic indication of this argument is the s 8 (2) application provision of the 1996 South African Constitution, which states: 'A provision of the Bill of Rights binds a natural or juristic person if, and to the extent that, it is applicable, taking into account the nature of the right and the nature of any duty imposed by the right.' While generally regarded as moving beyond the traditional model, and giving some horizontal dimension to the new Constitution (see H Cheadle and D Davis, 'The Application of the 1996 Constitution in the Private Sphere' (1996) 12 *South African Journal of Human Rights* 44, 54–55), it is important to note both the qualifications placed on this, and also how it confirms that the 'standard' model is direct applicability against governmental institutions.

[46] *Jackson v Metropolitan Edison Co* 419 US 345 (1974).

[47] *Lloyd Corp v Tanner* 407 US 551 (1972).

[48] *San Francisco Arts & Athletics, Inc v United States Olympic Committee* 483 US 522 (1987).

[49] *Evans v Abney* 396 US 435 (1970).

[50] *RWDSU v Dolphin Delivery* (1986) 33 DLR (4th) 174. See also *BCGEU v Attorney-General (British Columbia)* (1988) 53 DLR (4th) 1.

[51] *Stoffman v Vancouver General Hospital* (1990) 76 DLR (4th) 700 (hereafter, *Stoffman*).

[52] *Young v Young* (1994) 108 DLR (4th) 193.

one of its first decisions that the Bill of Rights, in speaking principally to state-individual relations, did not apply to the common law of defamation.[53] The English courts[54] have also invoked the idea of some 'natural' private sphere to exclude from review a private regulatory body which otherwise was amenable to the courts' supervisory jurisdiction.[55]

The obverse of the state action doctrine has been to equate corporations with rights-bearing individuals: in this regard, courts around the world have emulated the US approach and have conferred a range of benefits on corporate litigants. In Canada, for example, the Charter has been employed by corporations: to overturn a statutory ban on the advertising of cigarettes;[56] to strike down legislation granting special search and seizure powers to inspectors investigating restrictive practices;[57] and to gain a religion.[58] The European Court of Human Rights has similarly entertained applications from corporate plaintiffs[59]: in upholding a company's Article 10 freedom of expression rights,[60] it stated that this Article 'applies to "everyone", whether natural or legal persons'[61] and could not be denied on the basis of the applicant's status as a limited company or its commercial nature. In Australia, the High Court of Justice, even in the absence of a constitutional charter of rights, has sustained complaints by corporations that their freedom of political communication was infringed, setting aside, for example, laws limiting political advertising during election campaigns.[62] It is striking that each time these courts first upheld the constitutional claims of corporations, the appropriateness of extending 'human' rights in this way was not considered relevant for judicial comment.[63]

---

[53] *Du Plessis v De Klerk* (1996) 3 SA 850 (CC). Although this ruling was given under the interim Constitution, and so before s 8 (2) came into force (above n 45), the Constitutional Court has not yet taken the opportunity to revise this decision: J van der Walt, 'Blixen's Difference: Horizontal Application of Fundamental Rights and the Resistance to Neo-Colonialism' (2003) 5 *Law, Justice and Global Development*: http://elj.warwick.ac.uk/global/issue/2003-1/vanderwalt.htm).

[54] In pre-Human Rights Act administrative law cases: see N Bamforth, 'The Scope of Judicial Review: Still Uncertain' [1993] *Public Law* 239.

[55] *R v Disciplinary Committee of the Jockey Club, ex parte His Highness the Aga Khan* [1993] 1 WLR 909.

[56] *RJR-MacDonald Inc v Attorney General of Canada et al* (1995) 127 DLR (4th) 1.

[57] *Hunter v Southam Inc* (1984) 11 DLR (4th) 641.

[58] *R v Big M Drug Mart* (1985) 18 DLR (4th) 321.

[59] See *Air Canada v United Kingdom* Series A no 316 (1995) 20 EHRR 150 and *British American Tobacco Company Ltd v The Netherlands* Series A no 331-A (1996) 21 EHRR 409. Although the applicant companies' cases were rejected on the merits, in neither case was their corporate status an issue before the Court.

[60] *Autronic AG v Switzerland* Series A no 178 (1990) 12 EHRR 485.

[61] *Ibid* at para 47.

[62] *Australian Capital Television Pty Ltd v Commonwealth* (1992) 177 CLR 106.

[63] See *Santa Clara Co. v Southern Pacific Railroad* 118 US 394 (1886); *Hunter v Southam Inc*, above n 57; *Sunday Times v United Kingdom* Series A no 30 (1979–80) 2 EHRR 245; and *Nationwide News Pty Ltd v Wills* (1992) 177 CLR 1.

REMAKING RIGHTS CONSTITUTIONALISM?

This account of the hold of classical liberal politics of definition in modern constitutionalism is necessarily impressionistic. Given the argument from internal legal pluralism, it should not be taken as suggesting that this is a monolithic picture, and as I will shortly discuss, there are important counterexamples in the doctrinal record. However, the sway of classical liberal constitutionalism, identified by a number of scholars across various jurisdictions,[64] is an important clue in delineating the parameters of debate for rights constitutionalism's engagement with private power. This view appears to be vindicated by those agitating for a reformulated rights constitutionalism, who acknowledge that their goal is to transcend the dominant classical liberal narrative. For example, Andrew Clapham's case for a 'rights-based strategy to social change'[65] accepts that rights have protected private power, but that this can be overcome:

> [I]f fundamental rights come to operate in the private sphere, the critique which labels them as vacuous bourgeois tools of legitimization whose function is to deceive citizens into believing in the justness of the system begins to lose some of its force.[66]

Here, I put this argument to the test, by discussing the two principal means proposed for moving to counterhegemonic constitutional adjudication. The first focuses on extending the reach of constitutional rights by redefining who or what counts as the state, the second on deepening their scope by redefining the nature of constitutional obligations. When we consider how these doctrinal positions have been employed in actual adjudication, this has not effected any significant shift in the parameters of constitutional discourse, and so confirms the difficulty in practice of transcending the classical liberal default. Accordingly, we must doubt the counterhegemonic potential claimed on their behalf.

The Application to State Institutions (ASI) Model

The first proposed reworking takes its bearings from North America where the operative idea is that constitutional rights only speak to the institutions of the

---

[64] For a representative sample see: M Tushnet, *Red, White and Blue: A Critical Analysis of Constitutional Law* (Cambridge, MA, Harvard University Press, 1988); J Bakan, *Just Words: Constitutional Rights and Social Wrongs* (Toronto, University of Toronto Press, 1997); KD Ewing, 'Human Rights, Social Democracy and Constitutional Reform' in CA Gearty and A Tomkins (eds), *Understanding Human Rights* (London, Mansell, 1996) 40; Mandel, above n 41; DP Currie, 'Lochner Abroad: Substantive Due Process and Equal Protection in the Federal Republic of Germany' (1989) *Supreme Court Review* 333; T Campbell, 'Democracy, Human Rights, and Positive Law' (1994) 16 *Sydney Law Review* 195; and Woolman and Davis, above n 42, at 382–85.
[65] A Clapham, *Human Rights in the Private Sphere* (Oxford, Oxford University Press, 1993) 151.
[66] *Ibid.*

state. As such, constitutional rights do not apply to conduct which is 'fundamentally a matter of private choice and not state action.'[67] The central doctrinal issue of the *Application to State Institutions* (ASI) approach is, having fixed a putative constitutional violation onto a discrete act, to ask if that act can be attributed to the state. Analytically, this approach breaks down into four categories:

1. The alleged unconstitutional action is carried out by a body which, by definition, is manifestly a state institution, so the constitution applies.[68]
2. The action is executed through a body whose 'public' status is more ambiguous, but which on closer examination can also be seen to be a state actor.[69]
3. The violation is committed by a private entity, but, because there is sufficient implication by the state in the 'private' action, the constitution applies.[70]
4. The violation is by a private entity, but here there is insufficient implication of the state to invoke the constitution.

It is the cases in the fourth category where classical liberal politics of definition are most visible, as under this rubric both Supreme Courts have shielded a significant proportion of social life from constitutional review. For example, each Court has held that where an action is carried out by a private body under statutory authority, this may not in itself be enough to attach constitutional interest. In Canada, where a university had been created by, and exercised its powers (including its employment policies) pursuant to, statute, the Charter was held not to apply to its mandatory retirement scheme as this was neither instituted under statutory compulsion nor was it 'following the dictates of the government.'[71] In *Flagg Bros v Brooks*,[72] the US Supreme Court found that the granting of a lien under a legislative property code was not state action, as the state's providing the background statutory framework was no more than 'acquiescence in a private action.'[73] The US Supreme Court has also held that

---

[67] O'Connor J in *Edmonson v Leesville Concrete Co* 500 US 614, 632 (1991).

[68] Non-problematic cases include: where a constitutional right has been limited by the direct action of a government agency (*Brown v Board of Education of Topeka* 347 US 483 (1954)), and where legislation is the direct source of a constitutional infringement (*RJR-Macdonald v Attorney General of Canada et al*, above n 56).

[69] Eg, in *Douglas/Kwantlen Faculty Assn v Douglas College* [1990] 3 SCR 570, the Supreme Court of Canada considered whether a British Columbia community college was included in the term 'government'. Taking into account the control exercised over the college by the government, including the power of the education minister to appoint its board of governors, it answered this in the affirmative. See also *Lebron v National R R Passenger Corp* 513 US 374 (1995).

[70] See *Burton v Wilmington Parking Authority* 365 US 715 (1961) for the position that a public body which has not directly committed any constitutional violation may nonetheless be liable for breaches of constitutional rights carried out by a private actor. In that case, the US Supreme Court held that the Fourteenth Amendment applied where the owner of a private restaurant refused to serve blacks as the (public) parking authority who leased the restaurant had 'so far insinuated itself into a position of interdependence' (per Clark J at 725) with the owner that it was equally liable in constitutional terms.

[71] *McKinney v University of Guelph* (1990) 76 DLR (4th) 545, 639 (per La Forest J).

[72] 436 US 149 (1978).

[73] *Ibid* at 164, per Rehnquist J.

the failure of state-employed social workers to prevent a boy from being beaten and seriously injured by his father was not state action as the Constitution did not require the state 'to protect the life, liberty, and property of its citizens against invasion by private actors.'[74] The question of the courts' status as constitutional actors has also arisen, with the Supreme Court of Canada, in *RWDSU v Dolphin Delivery*,[75] adopting the position that courts are not covered by the reference to legislatures and governments, and so the Charter does not apply directly to their decisions.[76]

We can see a number of classical liberal hallmarks running through this case law, whether in the characterisation of legislation as necessarily coercive (so that the absence of direct coercion equates to the absence of the state), or in casting courts as 'neutral arbiters'[77] providing the framework for disputes arising from the free interaction of private individuals. At the root of this doctrine is the disconnected social theory of classical liberalism, which believes that social life can be split between the (artificially created) state and (spontaneous and free) civil society.[78] This provides the conceptual apparatus which enables courts, for example, to regard economic activity, which requires state infrastructure to function, as private. However, we can also find counter currents in the jurisprudence, and we now turn to other decisions which appear to rest on a less atomistic, more interconnected, view of society, and open up potential routes for bringing private action within constitutional reach.

Extending the Reach of Constitutional Rights?

There are three counter-tendencies in the jurisprudence, which underline that we are again dealing here with a situation of internal legal pluralism. The first refocuses on courts as constitutional actors, and how their decisions should not be treated as something apart from the constitution. In the US, for example, the Supreme Court has had no issue in making the common law of libel conform to the First Amendment in a dispute between two private litigants.[79] In Canada, the *Dolphin Delivery* decision makes this more problematic in direct terms. However, McIntyre J's dictum in that case, that the common law should be developed in a manner consistent with Charter values, has been seen as the basis for 'connect[ing] constitutional rights to private law'[80] In this way, the Charter

---

[74] *DeShaney v Winnebago County Dept of Social Services* 489 US 189 (1989), 195, per Rehnquist CJ.

[75] Above n 50.

[76] 'While in political science it is probably acceptable to treat the courts as one of the three branches of government, that is, legislative, executive, and judicial, I cannot equate for the purposes of Charter application the order of a court with an element of governmental action' (*ibid* at 196, per McIntyre J).

[77] *Ibid.*

[78] See Santos, above n 3, at 363.

[79] See *New York Times v Sullivan* 376 US 254 (1964).

[80] LE Weinrib and EJ Weinrib, 'Constitutional Values and Private Law in Canada' in D Friedmann and D Barak-Erez (eds), *Human Rights in Private Law* (Oxford and Portland, OR, Hart Publishing, 2001) 43, 43.

can indirectly influence private action: in this regard, the Court held in *Dagenais v CBC*[81] that common law rules on publication bans in criminal trials had to be reformulated to accord with Charter values, and in *Pepsi-Beverages (West) Ltd v RWDSU, Local 558*[82] that the right to free expression meant that the common law could not be interpreted as making secondary picketing illegal per se.

A second strategy has been to separate out the private nature of an entity from the public character of its actions. This has been the rationale behind the US public function cases,[83] and has recently found favour with the Supreme Court of Canada in *Eldridge v British Columbia*.[84] This was a claim that the denial of sign language interpreters to a deaf patient infringed the equality provisions of the Charter. Notwithstanding that this hospital had been regarded as a private body in *Stoffman*,[85] the Court held the Charter was applicable. Its solution was to contrast the definitional status of the hospital with the public nature of its action: here, the hospital had been delegated the statutory authority to decide which services should receive social insurance funding, which was a public act as it was in furtherance of a specific governmental objective.[86]

The third, and potentially most far reaching jurisprudential innovation, deals with the constitutional consequences of state *in*action. Over seventy years ago, the US Supreme Court, in the classic 'apple v cedar trees' controversy in *Miller v Schoene*,[87] held that where a legislature elects to do nothing, this can be 'none the less a choice' for constitutional purposes. More recently, in *Vriend v Alberta*,[88] the Canadian Supreme Court followed this reasoning when, in hearing a complaint by a teacher dismissed because he was gay from a private college, it considered the Alberta legislature's omission of sexual orientation as a forbidden ground of discrimination in its human rights code. The Court decided that the Charter applied, stating that it was not only engaged through positive acts, but also where a statute's under-inclusiveness failed to fulfil its enacting legislature's positive constitutional obligations.

These doctrinal moves echo critiques of a restrictive constitutional public–private divide within the legal academy. The idea that the courts are not state actors has been rejected as this 'necessarily transforms [the] judiciary into

---

[81] (1994) 120 DLR (4th) 12.

[82] *Pepsi-Cola Canada Beverages (West) Ltd v RWDSU, Local 558* [2002] 1 SCR 156 (hereafter *Pepsi-Cola v RWDSU*).

[83] Eg, in *Marsh v Alabama* 326 US 501 (1946) it was held that where a company-owned town had opened up its property for public use, it was performing a public function, and so was barred by the First Amendment from prosecuting distributors of religious pamphlets.

[84] (1997) 151 DLR (4th) 577 (hereafter *Eldridge*).

[85] Above n 51.

[86] The contrast here is with the same hospital's decision to institute a mandatory retirement scheme which was seen as internal to the hospital's management.

[87] 276 US 272 (1928). Here, the Virginia legislature was faced with a threat to the State's apple industry from a plant disease which was spread from cedar to apple trees. Its response was to enact legislation empowering, upon petition of the apple tree owners to a state official, the destruction of cedar trees growing close to apple orchards if they were found to be infested with the disease. The cedar tree owners alleged that this was a violation of the 'takings clause' of the US Constitution.

[88] [1998] 1 SCR 493.

an elitist and anti-democratic branch of government.'[89] Also, a 'formulaic' approach to labelling entities 'public' and 'private' has been attacked for 'insulating from constitutional scrutiny behavior fairly attributable to the state'[90]— instead it is suggested that focusing on whether an entity furthers 'governmental objectives' provides 'more accurate state action determinations.'[91] Further, the notion that positive state action is required to invoke constitutional review has been criticised because while 'it imagines that the state can abstain from decisions involving the content of the law,' in reality 'the state cannot abstain.'[92] Various benefits are assigned to extending the reach of constitutional application: for example, where it is properly guided by constitutional values, private law can play a part in 'fulfilling . . . constitutionally enshrined aspiration[s] [to a] free and democratic society.'[93] A more assiduous search for the performance of governmental objectives is said to show the constitutional relevance of activity previously deemed private, and so can extend the protection of constitutional rights to groups to which it has been arbitrarily denied.[94] The idea that rights impose positive duties on the state, which cannot be avoided through legislative and governmental inaction, can be seen as 'laying down certain principles that are fundamental . . ., and that operate as standards for the conduct of private persons and public bodies alike.'[95]

The Politics of Adjudication: Pluralist v Classical Liberalism

Underlying these positions is the idea that (to varying degrees) a more expansive ASI model can prevent the abuse of constitutional rights by private power[96]— what has been described as 'human rights at their most vulnerable point.'[97] This gives us the opportunity, in the context of the broader discussion, to consider the counterhegemonic potential of a reformulated constitutionalism. My point of departure is to question the assumption, implicit in all the above approaches, that we are dealing here with an interpretive issue, to which there are 'better' or 'correct' responses, and which, if implemented, can remove the problem of

---

[89] D Beatty, 'Constitutional Conceits: The Coercive Authority of Courts' (1987) 37 *University of Toronto Law Journal* 183, 190.

[90] RJ Krotoszynski Jr, 'Back to the Briarpatch: An Argument in Favor of Constitutional Meta-analysis in State Action Determinations' (1995) 94 *Michigan Law Review* 302, 305: this is because courts 'would be put to the burden of explaining their [determinations] with particularity and care.' See also RJ Glennon Jr and JE Nowak, 'A Functional Analysis of the Fourteenth Amendment "State Action" Requirement' (1976) *Supreme Court Review* 221.

[91] Krotoszynski, *ibid* at 345.

[92] R Elliot and R Grant, 'The Charter's Application in Private Litigation' (1989) 23 *University of British Columbia Law Review* 459, 479.

[93] Weinrib and Weinrib, above n 80, at 72.

[94] See D Beatty, 'Canadian Constitutional Law in a Nutshell' (1998) 36 *Alberta Law Review* 605, 614–17.

[95] B Slattery, 'Legislation' (1985) 63 *Canadian Bar Review* 148, 161.

[96] *Ibid.*

[97] F Raday, 'Privatising Human Rights and the Abuse of Power' (2000) 12 *Canadian Journal of Law and Jurisprudence* 103, 104.

doctrinal inconsistency. Rather, in adjudication on the reach of constitutions, we are dealing with the clash of different political ideas—specifically, between visions of the minimal and maximal state—and that, a fortiori, we should expect to find that this jurisprudence, in the words of O'Connor J of the US Supreme Court, 'ha[s] not been a model of consistency.'[98]

We can approach the political context of constitutional application jurisprudence by considering the seminal US case of *Shelley v Kraemer*.[99] The Supreme Court held there that the Fourteenth Amendment applied as the actions of courts in enforcing racially motivated restrictive covenants in real property bore 'the clear and unmistakable imprimatur of the state.'[100] The case has attracted considerable interest, not least because of its potentially far-reaching impact, as 'all private action ultimately rests on the state's willingness to enforce the civil and criminal rules that facilitate that action.'[101] However, the Supreme Court has not extended this rule to the enforcement of discriminatory wills,[102] and for some, it is impossible to imagine it applying to court orders enforcing a racially-motivated ban on trespass.[103] There have been various attempts to reconcile *Shelley* with other parts of the state action doctrine,[104] to show either that it is an anomaly[105] or contains a broader principle, but poorly expressed by the Court.[106] However, these contradictions are further evidence of internal legal pluralism, and are more plausibly explained by pointing to the different political values at stake in each instance, ie that the Supreme Court was less troubled about the private disposition of testamentary property than it was about the public sale of property tainted by racist restrictions.[107] (This point perhaps explains our intuitive sense that had the university and hospital, in *McKinney*

---

[98] In *Edmonson v Leesville Concrete Co* above n 67, at 632. See also D Gibson, 'Distinguishing the Governors from the Governed: the Meaning of "Government" under Section 32 (1) of the Charter' (1983) 13 *Manitoba Law Review* 505, 509.

[99] *Shelley v Kraemer* 334 US 1 (1948).

[100] *Ibid.*

[101] LM Seidman and M Tushnet, *Remnants of Belief: Contemporary Constitutional Issues* (New York, Oxford University Press, 1996) 61. See also, LH Tribe, *American Constitutional Law*, 2nd edn (New York, Foundation Press, 1988) 1697.

[102] *Evans v Abney*, above n 49.

[103] M Tushnet, 'Living with a Bill of Rights' in Gearty and Tomkins (eds), above n 64, 3 at 19, n 29.

[104] See, eg, PE Quint, 'Free Speech and Private Law in German Constitutional Theory' (1989) 48 *Maryland Law Review* 247, who argues (*ibid* at 272) that *Shelley v Kraemer* has a reasonably tight ratio and that the Fourteenth Amendment applied here because the restrictive covenants performed the 'public function of zoning.'

[105] See SG Calabresi, 'The Crisis in Constitutional Theory' (1997) 83 *Virginia Law Review* 247, 256.

[106] See Tribe, above n 101, at 1697–98, and L Henkin, '*Shelley v Kraemer*: Notes for a Revised Opinion' (1962) 110 *University of Pennsylvania Law Review* 473.

[107] As Tushnet remarks (above n 103), these are 'extremely difficult' distinctions to draw, and should also be located in historical context: *Shelley* coming just as the Court was awakening to the problem of official racial discrimination in the postwar years (see also *Sweatt v Painter* 339 US 629 (1950) and *McLaurin v Oklahoma State Regents* 339 US 637 (1950)); whereas by 1970, when *Evans v Abney* (above n 49) was decided, there were already signs of retrenchment reflecting the mood that formal equality had perhaps gone far enough.

and *Stoffman* respectively, discriminated on the basis of race not age, the Supreme Court of Canada may well have found that the Charter applied.)

Focusing on the underlying political contests clarifies that the fault lines of constitutional application doctrine can be traced to two competing visions of the role of the state. One is the classical liberalism discussed above which views social life in atomistic terms. The other, following Patrick Macklem, we will style 'pluralist liberalism'.[108] This differs from the classical liberal view that rights are protections 'accorded by law primarily to individual economic activity,'[109] and instead 'pays service to the interdependence and complexity of social life,'[110] and so under pluralist liberalism, the economic sphere:

> is no longer seen as the means by which individual initiative and self-reliance will be axiomatically rewarded in a fair and just manner; pluralist liberalism acknowledges that if left on its own, the economic market will generate injustice and inequality.[111]

In other words, pluralist liberalism is both more likely to see the state implicated in 'private' activity, and to regard violation of rights by private power as deserving of constitutional remedy. These different political perspectives can be seen to animate the doctrinal incoherence in this area. For example, under classical liberalism, courts can be depicted as the enablers of free interaction between individuals,[112] whereas under pluralist liberalism, the question of their provenance in state action cannot be avoided.[113] For pluralist liberalism, the delegation of political power can be more readily attributed to the state,[114] whereas classical liberalism can regard its constitutional significance as attenuated by the delegate's autonomy.[115] Questions of power are more to the fore of a pluralist liberal inquiry into the presence of state action, whereas matters of form tend to dominate a classical liberal one.[116] The constant ebb and flow between these different political perspectives partly explains why different conclusions seem to apply to very similar situations. However, focusing on the nature of these differences also explains the limits of pluralist liberal approaches, by highlighting important points of overlap with classical liberalism. In doctrinal terms, this means that it operates within the same framework that produces classical liberal results, and so always includes the kernel of a more restrictive jurisprudence.

---

[108] P Macklem, 'Constitutional Ideologies' (1988) 20 *Ottawa Law Review* 117, 129, 133.

[109] *Ibid* at 131.

[110] *Ibid* at 135.

[111] *Ibid* at 134.

[112] See AC Hutchinson and A Petter, 'Private Rights/Public Wrongs: The Liberal Lie of the Charter' (1988) 38 *University of Toronto Law Journal* 278, 290.

[113] See Slattery, above n 95, at 153.

[114] See, eg, *Slaight Communications Inc v Davidson* (1989) 59 DLR (4th) 416.

[115] See, eg, *McKinney v University of Guelph*, above n 71.

[116] Cf majority judgment of Rehnquist CJ and Blackmun J's dissent in *DeShaney*, above n 74.

The Politics of Definition: The Enduring Hold of Classical Liberalism

If we take first the argument that courts are under a duty to interpret private law in accordance with constitutional values, this does not necessarily lead to a different outcome than where courts are excluded from the definition of government. In the post-*Dolphin Delivery* case of *Dagenais*,[117] we saw the Supreme Court hold that common law bans on publicity in criminal trials offended the Charter, seemingly going beyond its previous non-application stance.[118] However, in the *Hill* case,[119] it considered that the common law of defamation was consistent with constitutional freedom of expression, maintaining in place the classical liberal 'fence of privacy'[120] around the reputation of the individual. In *Dolphin Delivery* itself, the Court (in obiter dicta) cast the relationship between the union and employer in terms of a contract between formally equal parties,[121] and held that an injunction against secondary picketing complied with the Charter as secondary employers could not make contractual concessions.[122] While in *Pepsi-Cola v RWDSU, Local 558*, the Court held that protection from economic harm had no pre-eminent status, and that here the presumption that the common law would uphold the right to free expression meant that an injunction restraining picketing could not stand, it kept open the possibility that this delicate balance would be struck in different ways in later cases, for example, where the economic harm to third parties was 'undue'.[123] Thus, to regard courts formally as constitutional actors does not guarantee that at a substantive level classical liberal ideas will not continue to inform the outcome of cases.[124] These cases show that courts may tend to find constitutional rights consonant with the private law values that they themselves (particularly in common law systems) have helped to shape[125]: we should

---

[117] Above n 81.

[118] A Barak, 'Constitutional Human Rights and Private Law' in Friedmann and Barak-Erez (eds), above n 80, 13 at 19.

[119] *Hill v Church of Scientology* (1995) 126 DLR (4th) 129.

[120] H Lessard, B Ryder, D Schneiderman and M Young, 'Developments in Constitutional Law: the 1994–95 Term' (1996) *Supreme Court Law Review* (2d) 81 at 130.

[121] Above n 50, at 189.

[122] *Ibid* at 190.

[123] Above n 82, at para 44.

[124] Lessard et al suggest that a classical liberal approach underpins both *Dagenais* and *Hill*: '. . . thinking about individuals in the classical liberal sense, as having the proverbial fence of privacy erected around them, helps to understand the different results in these two cases. In the context of a criminal trial (as in *Dagenais*), the accused is presumed to have lost those rights of dignity and privacy which attach to him or her in private civil society. Having been implicated in the criminal process, individual rights are circumscribed and the protection of reputation lost to exigencies of the open court. Yet, in the usual case of a suit for defamation (the *Hill* situation), the individual is presumed not to have lost the semblance of privacy and regard for reputation which attaches to the individual' (above n 120, at 130–31).

[125] See D Oliver, 'Common Values in Public and Private Law and the Public/Private Divide' [1997] *Public Law* 630. For example, in *Pepsi-Cola v RWDSU, Local 558* (above n 82) the Supreme Court of Canada stated that one of the clear grounds where picketing will be impermissible (and so the presumption in favour of the right to free expression would be rebutted) is when it breaches specific torts such as 'trespass, nuisance, intimidation, defamation or misrepresentation' (*ibid* at para 77).

therefore bear in mind that these have generally been in the service of maintaining classical liberal ideals of individual freedom,[126] through, for example, privity of contract and the protection of private property. As the history of trade unions and minorities'[127] engagement with the courts shows, such values have not tended to be rich sources of counterhegemonic constitutional politics.

We can see the further hold of classical liberalism on judicial thought if we turn to the second strategy for extending constitutional application, ie to focus on the public nature of the acts of private entities. We can illustrate the limitations of this approach by returning to *Eldridge* in more detail. It will be recalled that this concerned whether a hospital's denial of sign interpreters infringed deaf patients' equality rights. As the *Hospital Insurance Act*[128] under which medical care was provided did not preclude such services, the Supreme Court found category 1 of the ASI model inapplicable, as it was 'not the impugned legislation that potentially infringes the Charter.'[129] It also found the hospital did not fall into category 2, as (repeating its reasoning in *Stoffman*) it was not sufficient that it carried out 'what may be loosely termed a "public function." '[130] It was therefore under category 3 that the Charter applied, as the definitionally private hospital, in 'providing medically necessary services,' was carrying out 'a specific governmental objective.'[131]

This approach has been favourably contrasted with *Stoffman* (showing why constitutional rights should apply equally to the providers as well as the recipients of publicly-funded hospital services).[132] However, my argument is that both cases fall within the same broad framework, and so the *Eldridge* approach is of limited potential in doctrinal terms. At the heart of the act–entity distinction is the idea that the state is only complicitous in some private acts: a public–private divide is still in place, the difference in *Eldridge* being that the Court draws the line closer to the pluralist liberal end of the spectrum. However, a future court following *Eldridge* would gain little guidance on how to answer questions such as how we differentiate between generic state functions, like health and education, where the Charter does not automatically apply, and specific governmental objectives, like providing medically necessary services, where it does. Such questions are left open by the *Eldridge* approach,

---

[126] See Weinrib and Weinrib, above n 80, at 72.

[127] See CA Gearty and KD Ewing, *The Struggle for Civil Liberties: Political Freedom and the Rule of Law in Britain, 1914–1945* (Oxford, Oxford University Press, 2000).

[128] Hospital Insurance Act, RSBC 1979, c 180.

[129] Above n 84, at 593 (per La Forest J).

[130] *Ibid* at 607.

[131] *Ibid* at 610.

[132] See Beatty, above n 94, who argues that had the search for 'inherently governmental actions' been consistently applied, eg, between *Stoffman* and *Eldridge*, or between *Dolphin Delivery* and *Eldridge*, then this would have had, for him, the beneficial effect of extending the Charter's protection to, in the first case, the providers of medical services as well as their recipients and, in the second, to show that 'judges and courts are the vehicles the legislature has chosen to deliver its system of dispute resolution' (*ibid* at 621).

and are postponed rather than answered. How they are answered, in immediate doctrinal terms, depends on the adjudicative contest between classical and pluralist liberalism: in *Eldridge*, the latter wins out (perhaps suggesting that the Court regards disability discrimination as more offensive to formal equality than age discrimination). This though leaves in place a framework which enables courts to draw the line in a different place, and the record shows that they frequently do in a manner that reflects classical liberal ideas of carving out a broader realm of individual autonomy.[133]

However, even were a pluralist liberal approach to prevail, there is a strong sense, as in the response to *Shelley*, of inbuilt limits to its effectiveness in reaching private power. These limits were articulated by La Forest J in *Eldridge* when he discussed the constitutional position of corporations: while they are 'entirely creatures of statute,' the Charter does not apply to them because legislatures 'have not entrusted them to implement specific governmental policies.'[134] In its own terms, this is not self-evident—as discussed in chapter two, in the age of the global economy, state and corporate objectives are often closely intertwined. However, it does make sense when placed against the overarching hegemonic politics of constitutional definition, which reveals important points of commonality between classical and pluralist liberalism. Both are premised on the primacy of the constitutional protection of individual freedom,[135] but divide on the state's orientation thereto. This dichotomy falls squarely within the framework of the state–civil society divide, which, as Santos notes, encompasses:

> both the idea of a minimum and a maximum state, to the same extent that state action [is] simultaneously conceived as a potential enemy of individual freedom and as the condition of its exercise.[136]

Thus, social life is divided between the state—whose conduct determines the condition of liberty[137]—and everything else, which is placed in the realm of civil society. Crucially, this also includes economic activity, which is thereby separated from the political, and assumed to pose no inherent threat to individual freedom. Under pluralist liberalism, the state will sometimes be regarded as enhancing freedom, but such action is seen as necessary to correct malfunctions in civil society, which is then returned to its natural state of equilibrium. In this way, classical and pluralist liberalism agree that economic power should not be subjected to the same direct constitutional scrutiny as state power.

---

[133] See Stoffman, above n 51; *McKinney*, above n 71; *Lloyd Corp v Tanner*, above n 47; *Hudgens v NLRB* 424 US 507 (1976); *San Francisco Arts & Athletics, Inc v United States Olympic Committee*, above n 48.

[134] Above n 84, at 603.

[135] Macklem, above n 108, at 137.

[136] Santos, above n 3, at 363.

[137] It is important to note that pluralist liberalism therefore may, and does, side with classical liberalism in finding that the state is oppressive to freedom in individual cases. It is this dualism which runs through the constitutional application discourse, and which shows how within every apparently expansive holding, in terms of crossing the formal threshold, lies the potential for its reverse.

We can now see that focusing on courts as constitutional actors, or imputing governmental objectives to the acts of private entities (as defined by the courts), does not necessarily lead to a more expansive constitutional application jurisprudence. This conceptual doubt is corroborated by the record of courts following these tests, which as often as not rely on a formal public–private divide to hold the constitution inapplicable to private relations. We can thus enter the interim conclusion that the hold of classical liberal politics of definition remains strong in the judicial mindset. What though of the third strategy for reaching private action outlined above, ie, applying the constitution to legislative and governmental omissions to protect rights? As previously stated, this seems to hold out the greatest prospect for counterhegemonic adjudication, as it has the potential to impose positive constitutional obligations on states to protect rights, whether or not these were initially infringed by non-state actors (as in the private community college in *Vriend*). In fact, it seems to mark a conceptual shift, in moving beyond asking 'who did it?' to 'what was done?' As such, it regards the constitution as applying to inconsistent laws rather than the actions of (constitutionally responsible) actors.

The Application to Law (LAW) Model

The LAW model has its roots in European traditions of constitutionalism, and regards the central application issue as whether the positive law of the state fully respects constitutional rights. Here, drawing on the jurisprudence of the European Court of Human Rights[138] and the *Bundesverfassungsgerichts*, I outline the principal features of the LAW model which some commentators see as providing the means of imposing basic constitutional limitations on private power. While, in terms of the outcome of cases, the LAW model can often be commended over the ASI approach, I conclude that it shares many of the latter's shortcomings, limiting its potential for advancing a counterhegemonic form of constitutional politics.

---

[138] The European Convention on Human Rights would appear to be unpromising ground on which to build an account of the broader application of human rights vis-à-vis private parties. It is an international treaty binding only on the contracting states to which it is specifically addressed; applications brought against private parties would be inadmissible *ratione personae* (see DJ Harris, M O'Boyle and C Warbrick, *Law of the European Convention on Human Rights* (London, Butterworths, 1995) 21). However, despite this obvious objection to its direct application against private parties, some commentators speak approvingly of the *Drittwurking* (or third party application) of the Convention (see A Clapham, 'The "Drittwurking" of the Convention' in RStJ Macdonald, F Matscher and H Perzold (eds), *The European System for the Protection of Human Rights* (Dordrecht, Martinus Nijhoff, 1993) 163, and AZ Drzemczewski, *European Human Rights Convention in Domestic Law: A Comparative Study* (Oxford, Clarendon Press, 1983) 199–228). This reflects the reality that the European Court of Human Rights is the author of now a quite developed jurisprudence on the Convention's relevance in disputes between private parties.

Expanding the Scope of Constitutional Rights?

We can illustrate the major point of difference between the LAW and ASI approaches by considering the case of *Costello-Roberts v United Kingdom*.[139] This involved a European Convention challenge under Articles 3 and 8 to corporal punishment administered to a seven-year-old boy at an independent school, which was financed from private tuition fees and received no direct government funding. The issue was whether and how this engaged the UK's responsibility under a system of rights protection that speaks only to states. The European Court of Human Rights stated its general approach as follows:

> The Court has consistently held that the responsibility of a State is engaged if a violation of one of the rights and freedoms defined in the Convention is the result of non-observance by that State of its obligation under Article 1 to secure those rights and freedoms in its domestic law to everyone within its jurisdiction.[140]

The Court thus concluded that the school's actions could engage the UK's responsibility under the Convention. Thus, what was crucial was not the quality of the institutional or functional link of the private school in relation to the state[141] (as, for example, in *McKinney*), but rather that the Convention placed a positive obligation on the state to secure, through law, the protection of its rights. Article 11 jurisprudence gives further examples of this approach, with the Court applying the Convention to the dismissal of workers under a 'closed shop' agreement, made lawful by domestic law, irrespective of the public or private nature of the employer.[142] In Germany, the *Bundesverfassungsgerichts*, in the seminal *Lüth* case,[143] has echoed this broad approach:

> . . . far from being a value-free system, the Constitution erects an objective system of values in its section on basic rights, and thus expresses and reinforces the validity of the basic rights. This system of values, centring on the freedom of the human being to develop in society, must apply as a constitutional axiom throughout the whole legal system: it must direct and inform legislation, administration, and judicial decision. It naturally influences private law as well: no rule of private law may conflict with it, and all such rules must be construed in accordance with its spirit.[144]

This focus on how rights constrain the operation of all (state) laws has two important practical effects which seem to extend the scope of the application of

---

[139] Series A no 247–C (1995) 19 EHRR 112.

[140] *Ibid* at para 26. On the merits, the Court found for the UK that there had been no violation of the Convention.

[141] Thus there was no practical difference between this case and the Court's previous decision in *Campbell and Cosans v United Kingdom* Series A no 48 (1982) 4 EHRR 293, concerning corporal punishment in publicly funded state schools; see also the Opinion of the Commission in *Y v United Kingdom* Series A no 247–A (1994) 17 EHRR 238.

[142] *Young, James and Webster v United Kingdom* Series A no 44 (1982) 4 EHRR 38. See also *Sibson v United Kingdom* Series A no 258–A (1994) 17 EHRR 193. Cf *Lavigne v OPSEU* (1991) 81 DLR (4th) 545.

[143] Above n 38.

[144] *Ibid* (translated in Kommers, above n 38, at 355).

rights significantly beyond the ASI model. First, the position of courts is much less contentious as attention centres on the law they interpret and apply, rather than their status as constitutional actors. In the *Sunday Times*[145] case, there was an Article 10 challenge that an injunction against publication issued on the basis of the common law of contempt of court violated the newspaper's freedom of expression. For the European Court of Human Rights, the English court's institutional status was irrelevant; rather, it regarded the issue before it as 'whether the rules of contempt of court as applied in the decision of the House of Lords granting the injunction are a ground justifying the restriction under Article 10 § 2.'[146] Similarly, in Germany the Constitution is said to have a 'radiating effect'[147] on private law, so that a judge 'is constitutionally bound to ascertain whether the applicable rules of private law have been influenced by basic rights . . . : if so he must construe and apply the rules as so modified.'[148]

The second, and potentially more far-reaching, consequence of this approach, is its implication of positive obligations on the state to protect fundamental rights, whether or not they are being infringed by public or private actors. For example, in *Plattform 'Ärtze für das Leben' v Austria*,[149] the European Court of Human Rights held that the Article 11 right to freedom of association required Austria to amend its positive law to ensure that private individuals could hold demonstrations without fear of physical attack from other private individuals.[150] Such positive obligations can apply even in the 'private' sphere of family relations, with the European Court stating that, for example, the Convention's Article 8 right to respect for family life could require 'the adoption of measures designed to secure respect for private life even in the sphere of relations of individuals between themselves.'[151] On this basis, the Court has found that a wife who had been the victim of domestic violence was deprived of respect for her family and private life when the Irish legal system denied her legal aid to petition for judicial separation.[152]

There are limits, though, to how far the European Court of Human Rights is prepared to go in imposing positive obligations on states to remedy violations

---

[145] See above n 63.

[146] *Ibid* at para: 43. See also *Observer and Guardian v United Kingdom* Series A no 216 (1992) 14 EHRR 153, and *Tolstoy Miloslavky v United Kingdom* Series A no 316–8 (1995) 20 EHRR 442.

[147] Kommers, above n 38, at 49.

[148] BS Markesinis, *A Comparative Introduction to the German Law of Torts*, 3rd edn (Oxford, Clarendon Press, 1994) 355–56.

[149] Series A no 139 (1991) 13 EHRR 204.

[150] *Ibid* at para 32. However, the Court also stated (at para 34) that this was an obligation 'as to measures to be taken and not as to results to be achieved.' As such, the Court found that Austrian authorities had taken reasonable and appropriate measures to secure the applicants their rights.

[151] *X and Y v The Netherlands* Series A no 91 (1986) 8 EHRR 235, at para: 23. See also *Marckx v Belgium* Series A no 31 (1979–80) 2 EHRR 330, where the Court applied the Convention in the context of legal issues in the parent–child relationship. Here, it found that Art 8 had been violated when Belgian law refused to recognise a child born outside a marriage relationship as the full daughter of her mother, referring to the state's obligations, in determining a domestic legal regime for parent–child ties, to ensure respect for family life.

[152] *Airey v Ireland* Series A no 32 (1979–80) 2 EHRR 305.

of rights committed by private parties. In *Hatton v United Kingdom*,[153] the Grand Chamber rejected the applicants' claim that their Article 8 rights to respect for their private and family life were infringed by aircraft landing at night at Heathrow Airport, and so disturbing their sleep. At issue was the UK Government's scheme which permitted airlines to land aircraft at night provided a certain noise quota was not exceeded. While the Court reaffirmed the principle that the Convention may impose obligations on states to take measures to protect citizens' Article 8 rights where the immediate violation is by a private party, in the instant case it found that these rights could be restricted, inter alia, in the interests of the economic well-being of the country. Similarly, in *Appleby v United Kingdom*,[154] the Court held that the United Kingdom did not fail to fulfil its positive obligations to protect the applicants' rights to freedom of expression where the positive law enabled a privately owned shopping centre to refuse access to a group collecting signatures for a petition against the development of nearby public playing fields.

However, notwithstanding these reverses, the general framework of the LAW model can be seen to go considerably beyond the approach of the North American courts. As one commentator depicts the contrast between US and German constitutionalism, the former is based on 'the withdrawal of the Constitution from society,' while the latter rests on a 'general acknowledgement of affirmative constitutional obligations affecting society.'[155] This more expansive approach, perhaps reflecting the broader social theory of European political traditions,[156] has been favourably contrasted with the ASI model: for example, David Beatty has stated that under the former 'few interests . . . are put beyond the reach of [courts'] powers of review,'[157] thus extending the range of laws that have to be justified against standards of rationality and proportionality.[158] The LAW model has also been commended as the better approach to the question of the application of rights in new constitutionalist jurisdictions, including the UK[159] and South Africa.[160] Others have emphasised how the European approach can meet the critical views that rights are empty and formal by shifting the focus from the state to the victims of human rights abuses,[161] and so deal with the threat to human rights that 'also lies in wait from the conduct of other private parties.'[162] One writer sums up the social policy underlying the LAW jurisprudence as resting on 'the protection of human rights of weaker

---

[153] (2003) 37 EHRR 28.

[154] (2003) 37 EHRR 38.

[155] Quint, above n 104, at 347.

[156] See Kommers, above n 38, at 34–38.

[157] D Beatty, *Constitutional Law in Theory and Practice* (Toronto, University of Toronto Press, 1995) 134.

[158] *Ibid.*

[159] M Hunt, 'The "Horizontal Effect" of the Human Rights Act' [1998] *Public Law* 423, 438.

[160] van der Walt, above n 53.

[161] Clapham, above n 65, at 353.

[162] A Barak, 'Constitutional Human Rights and Private Law' (1996) 3 *Review of Constitutional Studies* 218, 258.

individuals against infringement by private parties who wield systemic socio-economic power over them.'[163]

The Counterhegemonic Limits of the LAW Model

While the LAW model transcends some aspects of the public–private divide at a formal level, it is more similar to the ASI approach than the arguments outlined in the preceding paragraph would indicate. The LAW model also operates within the framework of the state–civil society divide, and so in a number of important respects also takes its bearings from classical liberal constitutional politics of definition. Accordingly, this limits its doctrinal scope for engaging with private power in substantive terms; moreover, this suggests that symbolically, it is more likely to leave in place, rather than disturb, political attitudes that private actors are not a source of political authority. The first point of similarity between the ASI and LAW models is that the latter still sees the protection of constitutional rights primarily in negative terms. If we return to the case of *Plattform 'Ärtze'*, discussed above: while this seems to extend association rights beyond a strictly vertical relationship with the state, it is important to note the similarities of approach with the ASI model. Society is still viewed in terms of liberal social theory as a 'competition among individuals and groups seeking to further their interests and conceptions of the good,'[164] and the benefits conferred by rights are to protect such groups from interference in their private sphere, here manifested in their expression of political views. A fortiori this is the case where the European Court of Human Rights has applied Article 8, for example, to require the state to provide redress for a mentally retarded woman who had been sexually assaulted in a private nursing home.[165] Again, here the Court's application of the Convention to private relationships is principally concerned with enhancing individuals' private spheres.

This is not to deny that the LAW model can bring important benefits to the parties in individual cases, but rather to argue that the 'deep grammar'[166] of judicial thought which accompanies it is not indicative of a significant change of approach from the ASI model. We can further highlight these similarities by considering some of the German cases on freedom of expression in private law cases. In *Lüth*, an injunction had been issued against the plaintiff's call for a boycott of the films of an anti-Semitic director on the basis of the damage to the latter's reputation. The Constitutional Court applied Article 5 of the Basic Law, protecting freedom of speech, to rescind the order, referring to both the

---

[163] Raday, above n 97, at 118.
[164] Macklem, above n 108, at 133.
[165] *X and Y v The Netherlands*, above n 151.
[166] J Fudge, 'The Canadian Charter of Rights: Recognition, Redistribution and the Imperialism of the Courts' in T Campbell, KD Ewing and A Tomkins (eds), *Sceptical Essays on Human Rights* (Oxford, Oxford University Press, 2001) 335, 351.

importance of 'intellectual exchange and the contest among opinions,'[167] and the collective interest in breaking with Germany's Nazi past.[168] In *Blinkfüer*,[169] a newspaper company threatened to withhold its products from vendors who stocked the plaintiff's pro-communist weekly publication. The federal High Court found the boycott protected by Article 5, but the Constitutional Court reversed this holding, stating that the use of the company's economic power could deprive people 'of their ability to draw their conclusions freely.'[170]

Both decisions are strong examples of how German courts, in adjudicating actions between private parties raised under the Civil Code, will expressly weigh private law rights against constitutional values. However, while on the surface this can be contrasted with the formal exclusion of private disputes under the ASI model, at a deeper level there are various aspects common to both approaches. Johan van der Walt characterises the distinction between *Lüth* and *Blinkfüer* as follows:

> The boycott in *Lüth* won the favour of the court because the political manner in which the politically motivated economic boycott was conducted could be reconciled with the court's subordination of the economic to the political. The boycott in *Blinkfüer* failed to win the court's favour because the economic manner in which the politically motivated boycott was conducted, constituted an economic distortion of the political.[171]

However, he questions whether these terms have quite the singular meaning implied by the Constitutional Court,[172] and concludes that these cases reinforce 'the instability of the distinction between the public and the private, the political and the economic.'[173] This highlights that the dualisms which marked ASI jurisprudence have not disappeared under the LAW model, but have simply been relocated. For example, in *Lüth*, we can see that the Court is choosing between pluralist liberal accounts of societal interdependence, so that some greater value may be served by enhancing Germany's reputation abroad, and the classical liberal view of the primacy of the individual, and his or her right to a reputation. Also, in *Blinkfüer*, the Court is choosing between classical liberal ideas that economic power is beyond the reach of state regulation and the pluralist liberal notion that where this is used to excess, the state may step in. Thus, saying that the Constitution applies to all state law does not answer how these dilemmas are to be resolved. As with the ASI model, it leaves open the possibility that courts may take a less expansive approach, and indeed German

---

[167] Kommers, above n 38, at 372.
[168] *Ibid* at 374–75.
[169] (1969) 25 BVerfGE 256, (translated in *ibid* at 381).
[170] *Ibid* at 383.
[171] Above n 53.
[172] *Ibid*: 'But was there ever a political goal that was pursued purely politically? Can an economic boycott really be as purely political as the *Lüth* decision seems to aver?'
[173] *Ibid*.

jurisprudence on expression later took a restrictive turn,[174] with the courts more prepared to uphold private law rights against constitutional challenge.[175]

Highlighting the common features between the ASI and LAW models returns us to the question of the broad parameters of constitutional debate that pertain to the latter. Of significance here is the LAW model's view of the state, which, it is suggested, still embodies a dichotomous view of the latter's relationship to individual freedom. While the state is seen as the potential guardian of rights when implementing its constitutional obligations, it is also seen as the ultimate perpetrator of rights violations, given its responsibility for the condition of the positive law. Thus, rights do not apply in private disputes because of the threat of a boycott by powerful economic actors (or the admission of beatings by a private school), but because the state permitted such breaches of individual freedom to occur. Linked to this is the important point that the LAW model rests on a distinction between, as the Supreme Court of Canada put it in *Vriend*, '"private activity" and "laws that regulate private activity." '[176] Only the latter is of constitutional significance, and this provides us with a clue as to the sorts of obligations we can expect to be imposed on the state: these will relate to matters within its authority, but not to matters which are deemed to fall in the free realm of civil society. Thus, while the state provides education, or health services, the LAW model can require it to ensure that the positive law treats everyone with equal dignity. However, as economic activity takes place in civil society, this is not a matter of state law, and this is why we do not see, and do not expect to see, the European courts imposing obligations on states to protect their citizens from the disabling effects of global capitalism (although we can expect to see them continuing to uphold corporate rights).

CONCLUSION

A legal pluralist approach enables us to stand back from normative debates over, for example, whether courts are included in the term 'government,' and instead to view the relationship between rights constitutionalism and private power in terms of how the former articulates with hegemonic or counterhegemonic forces. The first test that a counterhegemonic constitutionalism has to pass is to show that constitutional doctrine can be remade to subject private power to constitutional scrutiny. While the comparative jurisprudence shows that courts can move beyond a strict vertical approach, where rights are only exercised directly against state institutions, the cases also show that the courts

---

[174] See DP Currie, *The Constitution of the Federal Republic of Germany* (Chicago and London, University of Chicago Press, 1994) 192–201.

[175] See, eg, *Mephisto* (1971) 30 BVerfGE 173 (translated in Kommers, above n 38 at 427) and *Princess Soraya* (1973) 34 BVerfGE 269 (discussed in Barak, above n 162, at 251). Accordingly, we can see that the LAW model can also display the disordering features of internal legal pluralism.

[176] *Vriend*, above n 88, at para 66 (per Cory J).

operate within a broadly hegemonic politics of definition that inhibits them from seriously engaging with private power. Thus, while the more expansive ASI and LAW doctrine can insist that when the state acts to regulate private parties, it does so in a proportionate way, courts following these approaches do not, and as things stand, will not, require, for example, corporations to observe standards of environmental protection[177] or social equity.

Thus, in terms of the relationship between rights constitutionalism and private power, we can say that at present there is limited scope for the courts to promote a counterhegemonic form of constitutional politics. However, there is more evidence that hegemonic forces are articulating with rights constitutionalism to further their interests. We can see this, for instance, through the global spread of rule of law reforms which reinforce the changing perception of the state from a redistributive forum to a mechanism for ensuring the efficient functioning of the market economy. Or, for that matter, by the infusion of jurisprudence with the values of consumerism,[178] which reflects the values of possessive-individualism through which the market economy thrives. The most important artefact of the successful articulation of hegemonic globalization with rights constitutionalism remains the state–civil society divide, which lies at the heart of the prevailing constitutional politics of definition. This serves the crucial legitimating function of obscuring the broader constellation of law and political power—including corporate law-making and corporate political power—operating in society.[179] In this way, a politics of definition that equates law with state law, and constitutionalism with limits on state law, to the extent it takes hold in the political and legal imagination, is a powerful antidote to regarding corporations as sites of political power, and sources of constitutional law, which a critical approach to legal pluralism suggests they always have been.

None of the foregoing should be taken as arguing that a hegemonic constitutionalism is inevitable or irreversible—this would be to commit the same error as regarding the prevailing form of economic globalization in similarly determinist terms. Indeed, we can see within the hegemonic jurisprudence discussed above, the kernel of a counter-movement. However, the legal pluralist focus on the politics of definition reveals the deep-rooted assumptions in judicial thought which prevent that kernel from growing and developing to become an effective constitutional check on private power. Accordingly, if we wish to move to a counterhegemonic version of constitutional politics, these assumptions have to be 'unthought'.

---

[177] See *Hatton v United Kingdom*, above n 153.

[178] See D Schneiderman, 'Constitutionalizing the Culture-Ideology of Consumerism' (1998) 7 *Social and Legal Studies* 213

[179] As Santos puts it (above n 3, at 368): 'the conversion of the public place into the exclusive site of law and politics performed a crucial legitimating function by obscuring the fact that the law and politics of the capitalist state could only operate as part of a broader political and legal configuration in which other contrasting forms of law and politics were included.'

Conclusion: Towards a Legal Pluralist Constitutionalism

MODERN CONSTITUTIONALISM is in paradigmatic crisis. The rise of transnational corporations undermines the liberal legalist paradigm of constitutional law which regarded the state as the only form of political power and the only source of law. In the context of the global economy, multinational corporations must now be seen as major political actors and important sites of law production, whose decisions have an enormous impact on people's lives, affecting where they live, how they work, what they eat and the quality of their environment. Moreover, these decisions, reflecting narrow market-related concerns, often prevail in practice over broader notions of the public interest that are nominally in the keeping of national governments. Accordingly, we cannot properly engage with the central questions of constitutional law—who exercises political power, on what terms, and subject to what conditions and limits—without including corporations in our analysis. Confronting these developments places the adequacy of our received knowledge of constitutional law at the centre of scholarly debate.

In this book, I have begun the task of considering the basis of a new constitutional knowledge by highlighting the explanatory strengths of legal pluralism over liberal legalism. I have argued that legal pluralism enables us to make better sense of the nature of the paradigmatic transition, and that it provides a more illuminating account of the relationship between rights constitutionalism and private power. In doing so, I have sought to clear the ground for constructing a constitutional epistemology that can respond better to the challenges of globalization. While I have concentrated on the descriptive richness of legal pluralism, there is a necessary link between this and its prescriptive aspects. If, as legal pluralism contends, our knowledge of law builds and maintains realities, then discarding the old in favour of a new knowledge is a necessary first step in creating a new reality. I accordingly close now by tracing the outlines of what a legal pluralist constitutionalism, that might hold private power more effectively to account, might look like.

A legal pluralist knowledge of constitutionalism builds upon three principal insights of the critique of liberal legalism. It holds first that constitutionalism always involves questions of private, as well as public, power. This follows from the legal pluralist argument in favour of multiple sources of constitutional law, but this applies also to more formal manifestations such as rights constitutionalism. As the state is the source of but one form of power and one form of law, where constitutional texts single these out by prescribing the conditions under which their exercise is deemed legitimate, they are also necessarily addressing other forms of power and law, for example, by not insisting on such special conditions in their case. From its origins, rights constitutionalism has spoken volubly to private power, making clear that its exercise is not of significant political concern, whether by reserving higher law limits in the form of individual rights for state institutions and law, or by equating corporations with human beings capable of prosecuting rights against the state. As such, legal pluralism makes it clear that the relevant question is not whether, but how constitutionalism engages with private power.

Legal pluralism also opposes the idea that the state is the exclusive location of constitutional discourse, and highlights the need to go beyond the explicit constitution to gain a proper purchase on contemporary constitutional phenomena. As the state does not have a monopoly on generating constitutional law, then it is necessary to develop a focus of analysis that takes account of other sites of law production. This reveals that the formal constitution is often less important in structuring and regulating political power than the practices and actors of the global economy. In particular, the spread of the Washington consensus has played a key role in setting the terms of the public policy agenda in a manner favourable to the interests of global capital, notwithstanding that the texts of formal, national constitutions may appear, for example, to suggest a stronger commitment to the values of the welfare state. This doubts whether we can fully understand the constitutional dimensions of globalization without including private power as a source of constitutional law.

Related to the importance of the implicit constitution is the key legal pluralist argument that the instrumental capacities of rights constitutionalism are considerably overstated. Internal legal pluralism emphasises how the normal character of constitutional doctrine is incoherence, as judges, like other law-creating subjects, construct distinctive personal accounts of the legal world, whose mutual interaction necessarily leads to inconsistency and contradiction. External legal pluralism undermines the social engineering view of constitutionalism by outlining how social change is often attributable to factors other than adjudication, which in many cases produces unintended, and counterproductive, consequences. Accordingly, the disordering nature and effects of social life work against the idea that by designing the perfect constitution, or developing the best theory of interpretation, or appointing the most gifted and compassionate judges, we can reorder society according to some normative vision of the good life.

Thus, constitutional law is not solely what the state does, is not manifested exclusively through formal structures, and is not to be explained in terms of a simple command. For legal pluralism, this fuller understanding that takes account of constitutionalism beyond the state, that includes its semiformal and informal locations, and that acknowledges its instrumental limits, has always been necessary to give a more accurate description of constitutional phenomena. However, this broader conception of constitutionalism has been suppressed by the ascendancy of liberal legalist politics of definition which narrow the scope of our constitutional knowledge in general, and which, in its highest form as rights constitutionalism, represents a particularly singlular constitutional vision. Here, there is one form of social power operating in society (the state), one privileged methodology (normative argument directed to courts), and one optimum form of promoting autonomy (constitutional adjudication upholding individual rights).

However, the liberal legalist paradigm is coming under increasing pressure. The epistemological crisis provoked by globalization, by underscoring the contingent basis of our taken for granted knowledge, means that the politics of constitutional definition are no longer obscured, but are now brought to the surface. Moreover, the political crisis engendered by the realignment of power relations in the global economy, questions the adequacy of a state-based knowledge of constitutionalism to respond to the rise of transnational corporate power. This makes clear that the liberal legalist politics of definition, while masquerading as the whole, is a necessarily partial constitutional account. If we wish to move to a counterhegemonic form of constitutional discourse, it is therefore imperative to take advantage of the opportunity provided by the paradigmatic moment to advance a new form of constitutional knowledge.

At base, a legal pluralist constitutionalism stands for the idea that no form of social power should attract special constitutional protection or limitation on account of its provenance alone. Instead, it 'presumes that inquiries about legitimacy, due process, and substantive justification'[1] are relevant with regard to all exercises of political authority, whatever the source. This approach opens up many of the issues which liberal legalism prefers to keep closed. For example, the central divisions of liberal thought, between public and private, and the state and civil society, can have no a priori status, but must be interrogated as to whether they impede or enhance the accountability of power. This means that the politics of definition are now a central feature of the constitutional debate, and can have no presumptive validity on account of the historic victory of some factions and interests over others: rather, they can be sustained only if they can be justified in contemporary terms. In the case of liberal legalism and rights constitutionalism, I have argued that this substantive justification is wanting both at a descriptive and normative level.

This has potentially enormous implications for how we view the exercise of political power by corporations, as legal pluralism seeks to reclaim for public discourse questions concerning the operation of the marketplace that have been immunised from constitutional scrutiny. It challenges the idea that the questions of constitutional accountability which we ask of major political actors should depend on their formal classification as public or private by the liberal legalist

---

[1] RA Macdonald, 'Metaphors of Multiplicity: Civil Society, Regimes and Legal Pluralism' (1998) 15 *Arizona Journal of International and Comparative Law* 69, 79.

politics of definition. More specifically, it doubts whether the test of constitutional legitimacy can be satisfied when decisions that have enormous implications for how people conduct their daily lives are taken within the closed confines of the boardroom, or according to the market-based interests of the corporation. It suggests that such decisions require to be justified to, and in some form sanctioned by, those who are affected by their consequences, and moreover, that the content of these decisions should be informed more by considerations of the general welfare than narrow self-interest.[2]

For legal pluralism, the key to provoking debate over the criteria of legitimacy that should apply to all forms of power lies in opening up the meaning of constitutionalism to critical scrutiny. The message of this book has been that grand constitutional designs such as that offered by rights constitutionalism (whether in traditional or adapted mode) are both normatively objectionable—potentially suppressing other equally valid understandings of constitutionalism—and sociologically questionable, as they are unable to deliver the instrumental gains that they promise. Accordingly, the solution to the issue of private power does not lie in replacing one politics of definition with another, but rather in making them a constant feature of debate, keeping at the surface the question of why we apply the label 'constitutional' to some actions, but not others, and the consequences of doing or not doing so. It is by acknowledging, and placing to the fore, competing knowledges of constitutional law, that we can best emphasise the diverse sites of production of constitutional laws. This leads to the conclusion that it is only by rejecting the idea of overarching constitutional solutions to the accountability of private power that we can better address the question of how to hold private power to constitutional account.[3]

The task of legal pluralism is therefore to develop a constitutional discourse that symbolises the multiple forms of political authority in society, and that encourages wider notions of the accountability of power.[4] In the academy, there has been some important recent work attempting to retrieve a broader constitutional narrative. For example, James Tully has argued that even within the US, the tendency to regard constitutionalism in singular terms is historically misinformed, and sits ill with how Jeffersonian ideas of a continuing constitution have informed US political thought and action.[5] Others have sought to open up conceptual space by showing that constitutionalism has been used not

---

[2] See H Arthurs, 'The Re-constitution of the Public Domain' in D Drache (ed), *The Market or the Public Domain? Global Governance and the Asymmetry of Power* (London, Routledge, 2001) 85, 95.

[3] See RA Macdonald, 'The Design of Constitutions to Accommodate Linguistic, Cultural and Ethnic Diversity: the Canadian Experiment' in K Kulcsár and D Szabo (eds), *Dual Images: Multiculturalism on Two Sides of the Atlantic* (Budapest, Institute for Political Science of the Hungarian Academy of Sciences, 1996) 52, 53.

[4] Compare Macdonald, *ibid* at 75.

[5] J Tully, *Strange Multiplicity: Constitutionalism in an Age of Diversity* (Cambridge, Cambridge University Press, 1995) 93. For Tully, the error in regarding US constitutionalism in terms of 'an undiverse sovereign people and uniform institutions [as] a universal norm' (*ibid* at 91) is 'to accept

only to refer to a codified written document, but the general regime whereby power is exercised,[6] or as 'the organized form of a political society.'[7] I conclude by considering some of the ways (without in any way suggesting that the following is exhaustive) in which these ideas of constitutional plurality can be, and are being, implemented at a practical level.

One of the most important places where the liberal legalist politics of definition are symbolically reinforced is the classroom. Students are taught in the first week of law school that constitutional law concerns the institutions of state, and the focus of their study is increasingly on courts adjudicating claims of individual rights. Business or commercial law is where they encounter corporations. To the extent these ideas are ingrained in the minds of the next generation of lawyers, this is an effective means of perpetuating the liberal legalist myth. A legal pluralist constitutionalism entails significant rethinking of the basis of legal education. This requires more members of the legal academy to be conscious of the qualifying adjective of state—and the pluralising consequences of that adjective—which always should be placed before their everyday use of the word 'law.' Why not begin constitutional law classes by looking at a corporate charter rather than the formal constitutional text? Such an approach would symbolise that the politics of definition are an integral component of studying and understanding constitutional law.

For some, another way of diversifying our knowledge of constitutionalism is to rethink the uses and forms of constitutional litigation. Santos, one of the leading critics of liberal legalism, has argued that we should take advantage of the 'indeterminacy and ambiguity' of adjudication to make the political role of the courts 'an object of social struggle.'[8] He suggests that for courts to serve counterhegemonic ends, they have to connect the individual disputes before them to their underlying social conflicts.[9] One proposal for moving to a new understanding of adjudication draws on developments in US public law litigation that have been described as destabilization rights. These claims, designed 'to unsettle and open up public institutions that have chronically failed to meet their obligations,'[10] represent a move away from the command model where parties seek a specific remedy to the *lis* in question. Instead, the courts acknowledge their limitations in directing social change by setting the broad goals to be achieved, leaving the actors involved to decide how this is to be done.[11]

---

a partial framework in which the [Jeffersonian] tradition and its two hundred years of demands for recognition—from the popular opposition of the 1780s to abolitionists, suffragettes, labourites, African Americans and the politics of cultural recognition today—cannot be given a fair hearing' (*ibid* at 93).

[6] See J-E Lane, *Constitutions and Political Theory* (Manchester and New York, Manchester University Press, 1996) 5–13.

[7] D Castiglione, 'The Political Theory of the Constitution' (1996) 44 *Political Studies* 417, 421.

[8] B de Sousa Santos, *Toward a New Legal Common Sense* (London, Butterworths, 2002) 350, 348.

[9] *Ibid* at 346.

[10] CH Sabel and WH Simon, 'Destabilization Rights: How Public Law Litigation Succeeds' (2003–04) 117 *Harvard Law Review* 1016, 1020.

Assuming that we can find a constitutional nexus with private power, such an approach may present an avenue for scrutinising the ways in which corporations have been shielded from questions of political accountability. These innovations symbolise that the courts can only be one component of a broader counterhegemonic strategy, and also that powerful law-producing actors are responsible for the consequences of the normative regimes they help to create.

The emergence of social movements as sites of resistance to the Washington consensus can be seen as a form of legal pluralism in action. For some, this holds out the promise of shifting rights discourse 'from its narrow, state-centred, elitist basis to a grassroots-oriented praxis of the subalterns.'[12] The diverse tactics pursued by the various pressure groups often bypass official processes completely: for example, the campaign against electricity cut-offs in South Africa was mounted directly by activists against the privatised company in the form of 'illegal' reconnections.[13] These and other groups are simply regarding corporations as centres of political authority, and devising means of holding that power to account, unconcerned with whether or not the official narrative catches up. In some case, the successes have been quite striking, whether in reversing water privatisation in Bolivia,[14] or in agitating for land reform in Brazil.[15] As with the innovations in litigation, these developments can be seen as one part of promoting legal pluralist ideas of constitutionalism—if seen as the exclusive means, this carries the risk that power politics will eventually prevail. However, as part of a broader strategy, the social movements symbolise that the state is not the only source of constitutional discourse, and also underscore the transformative law-creating capacity of individuals.

Another response to the pressures on state-centred accounts of constitutionalism is to recover the narrative at the supranational level. This important line of scholarship, under the rubric of postnational constitutionalism, rests on two premises: that constitutional law is 'an internal and intrinsic characteristic of a polity' and that in contemporary terms, a polity is not coterminous with the nation-state.[16] This asks how we devise constitutional language for entities like the EU, raising the question of how to translate key constitutional criteria, such as foundational authority, jurisdictional delineation and representation, in their new setting. However, the lack of fit with traditional constitutional categories is the very strength of postnational constitutionalism, as it takes as its

---

[11]   Eg, by setting general performance standards for the health care of prisoners: *ibid*, at 1035–6.

[12]   B Rajagopal, *International Law from Below: Development, Social Movements and Third World Resistance* (Cambridge, Cambridge University Press, 2003) 271.

[13]   P Kingsnorth, *One No, Many Yeses: A Journey to the Heart of the Global Resistance Movement* (London, Free Press, 2003) 89–90.

[14]   J Bakan, *The Corporation: The Pathological Pursuit of Profit and Power* (New York, Free Press, 2004) 164–66.

[15]   Kingsnorth, above n 13, at ch 7.

[16]   N Walker, 'The EU and the WTO: Constitutionalism in a New Key' in G de Búrca and J Scott (eds), *The EU and the WTO: Legal and Constitutional Issues* (Oxford and Portland, OR, Hart Publishing, 2001) 31, 34, 35.

central problematique that these new constitutional entities 'are not anchored in any of the conventional forms or symbols of legitimacy.'[17] Accordingly, this opens debate on many of the assumptions left untouched by liberal legalism— not least, what constitutes a polity—asking questions, as James Tully puts it, not just about, but within, the rules.[18] If we can overcome the continuing tendency to focus on (now supranational) public institutional forms, this approach asks the sorts of questions which legal pluralism argues can and should be asked of corporations. To the extent that we can shift the level and location of constitutional discourse, this symbolises that the meaning of constitutionalism can never be fixed, but has to be subject to constant re-examination and re-evaluation in terms of its contemporary relevance and value.

These different ways of imagining constitutionalism emphasise that the constitutional reality that we inhabit is our own doing, and so our own responsibility. There is nothing inevitable about the liberal legalist paradigm, or the Washington consensus that it facilitates and supports—just as these are created by humans, they can also be unmade. The emergence of multiple sites of governance which are breaking down old divisions, whether between public and private, state and civil society, law and non-law, highlight the urgent need to construct a new constitutional reality. The alternative is to struggle on with our existing concepts and ideas, tinkering here, modifying there, without facing up to how these concepts and ideas are a fundamental part of keeping hegemonic forces and interests in place. There is too much at stake here for us to follow this option by default. Instead, we require a paradigm shift. The argument of this book is that legal pluralism can provide this new way of thinking, and so enable us to move to a constitutional discourse that prosecutes the accountability of all forms of power.

---

[17] J Shaw, 'Postnational Constitutionalism in the European Union' (1999) 6 *Journal of European Public Policy* 579, 585.

[18] See J Tully, 'The Unfreedom of the Moderns in Comparison to their Ideals of Constitutional Democracy' (2002) 65 *Modern Law Review* 204, 223.

Index